THE DEVELOPMENT OF
ADMIRALTY JURISDICTION
AND PRACTICE SINCE
1800

F.L.WISWALL Jr

Yorke Prizeman of the University of Cambridge
Proctor and Advocate in Admiralty

THE DEVELOPMENT OF ADMIRALTY JURISDICTION AND PRACTICE SINCE 1800

AN ENGLISH STUDY WITH AMERICAN COMPARISONS

CAMBRIDGE

AT THE UNIVERSITY PRESS

1970

CAMBRIDGE UNIVERSITY PRESS
Cambridge, New York, Melbourne, Madrid, Cape Town, Singapore, São Paulo, Delhi

Cambridge University Press
The Edinburgh Building, Cambridge CB2 8RU, UK

Published in the United States of America by Cambridge University Press, New York

www.cambridge.org
Information on this title: www.cambridge.org/9780521077514

First published 1970
This digitally printed version 2008

A catalogue record for this publication is available from the British Library

Library of Congress Catalogue Card Number: 77–108113

ISBN 978-0-521-07751-4 hardback
ISBN 978-0-521-08991-3 paperback

CONTENTS

PREFACE

WITH a few subsequent alterations and additions, this work is the Yorke Prize essay originally submitted in 1968, which was in turn largely derived from my doctoral dissertation of the previous year. It is published at the behest of the Faculty Board of Law of the University of Cambridge.

I wish to express my sincere appreciation to the following persons who have given me generous assistance in the procurement of books and materials for research:

W. A. F. P. Steiner, Esq., and the Staff of the Squire Law Library, Cambridge;

K. C. McGuffie, Esq., the Admiralty Registrar and P. V. Gray, Esq., the Admiralty Marshal, for the loan of books and materials from the Admiralty Registry, Royal Courts of Justice;

D. V. A. Sankey, Esq., Librarian and Keeper of the Records of the Honourable Society of the Middle Temple, for the loan of books from the Middle Temple Library;

C. L. Fisher, Esq., Librarian of the Bar, Probate and Supreme Court Libraries, for the loan of books from the Bar Library and storage rooms, Royal Courts of Justice;

The Rt Hon. Sir Jocelyn E. S. Simon, President of the Probate, Divorce and Admiralty Division of the High Court of Justice and B. H. Erhard, Esq., the President's Clerk, for the loan of books from the President's Room, Royal Courts of Justice;

The late K. H. Drake, Esq., Secretary of the Selden Society, for access to books in the Library of the Institute of Advanced Legal Studies, London;

The Hon. E. T. Gignoux, United States District Judge for Maine and the Maine Historical Society, for references and duplicated materials;

The Staff of the Library of the United States Court of Appeals for the Second Judicial Circuit, New York, for access to books and materials;

M. J. Prichard, Esq., of Gonville and Caius College, Cambridge and D. E. C. Yale, Esq., of Christ's College, Cambridge, for the loan of books and duplicated materials;

Lord McNair, Q.C., for the loan of a book; and

The Fellows of Doctors' Commons, who, though having long since departed this life, once assembled the great Library of the College of Advocates, many of the remnants of which have been of valued use to me.

I wish also to give my particular thanks to the following persons:

M. J. Prichard, Esq., for his guidance and generous assistance;

The Rt Hon. Lord Gardiner, Lord High Chancellor, K. C. McGuffie, Esq., Admiralty Registrar, and L. Bell, Esq., Assistant Keeper of the Public Record Office, for providing information cited in the body of this work;

Professor G. R. Elton, M. J. Prichard, Esq., Professor C. Parry, D. E. C. Yale, Esq., and K. C. McGuffie, Esq., for reading portions of the mss., and giving to me the benefit of their criticism;

The Editorial Staff of the Cambridge University Press, both in Cambridge and at the American Branch in New York;

Messrs. Burlingham Underwood Wright White & Lord, New York, for forbearance and for the use of various facilities;

Dr G. H. Robinson, Cromwell Professor-Emeritus of International and Admiralty Law of Cornell University and Dr C. Parry, Professor of International Law in the University of Cambridge, who were each partially responsible for my studies in Cambridge; and

My wife, Priscilla Gwyn Wiswall, for her encouragement over more than six years of research and for her invaluable assistance in translation, typing, proof-reading and in jacket design.

Castine, Maine   F.L.W., JR.
June, 1970

ENGLISH ADMIRALTY JUDGES

When one is made admirall, hee must first ordaine and substitute for his lieutenant, deputies, and other officers under him, some of the most loyall, wise, and discreete persons in the maritime law and auncient customes of the seas which hee can any where find, to the end that by the helpe of God and their good and just government the office may be executed to the honour and good of the realme.

First Order of *The Black Book of the Admiralty.*

─────────

HIGH COURT OF ADMIRALTY

Sir William Scott, Lord Stowell	1798–1827
Sir Christopher Robinson	1828–33
Sir John Nicholl	1833–38
Dr Stephen Lushington	1838–67
Sir Robert Phillimore	1867–75

ADMIRALTY DIVISION
HIGH COURT OF JUSTICE

Sir Robert Phillimore	1875–83
Sir James Hannen, P.	1875–91
Sir Charles Butt, J.	1883–92
Sir Francis Jeune, P.	1891–1905
Sir Gorell Barnes, Lord Gorell, P.	1892–1909
Sir Samuel Evans, P.	1910–18
Sir Maurice Hill, J.	1917–30
Sir Henry Duke, Lord Merrivale, P.	1919–33
Sir Boyd Merriman, Lord Merriman, P.	1934–62
Sir Gordon Willmer, J.	1945–58
Sir Bushby Hewson, J.	1958–66
Sir Jocelyn Simon, P.	1962–
Sir Henry Brandon, J.	1966–

[only judges named in the body of the work are listed]

ABBREVIATIONS

A	Answer
A.C.	Appeal Cases [Reports], 1891–
A.C.A.	Admiralty Court Act
A. & E.	Admiralty & Ecclesiastical Cases [Reports]
Adm.	Admiralty
A-G	Attorney-General
aff'd.	affirmed on appeal
A.J.	Associate Justice
Am. L. Rev.	*American Law Review*
Ap.	Appendix
[App.]	Appeal in Court of Appeal
App. Cas.	Appeal Cases [Reports], 1875–90
Asp.	Aspinall's Maritime Law Cases
B.	Baron [of the Exchequer]
B.D.I.L.	*British Digest of International Law*
Bos. & Pul.	Bosanquet & Puller's [C.P.] Reports
Br. & Lush.	Browning & Lushington's Reports
c.	chapter
c.	*contra* [versus], *circa*
C.B.	Common Bench [C.P.] Reports
C.C.	Circuit Court [U.S.]
C.C.R.	Crown Case Reserved
cert. den.	certiorari denied [U.S.]
C.J.	Chief Judge, Justice
C.J.S.	Civil Judicial Statistics
C.P.	Common Pleas
C. Rob.	Christopher Robinson's Reports
Can.	Canadian
Car. & K.	Carrington & Kirwan's [N.P.] Reports
cf.	see for comparison
Ch.	Chancery
ch.	chapter [U.S.]
Ch.D.	Chancery Division Reports
Cir.	Circuit [U.S.]
cit.	citation omitted
cl.	clause
Cmd.	Command
Co.	Coke's [K.B.] Reports
col.	column
Comm.	Commission, Committee
Cons.	Consolidation

contra	see for contrast
Ct(s).	Court(s)
D.	District [U.S.]
D.A.B.	*Dictionary of American Biography*
D.N.B.	*Dictionary of National Biography*
Dall.	Dallas' [U.S.] Reports
D.C.L.	Doctor of Civil Law (*Oxon.*)
Deb.	Debate
Div.	Division of the H.C.J. or of U.S. Judicial District
Doc.	Document
Dod.	Dodson's Reports
Doug.	Douglas' [K.B.] Reports
E.D.	Eastern District [U.S.]
E.R.	English Reports Reprint
Ecc.	Ecclesiastical
ed.	edition
Edw.	Edwards' Reports
Ex.D.	Exchequer Division Reports
F.	Federal Reporter [U.S.]
F.2d	Federal Reporter, Second Series [U.S.]
F.R.C.P.	Federal Rules of Civil Procedure [U.S.]
F. Supp.	Federal Supplement [U.S.]
Fed. Cas.	Federal Cases [U.S.] [Reports]
Godb.	Godbolt's [K.B.] Reports
H.C.	House of Commons
H.C.A.	High Court of Admiralty
H.C.J.	High Court of Justice
H.E.L.	*History of English Law* (Holdsworth)
H.L.	House of Lords
H.L. Cas.	House of Lords' Cases [Reports]
H.L.R.	*Harvard Law Review*
Hag.	Haggard's Reports
Hob.	Hobart's [K.B.] Reports
How.	Howard's [U.S.] Reports
[Inst.]	instance proceedings
intro.	introduction
J.	Judge, Justice
J. & H.	Johnson & Hemming's [Ch.] Reports
J.C.L. & I.L.	*Journal of Comparative Legislation*
Jur.	*The Jurist*
K.B.	King's Bench
K.B.D.	King's Bench Division Reports
K.C.	King's Counsel
Kn.	Knapp's [P.C.] Reports

La.	Louisiana
L.C.	Lord Chancellor
L.C.J.	Lord Chief Justice
L.Ed.	Lawyer's Edition [U.S.] Reports
L.J.	Lord Justice of Appeal
L.J.	*The Law Journal*
L.J. Adm.	*Law Journal Admiralty*
LL.D.	Doctor of [Civil and Canon] Laws (*Cantab.*)
Ll.L.	Lloyd's List & Shipping Gazette
Ll.L.R.	Lloyd's List Law Reports 1919–50
Ll. Rep.	Lloyd's List Law Reports 1951–
L.M.L.	*Law of Maritime Liens* (Price)
L. Mag.	*Law Magazine*
L. Mag. & Rev.	*Law Magazine & Review*
L.Q.R.	*Law Quarterly Review*
L.R.	Law Reports, Law Review
L. Rev.	*The Law Review*
L.T.	*Law Times*
L.T.R.	Law Times Reports
Leo.	Leonard's [K.B.] Reports
Lush.	Lushington's Reports
m.	membrane of the roll
M. & W.	Meeson & Welsby's [Exchequer] Reports
M.L.A.U.S.	The Maritime Law Association of the U.S.
M.R.	Master of the Rolls
M.S.A.	Merchant Shipping Act
M.S.R.	Merchant Shipping Rules
Mass.	Massachusetts
Md.	Maryland
Me.	Maine
Mich.	Michigan
Moo.	Moore's [P.C.] Reports
n.	note
N.E. 2d	North Eastern Reporter [U.S.] (2nd series)
N.P.	Nisi Prius
(n.s.)	new series
N.Y. 2d	New York Reports (2nd series)
N.Y.S. 2d	New York Supplement (2nd series)
Not. Cas.	Notes of Cases [Reports]
O(O).	Order(s) in R.S.C.
O.-in-C.	Order in Council
Ore.	Oregon
P.	President, Probate Division Reports [Admiralty] 1891–

P.C.	Privy Council
P.D.	Probate Division Reports [Admiralty] 1876–90
P.D.A.	Probate, Divorce, and Admiralty
P.R.O.	Public Record Office
Pa.	Pennsylvania
Parl.	Parliamentary
[Prohib.]	proceeding for writ of prohibition
Q.	Question
Q.B.	Queen's Bench
Q.B.D.	Queen's Bench Division Reports
Q.C.	Queen's Counsel
r(r).	rule(s)
R.C.	Royal Commission
R.I.	Rhode Island
R.S.C.	Rules of the Supreme Court
R.S.C.	Revised Statutes of Canada
Reg'r.	Registrar
Rett.	Rettie, Court of Session Cases [Reports]
Rev.	Revised, Revision
rev'd.	reversed on appeal
Ric.	Richard
Rt	Right
S.	South(ern) [U.S.] [also So.]
S.C.	South Carolina
S.C.J.	Supreme Court of Judicature
S.C.R.	Shipping Casualties Rules
S.C.R.	Short Cause Rules
S.D.	Southern District [U.S.]
S.G.S.	Shipping Gazette Supplement
S.I.	Statutory Instruments
S.R.O.	Statutory Rules & Orders
Sel. Pl. Adm.	*Select Pleas in Admiralty* (Marsden)
Sp.	Spinks' Reports
subs. proc.	subsequent proceedings
Sumn.	Sumner's Reports [U.S.]
Sup. Ct.	Supreme Court
Swab.	Swabey's Reports
T.L.R.	Times Law Reports
T.R.	Term [K.B.] Reports
'took silk'	made Q.C. or K.C.
U.S.	United States [Reports]
U.S.C.	United States Code
unrep.	unreported
v.	*versus*

W.B.	H.C.A. Warrant Book
W.D.	Western District [U.S.]
W.L.R.	Weekly Law Reports
W. Rob.	William Robinson's Reports
W.W.	*Who's Who*
W.W.W.	*Who Was Who*
Wall.	Wallace's [U.S.] Reports
Wheat.	Wheaton's [U.S.] Reports

SYMBOLS

§(§)	section(s)
¶(¶)	paragraph(s)
x	unofficial short title

TABLE OF STATUTES

NOTE: statutes without official short titles have been assigned appropriate short titles by the author for convenience of citation. In the body of the work, these unofficial short titles are designated by the symbol 'x', thus: Admiralty Jurisdiction Act, x1389. In this table, statutes with no official short title are listed first by regnal year and chapter, and the substance is then noted in brackets, as in the first statute in the table below.

STATUTES OF THE UNITED STATES

STATUTES OF CANADA

TABLE OF CASES

It will be no wonder if all courts of justice should, on some future day, in their turns be revolutionized:— but it will be some satisfaction and a curiosity at least, that the traces of their existence remain; and which, like the monumental inscriptions of the illustrious dead, may serve as examples to show WHO *were once useful to mankind.*

SIR JAMES MARRIOTT, LL.D.

Formulare Instrumentorum, 1802

intro., p.vi

Opposite: Court sitting in the Common Hall of Doctors' Commons – lithograph by Rowlandson taken from Ackermann's *Microcosm of London,* 1808, vol. I, facing p. 224.

INTRODUCTION

THE object of this work, as the title indicates, is to convey the writer's impressions of the development of Admiralty jurisdiction and practice during the last and the present century. The natural vehicle for such study is the Admiralty Court itself, because it is and was so obviously the focal point for change; tracing the history of the Court during the period covered by this work is therefore the most convenient method of observing the development of jurisdiction and practice, and, in the last chapter of the work, a remarkable change in the jurisprudence and substantive Law of Admiralty brought about as a result of alterations in the structure, composition and practice of the Admiralty Court.

It is, however, important to realize at the outset that this work is not precisely a history of the Admiralty Court as an institution; it is to avoid this impression that the work bears a title which emphasizes Admiralty jurisdiction and practice rather than the Court itself. Thus consideration is given not only to jurisdiction and practice, but to procedure, jurisprudence, peripheral influences upon development, and the more important personalities associated with the Court and its practice. And because the work is not properly a history of the Court *per se*, I am obliged to omit mention of personalities such as Pilcher, Langton, Bateson, and Karminski, JJ., who have served the Court during the present century but have not been directly involved in developments of jurisdiction and practice noted in this work, and to include mention of such personalities as Lord Esher, M.R., Sir John Jervis, C.J., and Sir Gainsford Bruce, J., who, though not actually Admiralty Judges, nonetheless had a profound influence upon the development of Admiralty jurisdiction and practice.

As one who went to sea before he went to law, and whose affection for and fascination with Admiralty is born of a love of the sea and ships, I am mindful of the wisdom of a statement made over a century ago:

The Jurisdiction of the High Court of Admiralty, resting, as it now does, upon a basis so firmly established by our statute law, and independent of that authority which it has derived from ancient custom, renders any inquiry respecting its origin a subject more fit for the research of the antiquarian than for that of the lawyer.[1]

A mariner and lawyer but not an historian, I have endeavoured to avoid pronouncing upon those phases of the subject which I know to lie outside the sphere of my own competence and within that of the trained historian. Moreover, consideration is restricted to the Admiralty jurisdiction itself, and does not include the jurisdiction of the Court in such matters as prize and maritime crime, which are worthy of detailed study by those more knowledgeable and interested in them than I—'the Prize Court', said Lord Mansfield, 'is peculiar to itself; it is no more like to the Admiralty than to any [common law] Court in Westminster Hall'.[2] What will be the concern of this work is the Court's civil, or 'instance' jurisdiction —so called because suits therein are brought at the instance of a plaintiff[3]—not merely because 'the Instance (at least in these times of peace) deserves more consideration than the Prize Court',[4] but because within the instance jurisdiction is contained the jurisprudence of Admiralty, in which I enjoy a particular interest.

The chronological period covered by this work has been chosen for several reasons; because it was in the nineteenth century that the Admiralty jurisdiction, which had been for so long restricted by statute, began to be restored and broadened by counteracting statutes; because the period covered has seen the development of most of the jurisdiction and substantive and procedural Law of Admiralty which prevails in the present day; and because the Admiralty Law of the United States, in which I have had my professional training and experience, and with which there are many fascinating and useful comparisons to be drawn, underwent its greatest development during the same period.

As the development of English Admiralty has had such a great influence upon that of American Admiralty, with a consequent interest by American textwriters in the history of English Admiralty jurisdiction,[5] and because the reverse of these propositions is true to a somewhat lesser degree,[6] reference is made to developments in American Admiralty, where useful, to illustrate parallels with or divergencies from the development of English Admiralty, or to show some direct relationship.

---

[1] Edwards, p. 1.
[2] See *id.*, p. 224.
[3] See Conkling, p. 354, n. (*a*).
[4] Edwards, p. 31.
[5] See, *e.g.*, Conkling, pp. 35–51.
[6] See, *e.g.*, Roscoe, *Practice*, intro., p. 2, n. (*c*).

In the period of Admiralty history prior to the nineteenth century, I must acknowledge a general inexpertise and lack of training in historical research, which original study of that period requires; consequently, when it is necessary to give a general picture or establish a particular fact of that period (particularly in the first chapter), reference will be made to such sources as R. G. Marsden's 'Six Centuries of the Admiralty Court' or the Introduction to the fifth edition of E. S. Roscoe's *Admiralty Jurisdiction and Practice* —not because they are themselves the most original or authoritative works upon the subject, but because (for the sake of convenience) they encapsulate, with references, brief and usually reliable pictures of that period prior to and outside the scope of this work.

It must be made absolutely clear that this work views the development of English jurisdiction and practice through the eyes of an American Proctor and Advocate; I have made a conscious effort to avoid the pitfall of chauvinism, but it may be that the reader will judge this an unsuccessful attempt.

While two of the three lawyers from whom I have drawn my greatest enthusiasm for The Law are understandably my father and the great teacher to whom this book is dedicated, the third is Sir W. S. Gilbert. The reader is at least fairly warned.

Finally, I must confess a degree of nostalgia for the relatively halcyon days of the Admiralty Court under the civilians, and in this I may also deserve the judgment passed upon one of the old proctors who lingered about·the Court after the fall of Doctors' Commons: that he 'was steeped in Admiralty lore, and the main object of his life appeared to be to preserve the old Admiralty practice against the attacks of the Common Law. For this purpose he had always some precedent or point which he pressed on counsel, hoping to keep the court in the ancient ways'.[1]

For these failings, if such they be, I tender apology in advance.

[1] Roscoe, *H.C.A.*, pp. 12–13.

CHAPTER I

THE ERA OF STOWELL

IN ORDER to appreciate the position of the Admiralty Court at the time when Lord Stowell came to the bench, it is first advisable to make a brief foray into the Court's previous history.

As the name suggests, the High Court of Admiralty was in fact an instrument of the office of Lord High Admiral. The Crown having made a delegation of the Royal Prerogative in maritime affairs to the Admiral, the Court came into existence to deal with offences and disputes within the Admiral's jurisdiction. The Judge of the Court was traditionally styled 'Deputy' or 'Lieutenant' of the Lord High Admiral, and originally even held his appointment by letters patent from the Admiral rather than from the Crown,[1] though by Stowell's time the reverse was true.[2]

For reasons which ranged from petty jealousy to righteous indignation at real encroachment upon their jurisdiction, the courts of common law very soon became resentful of the power exercised by the civil law Court of Admiralty; as early as the year 1296, the authority of the Admiral to adjudicate disputes involving seizure at sea was denied by the Common Pleas,[3] and in the later decades of the fourteenth century the steady acquisition of Admiralty jurisdiction[4] became intolerable to the common lawyers. Their remedy was to obtain statutory restriction of the Admiral's jurisdiction to 'a thing done upon the sea'.[5] Later, to plug backwaters through which the civilians had since sailed, all matters, including 'contracts, pleas, and quarrels', which arose within the body of a county whether on land or water, were explicitly removed from the jurisdiction of the 'Admiral's Court' and declared triable only at common law.[6] This latter statute also contained a provision excluding the Admiralty from cognizance of 'wreck'—included, it is said, as a result of greedy infighting between the barons and the Lord High Admiral over claims to and confiscation of shipwrecks.[7]

---

[1] Marsden, 'Six Centuries', p. 86.   [2] A. Browne, vol. 2, p. 28.
[3] Marsden, *Select Pleas*, vol. 1, intro., p. xvii.
[4] See *id.*, pp. xlv–xlix.   [5] Admiralty Jurisdiction Act, [x]1389.
[6] Admiralty Jurisdiction Act, 1391.
[7] Hall, intro., pp. xii–xiv.

These statutes—13 Ric. 2, c. 5 and 15 Ric. 2, c. 3—were still in force during the second quarter of the nineteenth century, restricting even then the exercise of Admiralty jurisdiction.[1] For triple certainty, yet another enactment—2 Hen. 4, c. 11—was secured by the common lawyers, aimed not at the Court but at 'wrongful' suitors, levying a fine of ten pounds upon and making double damages recoverable from one who instituted in Admiralty a cause not within its jurisdiction, both fine and damages to be determined in an action at common law by the 'injured' defendant in Admiralty.[2] Though this statute remained in force until 1861,[3] no exercise of it is apparent in the nineteenth century.

If these Acts of Parliament put a stop to the jurisdictional encroachments of Admiralty upon the preserve of the common law, they did not, evidently, satisfy the appetite of the common lawyers for the Admiralty jurisdiction itself. Various devices, consisting chiefly of legal fictions, were employed in the common law courts to enable them to adjudicate maritime matters actually within the Admiralty jurisdiction; but when retaliation in kind was attempted by the civilians in the Admiralty Court, they were thwarted by common law writs of prohibition.[4] A plea was made to Elizabeth I to intervene against these depredations, but the result was unsuccessful; a similar plea to James I unfortunately not only failed, but so enraged were the common lawyers at the attempt [and most particularly Sir Edward Coke, then Lord Chief Justice of the Common Pleas (see the attack upon the Admiralty Court in his *Fourth Institute*)], that the frequency of prohibition was actually increased.[5]

That the civilians were driven in desperation to seek the aid of the Crown is understandable, if one considers the provocation which they had endured. Surely there could have been no more legitimate concern to the Admiral and his Court than the validity of the patents issued by him to Vice-Admirals of the counties; yet, in *Sir Thomas Bacon's Case*,[6] the High Court of Admiralty having issued an order to show cause why the patents of the Vice-Admirals of Norfolk and Suffolk ought not to be revoked following the death of the Lord High Admiral, Coke—even in 1588 a

---

[1] *The Public Opinion*, (1832) 2 Hag. Adm. 398.
[2] Admiralty Jurisdiction Act, ×1400.
[3] Repealed: Admiralty Court Act, 1861, §31.
[4] Roscoe, *Practice*, intro., p. 7.
[5] *Id.*, pp. 10–11. [6] (1588) 2 Leo. 103, 3 Leo. 192.

foe of the Admiralty jurisdiction—moved for and received a prohibition in the King's Bench upon grounds that the cause was properly determinable only at common law. Later, in *Sir Henry Constable's Case*,[1] the King's Bench was able to act even more effectively, judicially defining 'wreck' under the Act of 1391 as that cast at ebb tide upon the shelf below the flood mark, thereby removing all such cases from the Admiralty jurisdiction into that of the common law, though the Admiral had always theretofore exercised jurisdiction below the high-water mark; this case, together with other restrictive decisions of the common law courts, laid the foundation of modern Admiralty jurisdiction, which even today is more limited in some respects than it was prior to its pillage by the common lawyers.

It ought to be noted that, though Coke may properly be classed as the chief antagonist of the Admiralty jurisdiction, the side of the common law was well represented both before and after his time by other men of great ability and dedication to victory in a struggle which, at times, took on some of the aspects of a holy war. One of the most telling common law decisions was that of Hobart, C.J., in *Bridgeman's Case*,[2] which went far beyond the language of the statutes of Richard II in holding that contracts made at sea must be sued upon at common law if the debts thereby created were to be paid on land. In the eighteenth century this rationale was supported by Blackstone, and extended by him to restrict to the cognizance of Admiralty only those contracts both made and executed at sea.[3]

In 1632, at the urging of Attorney-General Noy, articles were drawn by Charles I and his council which restored a portion of the Admiralty jurisdiction; though these articles were ratified and subscribed by all the common law judges, however, they did not seem to avail.[4] During the Commonwealth, an ordinance was passed which defined and considerably broadened the Admiralty jurisdiction, but it was declared invalid at the Restoration and an attempt to persuade Parliament to re-enact the provisions was unsuccessful in spite of a determined civilian effort.[5]

Not surprisingly, the Admiralty Court fell into a decline following these rebuffs, and the civilians retreated into a state of semi-

[1] (1601) 5 Co. Rep. 106a.   [2] (1614) Hob. 11 [No. 23].
[3] A. Browne, vol. 2, p. 75.   [4] Roscoe, *Practice*, intro., pp. 11–12.
[5] *Id.*, pp. 13–14.

isolation which avoided open conflict with the common law. An occasional prohibition issued to the Court, but for the most part the civilians seemed content to allow the common law judges to set the boundaries of Admiralty jurisdiction,[1] though even the latter became critical, in time, of the oppressive behaviour of their predecessors.[2] It should not, however, be supposed that the civilians either forgot or forgave the attacks of the common lawyers; indeed, it was often necessary even in the nineteenth century to settle jurisdictional questions in the Admiralty Court by considering at length that phase of the historical development of the Admiralty jurisdiction.[3] 'Outnumbered and outgunned', it was wiser by far for the civilians to bide time, awaiting a more favourable climate in which to press the reforms which they desired.

When Stowell became Admiralty Judge, the instance jurisdiction of Admiralty was still restricted to its narrowest scope, and the instance Court was practically dormant. The naval wars were providing the Court with a considerable volume of prize adjudication, but the civil business occupied the Judge only for an hour or so, once or twice a week.[4] Nevertheless, it is important to note in some detail what, in fact, the instance jurisdiction was at the beginning of the nineteenth century, before noting the jurisdictional developments during Stowell's tenure as Judge.

Fortunately, a magnificent work on the Law of Admiralty, comprehending both jurisdiction and procedure, was published in 1802. The author, Arthur Browne, LL.D., was Professor of Civil Law in the University of Dublin; but his treatise was dedicated to Stowell and based upon the law and practice of the English Admiralty Court. Of course, as a civilian, Browne did not hesitate to refute the transgressors of the rightful jurisdiction of Admiralty at every opportunity. His arguments, however, are sound ones, and he freely ceded points to the common lawyers when he felt that their position was justified, even concerning interpretation of the statutes of Richard II.[5] Browne's work had an immense impact upon Admiralty, wherever practised; not only was it relied upon in the English Admiralty Court, but, scarcely five years after its publication, was also specifically cited

---

[1] See *LeCaux v. Eden*, (1781) 2 Doug. 594.

[2] See Buller, J., *Smart v. Wolff* (1789) 3 T.R. 323, 348.

[3] See, *e.g.*, *Lord Warden of Cinque Ports v. The King in his Office of Admiralty*, (1831) 2 Hag. Adm. 438.

[4] Marsden, 'Six Centuries', p. 174.   [5] A. Browne, vol. 2, p. 92.

as standard authority by Chief Justice John Marshall in an Admiralty appeal before the Supreme Court of the United States.[1] Indeed, Browne was so well received in America that a U.S. edition of his work was published in New York in 1840, and this edition was, in turn, relied upon by later American Admiralty textwriters.[2]

The instance jurisdiction at the dawn of the nineteenth century is summarized by Browne as: contract—for wages or hypothecation; tort—for assault, collision and spoil; and quasi-contract—for salvage and in actions by part-owners for security.[3] But Browne admits that the limits of the jurisdiction were confused,[4] and he goes into considerably greater detail on specific points. In fact, Browne did not include several points of instance jurisdiction at all, perhaps because they were in that day such commonplace matters that they were not considered important enough to dwell upon. With the aid of other sources, however, a reasonably complete jurisdictional picture may be drawn as follows:

DROITS: civil droits were the Admiral's *perquisites* [property rights] in wreck at sea.[5] 'Wreck', in this sense, included *jetsam* [shipwreck, and/or cargo and deck gear jettisoned to lighten a vessel *in extremis* and so prevent her from foundering]—whether found as *flotsam* [floating on the surface] or as *lagon* [sunken, but buoyed for retrieval],[6] *derelicts* [abandoned vessels],[7] and *deodands* [objects instrumental to death aboard ship, or goods and belongings found upon a corpse floating at sea or cast ashore].[8] Pirate goods and spoils were also droits of Admiralty after the pirate's conviction,[9] and certain kinds of 'Royal Fish' [sturgeon, grampuses, porpoises, and *sea-waifs* (stranded whales)] were perquisites of the Admiral.[10] Any droits could be claimed by the owner within a year and a day of finding, but he was liable for salvage.[11] In the case of wreck on shore, found and sold (except for deodands), the owner's sole remedy lay at common law;[12] but where wreck was

---

[1] *Jennings v. Carson*, 4 Cranch (8 U.S.) 2 (1807).
[2] Conkling, p. 376, n. (*a*).   [3] A. Browne, vol. 2, pp. 121–2.
[4] *Id.*, p. 71.   [5] *Id.*, pp. 45–7.
[6] See *id.*, p. 50.   [7] *Id.*, p. 51.
[8] *Id.*, p. 56.   [9] *Id.*, p. 54.
[10] See *Lord Warden of Cinque Ports v. The King in his Office of Admiralty*, (1831) 2 Hag. Adm. 438.   [11] A. Browne, vol. 2, p. 51.
[12] A. Browne, vol. 2, p. 51; see also *id.*, p. 49.
Sir Henry Constable's Case, (1601) 5 Co. Rep. 106a.

retrieved from the water and carried away, remedy was by suit in Admiralty.[1] In the event that no owner appeared, the wreck was sold by order of the Court and the finder awarded salvage out of the proceeds, the remainder being perquisites of Admiralty.[2] The apportionment of salvage, whether or not an owner appeared, was therefore the primary occupation of the Admiralty Court under the category of droits.[3] Pirate goods were something of a special matter, in that the owner could claim them only if they were brought to England,[4] but the Court had power both to condemn pirate goods as droits[5] and to decree their restoration.[6]

SALVAGE: civil salvage (as distinct from prize salvage) is part of the ancient 'inherent' jurisdiction of Admiralty.[7] Salvage could be earned (at that time) simply for towing a distressed vessel,[8] or for endeavour so heroic that it is unrivalled in fiction.[9] It is awarded at the suit of the salvor, in an amount proportional to the degree of service and the value of the property salved.[10]

CONTRACT: the Admiralty jurisdiction comprehended only unsealed contracts made upon the sea for a maritime consideration.[11] A partial exception was also made for contracts made abroad incident to a matter originating at sea.[12] The principal test was therefore locality, but even so the contract would not be cognizable in Admiralty unless the subject matter was maritime on its face.[13]

HYPOTHECATION: questions of hypothecation were brought before the Court upon the suit of a bondholder who supplied necessaries [provisions, stores, tackle, etc.] or loaned money for the voyage, usually to the ship's master, on the credit of the ship rather than that of the owner.[14] If the form of hypothecation was a *bottomry* bond, it pledged the ship's bottom (usually the

---

[1] A. Browne, vol. 2, p. 51.·
[2] *Id.*, p. 52.
[3] *Id.*, p. 53.
[4] *Id.*, p. 54.
[5] *The Marianna*, (1835) 3 Hag. Adm. 206.
[6] *The Hercules*, (1819) 2 Dod. 353.
[7] *The Calypso*, (1828) 2 Hag. Adm. 209; see also *The Gas Float Whitton (No. 2)*, [1896] P. 42, at pp. 47–53.
[8] See *infra*, p. 41.
[9] See *The Holder Borden*, 12 Fed. Cas. 331 (No. 6600) (D. Mass. 1847).
[10] See *The Calypso*, (1828) 2 Hag. Adm. 209, 217–18.
[11] A. Browne, vol. 2, p. 72.
[12] *Id.*, p. 84.
[13] *Id.*, pp. 75, 81, 88, 90, 91, 94.
[14] Robinson, §49, p. 370.

keel) as security.[1] The ship could not be hypothecated in her home port before commencing a voyage,[2] nor could Admiralty take jurisdiction of claims for necessaries supplied to foreign ships in English ports unless there was an express hypothecation.[3] But Admiralty always retained jurisdiction over hypothecation of English ships in foreign ports.[4] It ought to be noted that suit upon hypothecation could only be brought *in rem* [against the *res*, or thing hypothecated: the ship], a right unique to Admiralty, and that there could be no suit *in personam* [against the master or owners] as there was no personal liability upon any bond of hypothecation.[5]

FREIGHT: in the case of cargo brought to England, the master had a lien upon the cargo in his possession for payment of *freight* [charges for carriage by sea], and this lien was enforceable in Admiralty.[6]

WAGES: seamen had a right to sue in Admiralty for wages earned on a voyage, and they had a lien upon the ship for payment, which might be enforced by an action *in rem*.[7] But the master of a ship, though his contract of employment might satisfy the requirements for Admiralty jurisdiction, could not sue for his wages in Admiralty because his contract was held to rely upon the credit of the owner rather than upon the credit of the ship.[8]

TORT: in general, the Admiralty jurisdiction comprehended all torts at sea.[9] Actions for assault and personal injury were very common in the instance Court,[10] and suit could be instituted by either passengers[11] or crew.[12] Damage to property at sea, including collision, was also within the Admiralty jurisdiction,[13] though in cases of cargo spoil and damage, common law evidently had concurrent jurisdiction with Admiralty.[14]

POSSESSION AND RESTRAINT: in cases of wrongful possession of a ship, Admiralty had an equitable power to decree restitution; but there was no Admiralty jurisdiction if possession was

---

[1] Robinson, §49, p. 370.   [2] A. Browne, vol. 2, p. 80.   [3] *Ibid.*
[4] *Id.*, p. 84.   [5] *Id.*, p. 99.   [6] *Id.*, p. 82.
[7] See Holt, p. 44; on 'special contract' for wages, see *infra*, pp. 25–6.
[8] A. Browne, vol. 2, pp. 95, 104; Maxwell, p. 8.
[9] A. Browne, vol. 2, p. 110 [torts often called 'damage'].
[10] *Ibid.*   [11] *The Ruckers*, (1801) 4 C. Rob. 73.
[12] See, *e.g.*, *The Agincourt*, (1824) 1 Hag. Adm. 271.
[13] See A. Browne, vol. 2, pp. 110–11.   [14] *Id.*, p. 116.

taken within the body of a county.[1] The Court had no jurisdiction to try legal title or order sale of the ship upon application by part-owners, and so could not entertain petitory suits.[2] Part-owners could, however, bring suit in Admiralty to restrain their ship from commencing a voyage to which they did not agree, pending the deposit of a bond for safe return with the Court by the majority owners.[3]

MISCELLANEOUS: in addition to its instance jurisdiction, the Admiralty Court had power to revoke English privateers' letters of marque when ancillary to decision of civil questions involving privateers,[4] power to punish for contempt,[5] power to execute judgments of foreign Admiralty courts—including imprisonment impervious to *habeas corpus*,[6] and jurisdiction to hear cases on appeal from Vice-Admiralty courts.[7] It is also well to note one of the more serious jurisdictional defects— Admiralty had no cognizance of ship mortgages made ashore,[8] and did not exercise jurisdiction over those made at sea.[9] But as to some of the jurisdiction claimed by the common law, Browne says that if suit should be brought in Admiralty on a charter-party, for freight in general average, or to determine title to a ship, and a prohibition not issue to the Admiralty Court, 'I do not see how the [C]ourt could refuse to entertain it . . .'[10]

As to the exercise of the instance jurisdiction in that day, it is said that it was practically limited to the settlement of petty disputes between shipowners,[11] and the determination of such fundamental questions as whether Jersey was a 'foreign possession' for the purpose of sustaining a bottomry bond.[12]

From the jurisdiction of the High Court of Admiralty, it is well to turn to an outline of the practice in the Court at the time of Stowell's judgeship. In doing so, assistance is chiefly by two

---

[1] A. Browne, vol. 2, p. 117.
[2] *Id.*, pp. 114–15; Holt, pp. 204–5; *contra*, Parsons, p. 236.
   See also Betts, p. 16.
[3] See, *e.g.*, *The Apollo*, (1824) 1 Hag. Adm. 306.
[4] See *Die Fire Damer*, (1805) 5 C. Rob. 357, 360.
[5] See *The Harmonie*, (1841) 1 W. Rob. 179.
[6] A. Browne, vol. 2, p. 120.   [7] *The Fabius*, (1800) 2 C. Rob. 245.
[8] A. Browne, vol. 2, p. 95.   [9] See *The Portsea*, (1827) 2 Hag. Adm. 84.
[10] A. Browne, vol. 2, pp. 121–2.   [11] Holt, p. 206.
[12] So held in *The Barbara*, (1801) 4 C. Rob. 1.

works—Browne, and a collection of instruments then used in the Court which was also published in 1802, compiled by Sir James Marriott, Master of Trinity Hall, Cambridge, and Stowell's predecessor as Admiralty Judge.

It is interesting to note that, like Browne, Marriott exerted a great—and even more enduring—influence upon American Admiralty Law. The author of the first published collection of Admiralty forms in the United States candidly admits drawing it from Marriott,[1] as do later American textwriters;[2] and there can be little doubt that the striking similarity between many modern forms in England and the United States is directly traceable to Marriott's work.

In considering the procedure of the early nineteenth century, reference will be made to the location in Marriott's collection of some of the more important forms of instruments.

Proceedings in Admiralty are divisible into two categories: those *in rem*, and those *in personam*. By the time of Stowell's judgeship, actions *in rem* under the instance jurisdiction of the Court had become far more common than actions *in personam*;[3] the former, therefore, will be examined first.

The proceeding *in rem* was most frequently employed in suits for seamen's wages, on hypothecation, of possession, and in collision;[4] doubtless it was often used as well in cases of salvage and droits.

The first step in the proceeding *in rem* was for the plaintiff's proctor to secure an entry in the 'action book' kept in the Admiralty Registry, stating the name of the plaintiff, and giving a description of the ship to be sued and the amount of the claim.[5] Then the plaintiff executed an affidavit of the cause of action,[6] later to become known as the 'affidavit to lead warrant'[7] (this procedure was instituted in 1801, to curtail the frequency of vexatious arrests[8]), whereupon a warrant issued to the Admiralty Marshal from the Registry, directing him to arrest the ship and/or cargo, and citing the ship's master, and others having any interest in the vessel [the owners], to appear and defend upon a named day.[9] By 1800 the

---

[1] Conkling, intro., p. v, n. (*a*).   [2] See, *e.g.*, Dunlap, intro., p. viii.
[3] A. Browne, vol. 2, pp. 396, 397; and *cf.* Clerke, p. 3.
   See also *The Clara*, (1855) Swab. 1, 3.   [4] A. Browne, vol. 2, pp. 396–7.
[5] A. Browne, vol. 2, p. 397; Coote, 1st ed., pp. 10, 20.
[6] A. Browne, vol, 2, p. 397.   [7] Coote, 1st ed., p. 241.
[8] A. Browne, vol. 2, p. 402, n. (7).   [9] *Id.*, pp. 397–8; Marriott, p. 326.

warrant, and other process of the High Court of Admiralty, issued in the name of the King rather than that of the Lord High Admiral.[1]

The warrant was next served upon the vessel by the Marshal in the time-honoured manner of exhibiting the original and holding it to the mainmast, then nailing a copy in its place;[2] it is also a very ancient practice to chalk a fouled anchor, symbolic of the jurisdiction of the Admiralty Court, on some prominent space topsides in addition to the service of the warrant.[3] The Marshal then executed a certificate of service (commonly called the 'Marshal's return'), which was filed in the Registry together with the original warrant.[4]

The owner(s), in due course, either appeared or defaulted. Assuming the latter case, the persons cited in the warrant were publicly called to appear, three times on each of four successive court days, each non-appearance incurring a formal default. The plaintiff's proctor then filed a 'summary petition', praying possession of the *res*; the ship's defenders again having been called three times without appearing, the Judge admitted the petition on pronouncing contempt, and issued a 'first decree' giving the plaintiff possession.[5] Conditional upon securing the first decree, the plaintiff gave bail in the form of two sureties, in double the amount of the claim, to answer any 'latent demands' [claims of intervenors] which might arise within a year's time; unless this bail was given, the plaintiff had to wait for a year and a day before taking possession of the *res*.[6] Unfortunately for the plaintiff, the 'possession' thus secured gave no right of sale, and so it became necessary for his proctor to file an allegation of the ship's 'perishable condition', praying the issue of a commission to the Marshal to appraise and sell the ship and bring the proceeds into the Registry, upon which fiction the Court would, as a matter of course, decree a 'perishable monition' ordering all interested parties to appear and show cause why the ship should be be sold at auction.[7] The cause was then assigned for summary hearing, a commission of appraisement and sale decreed, the *res* sold, and

---

[1] Hall, p. 9.   [2] A. Browne, vol. 2, p. 398.

[3] See, *e.g.*, *The Jarlinn*, [1965] 1 W.L.R. 1098, 1100.

[4] A. Browne, vol. 2, p. 398.

[5] *Id.*, pp. 398–402.

[6] *Id.*, p. 402; Coote, 1st ed., pp. 97, 111.

[7] A. Browne, vol. 2, pp. 403–4; Marriott, p. 340.

the proceeds brought into the Registry and distributed in satisfaction of the claim or claims, according to their priorities, any
balance being decreed to the shipowner(s), saving latent demands.[1]
Remarkably, any interested party might appear and defend at
any time until a year after the first decree.[2]

If an interested party obeyed the warrant's citation, he might
enter an appearance 'under protest' [a *special* appearance] in
order to contest the Court's jurisdiction, or he might appear
'absolutely' [a *general* appearance]. In the former case, the protest
might be overruled and the appearance made absolute, should the
Court hold for jurisdiction.[3] Upon absolute appearance, the 'im-
pugnant' [defendant] gave a 'fidejussory caution' [bail of sureties]
which stipulated his personal liability for any judgment and undertook to appear when necessary in person.[4] Presumably, this bail
had the effect of releasing the ship from arrest.[5] The 'promovent'
[plaintiff] was then called upon to file his 'libel' [complaint],
with a bond of sureties, by the next court day—failing which the
action would be dismissed. Both parties were then required to
give further security in the form of 'cautions', which could equal
double the sum in which their respective sureties were bound;
but if the parties were unable to find sureties, then either or both
of them, at the discretion of the Judge, might be permitted to
give a 'juratory caution' [personal recognizance on oath].[6] The
plaintiff having filed his libel, the defendant then filed his answer,
which might be a general concession, a general denial, or formal
exceptions to particular articles of the libel; the exceptions might
be 'peremptory' [calling for summary judgment on the pleadings]
or 'dilatory' [objecting to the form of the libel]. The plaintiff
might then file a 'replication' [rebutter], to which the defendant
might reply with a 'duplication' [surrebutter].[7] Either party
might demand of the other that he answer each of the pleadings
on oath, which was then required on pain of personal attachment.[8]
Should the pleadings present the issues satisfactorily to both
parties, the cause might then be assigned for hearing; but if the
pleadings together with the personal answers of the adversaries
were not satisfactory to both, the cause then proceeded upon 'plea

---

[1] A. Browne, vol. 2, pp. 404–5. [2] *Id.*, p. 405.
[3] *Id.*, pp. 406–7. [4] *Id.*, pp. 407–10.
[5] *Id.*, p. 409, n. *October 9th*; Marriott, p. 355.
[6] *Id.*, pp. 410–11; *id.*, p. 354.
[7] *Id.*, pp. 414–15. [8] *Id.*, pp. 416–17.

and proof'. In the latter case the pleadings were first filed, and a 'term probatory' was granted to both parties, during which they might produce witnesses to prove or contradict allegations in the pleadings; a 'term probatory' was equivalent to one court day, and three were granted as a matter of form; in practice, however, continuances were easily obtained.[1]

Witnesses not appearing voluntarily could be served with a 'compulsory' process [subpoena] in person,[2] a citation *viis et modis* [by substituted service], or failing those, a warrant for 'personal apprehension'.[3] Once appearing, the witnesses were sworn,[4] whereupon they underwent a secret examination (in the normal course of the civil law) before an examiner commissioned by the Court, which resulted in a deposition signed by the individual witness and affirmed by him afterwards in open court before the Judge.[5] Either party might administer written interrogatories, via the examiner, to their adversaries' witnesses.[6] If any witnesses were incapable of appearing in London, they might be examined elsewhere by commission of the Court. The examiner so appointed was usually both an officer of the Court and a notary public; the parties' proctors were also required to be present at such an examination.[7] When either party had done examining witnesses, his proctor might move publication of the depositions; upon publication, exceptions and objections to the testimony might be offered, and, if necessary, corroborating or impeaching witnesses might then be called as before, new probatory terms having been granted for the purpose.[8] There was then a last opportunity for the introduction of documentary evidence, following which the cause was assigned for hearing.[9]

In 'trifling suits' the entire procedure just described might be dispensed with, the witnesses undergoing only a *viva voce* examination at the hearing.[10]

Upon a hearing, in open court before the Judge, the evidence was read and arguments heard by the parties' advocates; the Judge then assigned the cause for sentence, and issued a citation

---

[1] A. Browne, vol. 2, pp. 418–19; see also Coote, 1st ed., pp. 39–40.

[2] A. Browne, vol. 2, p. 419; Marriott, p. 344.

[3] *Ibid.*   [4] *Ibid.*; Marriott, p. 308.

[5] *Id.*, p. 421 [the office of Examiner in Admiralty yet exists].

[6] *Ibid.*

[7] *Id.*, pp. 422–5.   [8] *Id.*, pp. 425–6.

[9] *Id.*, p. 427.   [10] *Id.*, p. 428.

to the party against whom the decision had gone, to appear to hear the sentence and to show cause, if possible, why the sentence should not be pronounced and executed.[1] Following sentence, the Judge assigned costs,[2] which were absolutely within his discretion.[3]

If a want of Admiralty jurisdiction was apparent on the face of the libel, the defendant might obtain a prohibition at common law (usually from the King's Bench), despite his failure to contest the jurisdiction of the Admiralty Court, even *after* the Court had pronounced sentence.[4] If the libel was good on its face but a cause for prohibition still existed, the defendant had to except to the Admiralty jurisdiction in his answer or be afterwards ineligible to apply for a prohibition;[5] yet, all else failing, the defendant might obtain an injunction in Chancery after sentence to prevent enforcement of the decree of execution.[6]

The proceeding *in personam*—though infrequently used—might be employed in suits upon wages, injury, possession of proceeds, and ransom bills, although in the first two cases the Court was also able to exercise its jurisdiction *in rem*.[7] The proceeding *in personam* basically differed but slightly from that *in rem*. The warrant, when issued, was of course drawn for arrest of the person, and was executed by the Marshal exhibiting the warrant and taking the defendant into custody; the defendant remained in custody until providing a fidejussory caution [bail] in the sum of five hundred pounds.[8] Upon appearance, the defendant was obliged to produce new sureties or else go to prison, unless admitted to a juratory caution [personal recognizance];[9] in practice, it was evidently customary to waive even the juratory caution for seamen and paupers, unless demanded by the adverse party.[10] Thereafter, the prodecure *in personam* paralleled that of a suit *in rem* in which the defendant appeared collaterally to defend the *res*.[11]

In the case of an unfound or absent defendant, the ancient and

---

[1] A. Browne, vol. 2, pp. 428–9.   [2] *Id.*, p. 429.
[3] See *The Zephyr*, (1827) 2 Hag. Adm. 43.
[4] A. Browne, vol. 2, pp. 441–2.   [5] *Id.*, p. 442.
[6] See *The Jane and Matilda*, (1823) 1 Hag. Adm. 187, 196 n.
[7] A. Browne, vol. 2, p. 397.
[8] *Id.*, pp. 432–3; Marriott, p. 330.   [9] *Id.*, pp. 433–4; *id.*, p. 354.
[10] See *Polydore v. Prince*, 19 Fed. Cas. 950 (No. 11257) (D. Me. 1837).
[11] A. Browne, vol. 2, p. 434.
      Id., see pp. 406–29.

unique remedy of Admiralty attachment might have been applied
to seize goods of the defendant within the jurisdiction and thus
compel him to appear; but according to Browne, Admiralty
attachment had fallen into disuse prior to the nineteenth century.[1]
It has been suggested by textwriters in America, where Admiralty
attachment had become an important feature of the proceeding
in personam,[2] that its disuse in England resulted from the determination of the courts of common law, enforced by prohibition, to
restrict the Admiralty Court to the exercise of jurisdiction *in rem*.[3]

It is important to note that, although Admiralty attachment
superficially resembles the process of foreign attachment as
employed by the City of London Court, it is neither based upon
nor identical thereto.[4] The chief distinction between the two is
that Admiralty attachment effects the seizure of property (chattels
only; real property is not subject[5]) in the 'possession' of the defendant, while foreign attachment at common law effects the seizure of
a defendant's property while in the possession of a third party.[6]

In addition to two-party litigation, there was a procedure for
third-party intervention[7] and Browne even set out the procedure
in petitory suits,[8] though admitting that the Admiralty Court
did not decide questions of title.[9] When such detail abounds as
to matters seldom, if ever, coming before the Court, it is curious
indeed that Browne should omit all mention of at least two procedural points, particularly in discussing cases of collision, which
were common features of the Admiralty practice of his day.

It has been the custom of the Admiralty Court since the six-
teenth century, in cases of collision or salvage, for 'nautical assessors' to sit with the Judge at the hearing and later to give him the
advantage of their technical expertise in maritime affairs, thus
aiding his interpretation of the evidence. Most usually, these
assessors are two Elder Brethren of the London Trinity House,
an organization whose charter comprehended this function[10]
in addition to the regulation of Thames pilotage, maintenance of
navigational aids, and other duties. Though not attending in a

---

[1] A. Browne, vol. 2, pp. 434–5.   [2] Hall, p. 132; Conkling, pp. 478–85.
[3] See *Hall*, pp. 60–1.
[4] A. Browne, vol. 2, pp. 434–5; *cf.* Marriott, pp. 258, 350; *Manro v. Almeida*,
10 Wheat. (23 U.S.) 473, 490 (1825).
[5] *Miller v. United States*, 11 Wall. (78 U.S.) 268 (1870).   [6] See *infra*, p. 143.
[7] A. Browne, vol. 2, pp. 428–9.   [8] *Id.*, pp. 430–1.
[9] *Id.*, p. 430.   [10] See Roscoe, *Practice*, intro., p. 4 and n. (*k*).

majority of causes before the High Court of Admiralty, they had certainly become features of the Court before the nineteenth century. Interestingly, nautical assessors were once also used in American Admiralty courts, but in 1855 the practice was deemed improper by the Supreme Court, establishing the modern use of expert testimony instead.[1]

Another feature of the English Admiralty procedure which also had its American counterpart was the dual action. In some cases, the suit was entered both *in rem* against the vessel and *in personam* against her master;[2] a special form of warrant was served,[3] and bail for the ship released the master as well.[4] The dual action against ship and master died out during the nineteenth century, perhaps because masters became increasingly judgment-proof; but the practice continued for a time, particularly in cases of collision, of including the name of the master in parentheses following the name of the ship in the title of the cause given in the report; properly, the master's name should be omitted in the citation of such a case, but occasionally it was not, and cases such as *The Alexander*—(Larsen)[5] have since been cited quite incorrectly: *viz.*, '*The Alexander Larsen*'.[6]

An overall view of the Admiralty procedure of the early nineteenth century leaves one with mixed feelings. On one hand, a characterization of the proceedings as being analogous to arbitration (as opposed to actions at law or suits in equity) is probably fair, particularly in so-called 'trifling suits'.[7] On the other, both Browne[8] and his predecessor, Clerke,[9] take particular pains to impress upon the reader that the procedure in all causes in Admiralty was summary [informal] rather than plenary [formal]; not only, it has been observed, was this patently untrue[10] (save in the ecclesiastical sense of 'summary' procedure), but by modern standards the actual procedure was inefficient to say the very least. Moreover, the distinction between plenary and summary procedure was often productive of even further expense, delay,

---

[1] Parsons, vol. 2, pp. 438–9; however, assessors did sit in *The Jay Gould*, 19 F. 765 (E.D. Mich. 1884).

[2] *Id.*, p. 394; Conkling, p. 449; and see *The Newport*, 15 F. 2d 342 (9 Cir. 1926). [3] Marriott, p. 328.

[4] Conkling, p. 449. [5] (1841) 1 W. Rob. 288.

[6] See, *e.g.*, Williams and Bruce, 3rd ed., p. 191, n. (*n*).

[7] See Conkling, p. 565. [8] Vol. 2, p. 413.

[9] See *Praxis*, Title 19. [10] Conkling, p. 376, n. (*a*).

and confusion, because plenary [*e.g.*, personal injury] and summary [*e.g.*, wages] causes could not be joined in the same libel over the objection of the defence,[1] thereby necessitating two separate suits, often by plaintiffs who could least afford the expense and delay [*e.g.*, seamen].

As a brief examination of the Admiralty jurisdiction and procedure is necessary to an appreciation of the Court as an institution in any given period in its history, so almost equally important is at least a glimpse of the dominant personality of the Court, the Admiralty Judge.

Stowell's life was a wonderfully rich and fascinating one, which, in many respects, was not influential upon the Court and hence not within the scope of this work—but his biography is, in itself, very worthwhile reading.[2] Briefly, these are some notable points: he was born William Scott in 1745, in the County of Durham; he gained a scholarship to Corpus Christi, Oxford, and later became Camden Reader in Ancient History and a Fellow of University College; he was graduated D.C.L. in 1779 and became a Fellow of Doctors' Commons in the same year; he was called to the bar by the Middle Temple in 1780, but his practice remained in the civil law; he served as a Conservative M.P. from 1790 until 1821, latterly representing the University of Oxford, and was not considered an 'active' member of Parliament; he became Admiralty Advocate in 1782, Master of the Faculties in 1790, and Judge of the High Court of Admiralty in 1798; he was elevated to the peerage as Baron Stowell in 1821; he resigned the Admiralty Judgeship late in 1827, and died in 1836.[3] Socially, Stowell was a member of the highest intellectual circle of his day; he was a close personal friend of Dr Samuel Johnson, among others; Stowell's younger brother, John Scott, became Lord Eldon, the great Chancellor, and they were inseparable companions.[4] As a personality, Stowell was notorious not only for his brilliance, but for being 'parsimonious', and 'a great eater and a drinker of port';[5] indeed, Stowell's fondness for 'splicing the main brace' in good fellowship was so well known that it became the foundation for a social pun regarding his com**port**ment.[6] Stowell's career as

[1] *Pratt v. Thomas*, 19 Fed. Cas. 1262 (No. 11377) (D. Me. 1837); see also Parsons, vol. 2, p. 375; also *The Jack Park*, (1802) 4 C. Rob. 308, 309 [Dr Swabey].
[2] See Roscoe, *Lord Stowell, etc.*
[3] Holdsworth, *H.E.L.*, vol. 13, pp. 668–9; *D.N.B.* [4] *Ibid.*
[5] *Id.*, p. 675. [6] *Id.*, p. 611, n. 1.

Admiralty Judge will be considered in due course, but, undeniably, it was his adjudication in Prize for which he remains best known, and his authorship of the modern Law of Prize which is his monument.[1]

It is said that when Lord Stowell became Admiralty Judge, the paucity of the Court's instance business was such 'that it could be said to afford that great legal luminary little else than an occasional morning's occupation.'[2] This scarcely means, however, that Stowell sat idle upon the bench, because the volume of Prize causes accruing to the Admiralty Court from the naval warfare in which Britain was at the time engaged gave the Judge more business than at any previous time in the Court's history. In 1798, the year in which Stowell came to the bench, the total number of causes tried in both Admiralty and Prize was 880; the following year's total was 1,470; and in the peak year of 1806 the number of causes totalled 2,286 and the Court sat for business for 115 court days—a quite heavy docket even by present-day standards.[3]

It was during Stowell's tenure as Judge that the Admiralty Court experienced the stirrings of renascence, which later grew to the statutory expansion of the instance jurisdiction. The reason regularly advanced for the Court's later growth is that Stowell's adjudications, particularly in Prize, raised the Court to a position of far greater importance than it had theretofore enjoyed.[4] This explanation seems so cogent upon its face, that it does not appear ever to have been questioned or even considered in any detail. Indeed, there can be no doubt whatever that the number of Prize causes and Stowell's Prize decisions both brought about a new public interest in the Court; but the Second Peace of Paris in 1815 ended all Prize adjudication until the outbreak of the Crimean War, and even before 1815 the total number of Admiralty and Prize causes had fallen below the number entertained during Stowell's first year as Judge, and the Court likewise sat for business for fewer days (880 causes and 54 court days in 1798; 813 causes and 51 court days in 1812).[5] Moreover, eighteen years were to elapse between the last of the Prize business and the first official

---

[1] See Roscoe, *Lord Stowell, etc.*
[2] Coote, 1st ed., preface, p. v.
[3] See 1833 Return to H.C. by Swabey, Deputy Admiralty Reg'r.
[4] See, *e.g.*, Roscoe, *Practice*, intro., p. 14.
[5] See 1833 Return to H.C. by Swabey, Deputy Admiralty Reg'r.

consideration of an expansion of the Admiralty jurisdiction by a Parliamentary Committee in 1833, and the number of instance causes before the Court actually declined during that period; in 1822 a total of 64 Admiralty causes came before the Court, which sat for business for 38 court days during that year; and in 1832, the year prior to the Committee's Report, the total number of Admiralty causes dwindled to 37, and the number of court days for business was only 28.[1] Clearly, it is fallacious to assert that the sole or even the principal reason for the recommendations of the 1833 Committee and the Court's later growth was an eminence enjoyed by the Court over twenty years previously, and largely in a jurisdiction unexercised since 1815.

There is no single reason for the Court's jurisdictional expansion after the time of Stowell, but there are at least a few factors which were contributory and which are also traceable to origin in the period of Stowell's judgeship:

(1) the rapid development of maritime commerce following the naval wars, and the beginning of the age of the steamship, both pointing to the need for a Court which could give really effective application to the maritime law;

(2) the increasing awareness of the advantages of a suit in Admiralty (*viz.*, choice of remedy *in rem* or *in personam*, equitable protection of interests, absence of jury, increasing use of truly summary procedure) as opposed to an action at common law;

(3) the willingness of the common law courts to permit Admiralty a greater jurisdictional latitude than it had enjoyed since prior to the time of Coke;

(4) the undoubted respect, both public and legal, which accrued to the Court from Lord Stowell's administration of the Laws of Admiralty and Prize;

(5) the friends of the Court in Parliament (*e.g.*: Lushington, Nicholl, Robinson, and Stowell himself), and the impetus given by the passage, from 1813 to 1825, of a number of Acts affecting the Court's jurisdiction, however slightly.

The first and last of the factors previously mentioned are those most easily proven and illustrated, if not also the most important.

[1] See 1833 Return to H.C. by Swabey, Deputy Admiralty Reg'r.

During the eighteenth century, the growth of maritime commerce and the protection of shipping during the naval wars, especially in the West Indian trade, produced a number of statutes giving jurisdiction to the Admiralty Court over matters such as wilful disobedience in convoy[1] and hiding mariners from Royal Navy press gangs,[2] though they made no substantial addition to the Court's business. There was, however, one statutory provision of immense significance for the future of both the Court and Law of Admiralty; it introduced, upon considerations of public policy, the principle of limitation of a shipowner's liability in cases of cargo loss—through negligence or by fire—to the value of the ship and freight.[3] This was followed, in 1813, by an Act[4] extending the principle to cover both loss and damage in causes of collision. In no case, however, was jurisdiction under these Acts given to the High Court of Admiralty; instead, Chancery was declared to have sole jurisdiction under the Acts[5] to award limitation to shipowners upon their claim, actions having been instituted against them for recovery of damages either at common law or in Admiralty.[6] It would seem probable that this jurisdiction was originally awarded to Chancery because of its ability to enjoin the prosecution of a multiplicity of suits in the other courts—a power most useful in implementing the limitation procedure, and a power which would never have been given to the Admiralty Court. That the Court of Chancery continued to be awarded jurisdiction in limitation Acts well into the latter half of the nineteenth century can probably be ascribed to the principle of 'legislative inertia', in which later statutes tend to follow an earlier established pattern. Nonetheless, limitation of liability came to have its effect, both direct and indirect, upon the Admiralty Court.[7]

In 1813 a period began during which a succession of statutory enactments conferred miscellaneous bits of jurisdiction upon the Admiralty Court. That year saw questions of salvage occurring between the low and high water marks, and questions of damage done by foreign vessels to British vessels or navigational aids in

---

[1] See Maxwell, p. 63.
[2] See *The Jack Park*, (1802) 4 C. Rob. 308, 313.
[3] See Roscoe, *Practice*, p. 232.   [4] Responsibility of Shipowners Act, ×1813.
[5] Responsibility of Shipowners Act, ×1813, §7.
[6] See, *e.g.*, *General Iron Screw Collier Co. v. Schurmanns*, (1860) 1 J. & H. 180.
[7] See *infra*, pp. 178–80.

any 'Harbour, Port, River or Creek', come within the Admiralty jurisdiction, concurrently with any of the Courts of Record at Westminster.[1] This was a particularly remarkable gain because it gave to Admiralty a territorial jurisdiction which had been explicitly forbidden to it by the statutes of Richard II,[2] and restored even the jurisdiction once wrested from Admiralty in *Sir Henry Constable's Case*;[3] even more, it placed the Admiralty Court, which was not officially a court of record[4] (even though it possessed virtually all of the attributes of such a court), upon an equal jurisdictional footing with the common law. In 1819 a statute permitting seamen to sue for wages before Justices of the Peace included a provision giving the Admiralty Court appellate jurisdiction in matters arising under the Act, with certain evidentiary requirements.[5] Further appellate jurisdiction, concurrent with the Admiralty Court of the Cinque Ports, was given in 1821 in cases of awards by the Cinque Ports Salvage Commissioners, together with concurrent jurisdiction to order the sale of salved property to satisfy such awards.[6] The Admiralty Judge was given the power of summary adjudication in claims for bounty money in putting down the slave trade by an Act of 1824.[7] And in 1825 an Act made the exercise of Admiralty jurisdiction in cases of restraint more easy of application, for unless the part-owner bringing suit in the Admiralty Court (to restrain his ship's departure on a proposed voyage until the majority owners gave a bond for her safe return) could prove the amount of his shares, only the Court of Chancery had power to enjoin the sailing pending security;[8] the Registry Act arbitrarily divided ownership of every registered British vessel into sixty-four shares and compelled entry of the number of sixty-fourth shares with each owner's name upon the back of every Certificate of Registry,[9] and also restricted the number of owners of any one registered vessel to a maximum of thirty-two.[10] Thereafter, the part-owner of any registered vessel wishing to sue in Admiralty for restraint needed

---

[1] Frauds by Boatmen, etc., Act,×1813, §§6, 7.
[2] See Admiralty Jurisdiction Acts,×1389, 1391.
[3] (1601) 5 Co. Rep. 106a; see *supra*, pp. 6, 8.
[4] A. Browne, vol. 2, p. 417.
[5] Wages of Merchant Seamen Act,×1819, §§1, 2.
[6] Cinque Ports Act, 1821, §§4, 20.
[7] Slave Trade Act, 1824, §28.   [8] Holt, pp. 204–5.
[9] Act for the Registering of British Vessels, 1825, §§32, 2.
[10] Act for the Registering of British Vessels, 1825, §33.

only to submit a Certificate of Registry in order to give the Court jurisdiction.

The personal regard of the legal profession for Lord Stowell was far from the only advantage which he gave to the Admiralty Court; more important were the decisions in which he effectively increased the Court's jurisdiction. Stowell's decision in *The Favourite*,[1] given only months after his appointment to the bench, brought international admiration; he held in that case that despite the maritime nature of a shipmaster's service, his claim for wages was (according to the course of earlier prohibitions) non-maritime and therefore actionable only at common law; but, by way of dictum, he upheld the ability of the master to sue 'surplus and remnants' [unclaimed proceeds] remaining in the Admiralty Registry after sale by the Court, permitting recovery upon such a wage claim by the master where the suit was uncontested.[2] The effect of this decision was to found, in certain cases, an Admiralty jurisdiction over non-maritime claims. Soon thereafter in the United States, where masters did not until 1968 enjoy a maritime lien for wages,[3] Stowell's dictum in *The Favourite* was relied upon to establish a similar Admiralty jurisdiction.[4] Materialmen [ship's suppliers and repairers] were another class who had no lien upon the ship, and a suit *in rem* by them in the Admiralty Court would have been prohibited; but in 1801, following his earlier line of reasoning, Stowell held that materialmen might sue any balance of proceeds in the Admiralty Registry.[5] And in the same year Stowell gave greater importance to the Court's jurisdiction in hypothecation, holding for the first time that, in cases of extreme necessity, the master might give a bond for the entire cargo[6] as well as the ship and freight.

In a number of decisions spanning his tenure as Judge, Stowell reaffirmed the special status of the mariner to sue in Admiralty; whether the suit was for wages,[7] upon personal injury occasioned by the cruel treatment dispensed by a commercial[8] or prize master,[9]

---

[1] (1799) 2 C. Rob. 232.　　　　　　　　　　[2] 2. C. Rob. 232, 239
[3] See Price, *L.M.L.*, p. 127; Gilmore and Black, §9–20, p. 512; 46 U.S.C. §606.
[4] *Gardner v. The New Jersey*, 9 Fed. Cas. 1192 (No. 5233) (D. Pa. 1806).
[5] *The John*, (1801) 3 C. Rob. 288, 289; see also Browne, vol. 2, p. 81.
[6] *The Gratitudine*, (1801) 3 C. Rob. 240.
[7] See, *e.g.*, *The Jane and Matilda*, (1823) 1 Hag. Adm. 187.
[8] See, *e.g.*, *The Agincourt*, (1824) 1 Hag. Adm. 271.
[9] See, *e.g.*, *Die Fire Damer*, (1805) 5 C. Rob. 357.

or for a host of other specific causes, the seaman was [and is] considered a 'ward' of Admiralty.[1] This was not only because of his 'thoughtless character and ignorance'[2] which was provided for by automatically setting aside any statement or document in which the seaman purported to forfeit any claim or remedy for the recovery of his wages,[3] but also because the mariner was 'apt to be choleric in temper, and . . . rash and violent in language and conduct.'[4] The Admiralty Court therefore acted *in loco parentis* toward the seaman, not only protecting, as above, but sanctioning chastisement as well.[5]

Stowell's decisions also affected the Court's procedure, as, for example, the warrant's effect upon tackle previously removed from the ship;[6] other decisions pertained to evidence, as in the proof of necessity to hypothecate in order to uphold a bottomry bond;[7] but Stowell's most telling decisions, as far as development of the Admiralty Court was concerned, were those regarding the Court's jurisdiction—and not all of those decisions had the effect of increasing the cognizance of Admiralty.[8]

Alone, Lord Stowell's decisions tending toward a greater Admiralty jurisdiction could have had no effect. The other vital element was a passiveness on the part of the common lawyers which permitted the enlargement of the jurisdiction rather than strangling it with prohibitions. The reasons for this tolerant attitude appear to be diverse; probably the principal and least complex reason was that when Stowell came to the bench the Admiralty Court had been semi-dormant for well over a century, and was no longer seen as a threat to the jurisdiction of the common law; conversely, the little jurisdiction then exercised by Admiralty was not coveted by the common lawyers. This seems to be borne out by Browne, who commented that, in his day, 'the same irrational jealousy of the admiralty doth not exist'.[9] Then too, having bitten off one particular piece of the Admiralty jurisdiction, the courts of common law had undergone a severe attack of indigestion;

---

[1] See *The Juliana*, (1822) 2 Dod. 504; see also *Ramsay v. Allegre*, 12 Wheat. (25 U.S.) 611 (1827).

[2] Mr Justice Johnson in *Ramsay v. Allegre*, 12 Wheat. (25 U.S.) 611, at 620.

[3] See *The Juliana, supra*, n. 1.   [4] Conkling, p. 312.

[5] See, *e.g.*, *The Lowther Castle*, (1825) 1 Hag. Adm. 384.

[6] See *The Alexander*, (1811) 1 Dod. 278.

[7] See *The Nelson*, (1823) 1 Hag. Adm. 169.

[8] See *The Portsea*, (1827) 2 Hag. Adm. 84.   [9] A. Browne, vol. 2, p. 81.

this occurred when the common lawyers extended the principle that no contracts made on land were cognizable in Admiralty to include contracts involving seamen's wages. These claims were usually heard summarily in the Admiralty Court, the proceedings being further expedited by a joinder of the entire crew of a given ship in a single action *in rem*;[1] but the common law courts could not proceed *in rem*, could not give summary relief, and could not join several plaintiffs in the same action;[2] the resulting chaos, with the overburdening of court dockets and delay of many voyages, forced the common lawyers to recant in humiliation, and the jurisdiction of Admiralty over suits for seamen's wages was finally admitted by the courts of common law.[3] Memories of that experience may have encouraged the common lawyers in Stowell's day to let sleeping dogs lie.

Certainly any apathy of the common law courts that may have been evident at the dawn of the nineteenth century did not serve to lull the wariness of the civilians (as they continued to warn of the dangers of placing contracts and stipulations under seal[4]), nor had the earlier forays upon the Admiralty jurisdiction been allowed to lapse from memory (as the common lawyers were freely criticized for previously applying a one-sided logic to the question of the proper contract jurisdiction in Admiralty).[5] In Stowell's time, however, the common lawyers even seemed willing to accept reasonable arguments for the extension of jurisdiction by Admiralty over rivers and harbours,[6] the previous restriction of which was still being denounced by the civilians as a 'greater mischief' than the seizure of the contract jurisdiction.[7]

It must also be submitted that Stowell's decisions, though they tended on the whole toward an enlargement of the Admiralty jurisdiction, probably created no apprehension amongst the common lawyers. Indeed, they had reason to feel content, for in some decisions Stowell more than gave the common law its due; thus in *The Rendsburg*,[8] he for the first time applied the common law doctrine of *quantum meruit* to contracts cognizable in Admiralty, and in *The Frances*, he established the principle that the Admiralty Court would decline to adjudicate questions within its jurisdiction

---

[1] See A. Browne, Vol. 2, p. 85; see also Maxwell, p. 8.
[2] See Maxwell, p. 8.   [3] A. Browne, vol. 2, p. 85.
[4] See *id.*, p. 96.   [5] *Id.*, p. 95.
[6] See Frauds by Boatmen, etc., Act,ˣ1813, §7.
[7] A. Browne, vol. 2, p. 93.   [8] (1805) 6 C. Rob. 142.

where the matter might be more directly dealt with by a court of common law;[1] and, perhaps less surprisingly, Stowell saw fit to apply common law maxims in the increasing number of cases requiring statutory interpretation—*e.g.*, '*de minimis non curat lex*', applied to a technical breach of the revenue laws.[2] It would seem, therefore, that it was not only the respect of the common lawyers for the wisdom and integrity of Stowell, but also their satisfaction that to some degree common law principles were being acknowledged and even applied in the Admiralty Court which, toward the end of Stowell's judgeship, enabled the observation that: 'if a party, having a good ground of prohibition, shall, nevertheless, suffer the cause to proceed to a judgment upon its merits in the Court of Admiralty, the courts of common law will not interfere afterwards . . .'[3]

At the same time that Lord Stowell pondered and decided upon the questions of English Admiralty jurisdiction, many of the same questions were under heated consideration on the western side of the Atlantic. Law which had become law in other nations and under other codes had been in force in the English Admiralty Court for centuries,[4] and, from its inception, the Admiralty jurisdiction in America had been similarly governed; but even in admitting this, it was necessary to admit that the Admiralty Law of the United States, having been transplanted largely from the British system of Vice-Admiralty courts in the colonies, was virtually identical, in most respects, to the Admiralty Law of England.[5] Thus it was held in one of the State Courts of Admiralty established after the Declaration of Independence that the statutes of Richard II governed in the Admiralty of the new Nation,[6] and during the period of government under the Articles of Confederation, some States even went so far as to enact 15 Ric. 2, c. 3, as domestic law.

Later, when the prime grant of Admiralty jurisdiction was written into the Constitution of the United States as an exclusively Federal matter,[7] there arose the question whether the Admiralty jurisdiction of the new Federal District Courts could be as broad as the Colonial Vice-Admiralty jurisdiction had become just prior

[1] (1820) 2 Dod. 420, 431–2. [2] See *The Reward*, (1818) 2 Dod. 265.
[3] Holt, pp. 289–90. [4] See A. Browne, vol. 2, p. 29.
[5] See Roberts, p. 1.
[6] *Clinton v. The Brig Hannah*, 5 Fed. Cas. 1056 (No. 2898) (Adm. Ct. Pa. 1781).
[7] Article III, §2, cl. 1.

to the Revolution. The issue was settled in the first Admiralty appeal to the Supreme Court of the United States,[1] in which it was held that each of the District Courts possessed all of the powers of any of the previous Vice-Admiralty Courts. Prohibitions could also issue from the Supreme Court to restrain the exercise of Admiralty jurisdiction by an overzealous District Judge,[2] but the power had to be used with extreme discretion until the many remaining jurisdictional questions had been resolved by the highest tribunal.

The men most responsible for evolving, through judicial consideration, the American Admiralty jurisprudence were Chief Justice John Marshall and Associate Justices Joseph Story and Bushrod Washington of the United States Supreme Court, Chancellor James Kent of New York, Judge Ashur Ware of the United States District Court for Maine, and (in a later era) Judge Addison Brown of the U.S. District Court for Southern New York.

It is Mr Justice Story, a contemporary of Lord Stowell, who was undoubtedly the greatest champion of Admiralty Law in the United States. Born in Marblehead, Massachusetts, in 1779, Story was precocious enough to gain a scholarship to Harvard College and take his degree at the age of nineteen; he studied law in Marblehead and Salem offices, and served as a Representative both in his State Legislature (1805–7) and in Congress (1808–9), then becoming Speaker of the Massachusetts House in 1811; he was appointed to the Supreme Court by President Madison in 1812 at the age of thirty-two, and served until his death in 1845; in 1829 he became Dane Professor of Law in Harvard University, a post which he also held until his death.[3] Story versed himself in the civil law, and was a practitioner of Admiralty before his appointment as Associate Justice; in Admiralty causes, therefore, it is not surprising that he outshone even the brilliant Marshall, who was fond of saying: '[B]rother Story here can give us the cases, from the Ten Tables down to the latest term-reports.'[4] Story's greatest effect upon the development of American Admiralty was not, however, as an Associate Justice of the Supreme Court, but as Circuit Justice for the First Judicial Circuit,

---

[1] *Glass v. The Sloop Betsey*, 3 Dall. (3 U.S.) 6, 15 (1794).
[2] *United States v. Peters*, 3 Dall. (3 U.S.) 121 (1795).
[3] *D.A.B.*; Dunne, p. 240 *et seq.*   [4] Dunne, p. 247.

comprising the New England States of Maine, New Hampshire, Massachusetts and Rhode Island. In this capacity Story sat as an appellate judge in the Circuit Court, which was intermediate between the District Courts in the Circuit and the Supreme Court of the United States; occasionally, even though a member of his nation's highest judicial tribunal, Story would have the opportunity as Circuit Justice to hear Admiralty causes at the instance level, sitting in relief for a District Judge. It is highly ironic that, like Lord Stowell, Story earned his great reputation as an adjudicator of Prize causes—during the War of 1812 he condemned English prizes in America while Stowell condemned American prizes in England.

The history of the Admiralty jurisdiction in England was vital knowledge to Story, to whom fell the task of defining the Admiralty jurisdiction in America; his learning in Admiralty was great, as was his respect for Stowell's decisions in his later years on the bench—both points being well illustrated by his judgment in *The Draco*.[1] His knowledge was put to excellent use; he began to lay the foundation of the American Admiralty jurisdiction in contract in *The Emulous*,[2] and he expanded upon it in his greatest decision, *DeLovio v. Boit*, which is to this day the keystone of Admiralty jurisprudence in America. The basic question in *DeLovio v. Boit*[3] was whether policies of marine insurance were cognizable in Admiralty as maritime contracts; though it had long been established in England that despite their maritime character policies of marine insurance were actionable only at common law,[4] Story reasoned that the adoption of the English common law by the United States did not import those decisions by the common law courts which had the effect of restraining Admiralty from the exercise of jurisdiction over truly maritime matters, and that, likewise, the Statutes of Richard II were of no force against the Constitution's grant of jurisdiction in 'all civil cases . . . admiralty and maritime'.[5] Not only is Story's opinion in *DeLovio* cited by modern English Admiralty textwriters for its historical exposition of the English Admiralty jurisdiction,[6] but, as will later be seen, it forms the basis of the English line of

[1] 7 Fed. Cas. 1032 (No. 4057) (C. C. Mass. 1835).
[2] 8 Fed. Cas. 697 (No. 4479) (C. C. Mass. 1813).
[3] 7 Fed. Cas. 418 (No. 3776) (C. C. Mass. 1815).
[4] See A. Browne, vol. 2, pp. 82–3.   [5] Article III, §2, cl. 1.
[6] See, *e.g.*, Roscoe, *Practice*, intro., p. 2, n. (*c*).

decision on the subject of maritime liens;[1] and, together with his later opinion in *The Nestor*,[2] Story's rationale in *DeLovio* gives the theory of actions *in rem* in United States Admiralty.

Judges whose courts or circuits were located in centres of maritime commerce followed Justice Story's lead in varying degrees, slowly extending the Admiralty jurisdiction in America to cognizance of matters which, though marine in origin, were yet viewed by some as subjects proper for adjudication only at common law. But there was one who had the opportunity to act, and also the greatest ability in and thirst for knowledge of civil and Admiralty law possessed by any American judge—Ashur Ware.

Ware was born in Sherburne, Massachusetts, in 1782. He took his degree at Harvard College in 1804, was appointed a tutor in 1807, and became Professor of Greek at Harvard in 1811. He resigned his chair in 1815 and thought to prepare for the ministry, but decided instead upon the bar and studied law in Cambridge offices. He soon became a political writer and speaker of great renown in New England, and was an agitator for the separation of Maine, then a District of Massachusetts; when the battle was won he became, in 1820, the first Secretary of State for the State of Maine. In 1822 he was appointed Judge of the United States District Court for Maine—an appointment roundly condemned as 'political' and unqualified—but his classical mastery of Roman Law and his scholarly learning in the civil law, when given an opportunity for expression in Admiralty causes, soon brought him national recognition as the foremost maritime legal authority, and his reports were published and cited accordingly. He enjoyed one of the longest judicial tenures in American history—44 years —and resigned from the bench in 1866. He died in 1873.[3] He is perhaps best remembered today not only for his great legal scholarship, but, like Dr Lushington, also for his unremitting efforts to better the lot of the ordinary seaman.

Of all Ware's great decisions, his most influential was probably *The Rebecca*,[4] in which he delivered the finest exposition of the history and jurisprudence of the principle of limitation of liability which exists in the English language.[5] It has been held by the

---

[1] See *infra*, pp. 156–7.   [2] 18 Fed. Cas. 9 (No. 10126) (C. C. Me. 1831).
[3] *D.A.B.*; *W.W.W.*; Talbot, pp. 409–13.
[4] 20 Fed. Cas. 373 (No. 11619) (D. Me. 1831).
[5] Discussed *infra*, p. 178.

Supreme Court to be the foundation of American Admiralty law in this regard,[1] and citation of *The Rebecca* is not uncommon in the present day.[2] But in virtually every maritime decision, Ware undertook to show the relationship between Admiralty and the civil law[3]; indeed, Ashur Ware was America's foremost civilian, characterized by Mr Justice Story as the 'ablest and most learned' mind of United States Admiralty.[4]

The early drift of U.S. Admiralty decisions was clearly toward expanded jurisdiction, illustrated by Judge Ware's holding in *Steele v. Thacher*[5] that a suit might be maintained in Admiralty for the wrongful abduction of a child by a shipmaster, the rationale being that a Court of Admiralty could award damages for any tort committed principally upon the sea. And because the judicial expansion of jurisdiction went much further in a shorter period of time than in England, the reaction of those who sensed a threat to the common law was also more swift; Justice William Johnson spoke for many in declaring: 'I think it high time to check this silent and stealing progress of the admiralty in acquiring jurisdiction to which it has no pretensions.'[6] This particular statement so provoked Dr Henry Wheaton, Reporter of the Supreme Court of the United States, that he resorted to the unusual device of a long note following his report of the case, in which he undertook to rebut Johnson's opinion.[7] While it was perhaps the last public expression of that blunt view—essentially the same as that of Coke—the words of Mr Justice Johnson were a clear warning that the old enmity could be prodded into awareness once again.

With the great similarity between English and American Admiralty Law, and the early establishment of reciprocity in the enforcement of Admiralty judgments,[8] it soon became common for reasoning and precedents established in one country to be cited as authority in the other, and the balance seems, probably because of the greater number and variety of decisions, to have gone to the use of American authority in England. Not only were

---

[1] *Norwich Company v. Wright*, 13 Wall. (80 U.S.) 104, 116 (1871).
[2] *In re. Independent Towing Company*, 242 F. Supp. 950, 951 (E.D. La. 1965).
[3] See, *e.g.*, *Lane v. Townsend*, 14 Fed. Cas. 1087 (No. 8054) (D. Me. 1835).
[4] Talbot, p. 418.   [5] 22 Fed. Cas. 1204 (No. 13348) (D. Me. 1825).
[6] *Ramsay v. Allegre*, 12 Wheat. (25 U.S.) 611, 614 (1827).
[7] *Id.*, at pp. 640–3.
[8] See *Penhallow v. Doane's Administrators*, 3 Dall. (3 U.S.) 54 (1795).

American opinions heavily cited judicially,[1] but occasionally it also appeared that an argument presented to the Admiralty Court was almost entirely grounded upon American precedent.[2] In the matter of authority common to both lands, one visible pattern soon emerged as a permanent feature; there can be no stronger support for any original proposition in Admiralty than a joint citation of Stowell and Story in agreement, whether by counsel or by other great Admiralty judges, such as Ware[3] and Lushington.[4]

With a reputation which took firm root in Admiralty Law the world over, it is little wonder that Lord Stowell has come to be regarded as the greatest of the judges of the English Court of Admiralty; yet it is not entirely superfluous to examine reasons for that reputation, and to look at a few decisions which tell something of the man himself.

In fairness to his several illustrious predecessors, it must be pointed out that the availability of these decisions to the profession at large gave Stowell a tremendous advantage, for the first regular reports of causes determined in the Admiralty Court— Sir Christopher Robinson's—commence with Stowell's accession to the bench. As Chancellor Kent observed: 'The English maritime law can now be studied in the adjudged cases, with at least as much profit, and with vastly more pleasure, than in the dry and formal didactic treatises and ordinances professedly devoted to the science.'[5]

The names of Zouche, Jenkins, Dunn, Hedges, Penrice, and even (despite the labour of Marsden) Lewes and Caesar would undoubtedly have been enhanced by the transcription of their judgments in a regular series of reports. It would be dangerous, however, to place too heavy an emphasis upon the mere existence of reports of Stowell's decisions, for the quality of reporting in that day could and did vary; an edition, published in 1801, of Admiralty reports for the years 1776–9 was later held 'not executed in a satisfactory manner',[6] and even in the latter half of the nineteenth century, when a precedent was offered, it became necessary

---

[1] See, e.g., R. v. Keyn, (1876) 2 Ex. D. 63 [C.C.R.].

[2] See, e.g., argument of Gainsford Bruce in The Alexandria, (1872) L.R. 3 A. & E. 574, 577–9.

[3] See, e.g., Polydore v. Prince, 19 Fed. Cas. 950 [1 Ware 411] (No. 11257) (D. Me. 1837).

[4] See, e.g., The Fusilier, (1865) Br. & Lush. 341, 347.

[5] 3 Kent, p. 19.   [6] Reddie, vol. 1, intro., p. viii.

to estimate which of two earlier reports of the case concerned was the more accurate.[1] It is possible, therefore, that Stowell had a good deal to overcome as well as a great deal to gain from the publication of the Admiralty reports.

If Lord Stowell did have a chronic shortcoming as Admiralty Judge, it was perhaps a most understandable one: an intense fear of prohibition, which restrained him frequently from exercising jurisdiction over causes which could very reasonably be argued to have been within the legitimate compass of Admiralty. It cannot fail to strike the reader of many of Stowell's judgments how frequently he referred to the possibility of prohibition if he should allow the cause to proceed. The remarkable result of this phobia was that Stowell was never once prohibited in his entire judgeship;[2] and, in at least one instance, he candidly admitted fear of prohibition as a factor in his decision to refuse to entertain a suit in the Admiralty Court.[3] If this seems a new and isolated criticism of Stowell, it can be said that a similar observation was made in even stronger terms by no less an authority than Dr Lushington, who commented in the course of his judgment in *The Milford* that: 'Lord Stowell always stood in awe of a prohibition, and therefore, as I think, was too abstinent in taking any step which might, by possibility, expose him to such interference.'[4]

It was in considering the jurisdiction of the Admiralty Court to entertain claims by foreign suitors that Dr Lushington made the remark quoted above; and it is certainly true, whether from fear of prohibition or for less obvious reasons, that Lord Stowell showed a particular reluctance to entertain foreign claims, and especially so where both parties to the suit were foreign.[5] At a time in later years when American Courts of Admiralty were in the process of establishing a more open jurisdiction over suits between foreign parties,[6] the earlier decisions of Lord Stowell in this area were viewed with regret; but it is probable that American judges still harboured some bitterness at decisions of Stowell which dealt with the claims of American seamen in the

[1] See remarks of Sir R. Phillimore *re The Volant* in *The St. Olaf*, (1869) L.R. 2 A. & E. 360.

[2] See Advocate's argument in *The Neptune*, (1835) 3 Kn P.C. 94, 106.

[3] *The Courtney*, (1810) Edw. Adm. 239, 241.

[4] (1858) Swab. 362, 366.

[5] See, *e.g.*, *The Two Friends*, (1799) 1 C. Rob. 271, 280.

[6] See, *e.g.*, *The Bee*, 3 Fed. Cas. 41 (No. 1219) (D. Me., 1836).

High Court of Admiralty of England—indeed an American textwriter commented upon two particular cases[1] (decided at a time of great political tension between the two nations), in one of which Stowell refused to grant a wage recovery in accordance with the terms of a United States statute, while permitting a wage recovery in the other for a transaction illegal under the laws of the United States.[2]

It is also possible that Admiralty Courts in the great ports of northeastern America were adversely influenced by some of Stowell's decision involving the difficult problem of the slave trade; whether decisions in this area were especially agonizing for Lord Stowell it is impossible to say, but it is unfortunately true that in at least one case his decision on the law permitted a salved slaver to carry on her trade without arrest,[3] and that in another his decision was a strange precursor to that of Chief Justice Roger Taney in the case of Dred Scott, holding that a female slave—appraised value £125—had not become free by reason of her residence in a non-slavery territory, and that: 'no injury is done her by her continuance in a state of slavery . . .'[4] When Story rendered his great decision against the slave trade in *La Jeune Eugenie*,[5] his greatest and most painful difficulty, after a lengthy analysis, was the necessity of departing from Stowell's slave trade decisions.

Stowell was likewise prone to the prejudice of his time against working women, describing the wages suit of a lady seacook as 'a claim, which I have no particular wish to encourage, for man's work done by a female . . .'[6] Yet this same judgment, in *The Jane and Matilda*, is wonderfully illustrative of the qualities that made Stowell a truly great judge: his scholarship in the Law of Admiralty; his warm wit, especially present in a case with humorous aspects; and his wisdom in balancing the interests, often diverse, represented in each cause. If he evinced certain shortcomings, they were of the fundamentally human kind, and characterized the time as well as the man. Over all must stand his achievements

[1] *The Courtney*, (1810) Edw. Adm. 239.
   The Maria Theresa, (1813) 1 Dod. 303.
[2] Conkling, pp. 29–30, 31.
[3] *The Trelawney*, (1801) 3 C. Rob. 216n.
[4] *The Slave*, GRACE, (1827) 2 Hag. Adm. 94, 100.
[5] 26 Fed. Cas. 832 (No. 15551) (C. C. Mass. 1822).
[6] *The Jane and Matilda*, (1823) 1 Hag. Adm. 187, 188.

as the architect of the modern Laws of Prize and Salvage,[1] as a champion of the equitable powers of Admiralty,[2] and as a man of dedication and endurance, who during his last years on the bench was so weak in sight and voice that he had to have Dr Dodson or Sir Christopher Robinson read his judgments aloud in Court.[3] It is uniquely fitting that the greatest tribute paid to Stowell in his lifetime should have come from a letter written to him by the man perhaps best qualified of any then living to assess his contribution to the world of law, Mr Justice Story: 'In the excitement caused by the hostilities then raging between our countries, I frequently impugned your judgments . . . , but on a calm review of your decisions after a lapse of years . . . I have taken care that they shall form the basis of the maritime law of the United States . . .'[4] And so from the retrospective vantage of the present day, it is not difficult to agree with Holdsworth that 'The greatest of all the civilians in the whole history of English law is William Scott, Lord Stowell.'[5]

Upon the retirement of Lord Stowell, Sir Christopher Robinson became the Admiralty Judge. Robinson was born in 1766, and attended University and Magdalen Colleges, Oxford, graduating D.C.L. in 1796; in that same year he became a Fellow of Doctors' Commons; he was the first regular reporter of cases in the High Court of Admiralty (from 1798 until 1808), and a sometime Member of Parliament; he became King's Advocate in 1809, and served as Judge of the Admiralty Court from 1828 until his death in 1833.[6]

This five-year period in the Court's history was a completely tranquil one, business being solely limited to instance matters, and there being very little of it at all.[7] The jurisdiction and practice of the Court remained static, though quite inexplicably a new edition of a long-outdated treatise, the *Praxis Supremae Curiae Admiralitatis*, was published in 1829. This book, usually known as *Clerke's Praxis*, reflected the Admiralty practice and procedure which basically obtained in the Court during the Elizabethan era; the 1829 edition was merely a reprint of one published in the

---

[1] See Roscoe, *Practice*, pp. 127–8.
[2] See *The Minerva*, (1825) 1 Hag. Adm. 347.
[3] *D.N.B.*
[4] Reproduced in Holdsworth, *H.E.L.*, vol. 13, p. 679.
[5] *Id.*, p. 668.   [6] *Id.*, pp. 689–91; *D.N.B.*
[7] See *supra*, p. 21.

previous century, and, taking no account of the intervening change in emphasis from the proceeding *in personam* to that *in rem*, was wholly inferior to the edition of Dr Browne's work published in 1802.

Near the end of Robinson's office as Admiralty Judge, there was an alteration in the appellate structure of the civil law. The powers of the High Court of Delegates, which hitherto had heard all Admiralty and Ecclesiastical appeals, were transferred to the Privy Council,[1] and a Judicial Committee of the Privy Council was created to take cognizance of future appeals, including those from the Vice-Admiralty courts abroad, which had previously been taken to the High Court of Admiralty.[2] In terms of efficiency a change was certainly justified, for a separate commission had previously been required for each of these appeals 'to the King in Chancery', appointing *iudices delegati*—thus requiring, technically, a complete reconstitution of the Court of Delegates for each case brought before it.[3]

Appellate procedure, however, was basically unchanged; appeal lay from the Court of Admiralty only upon a definitive sentence[4] [final judgment] or a 'grievance' [material error], and the appeal was required to be specifically drawn in the latter case, whereas it might be asked *viva voce* in the former.[5] Appeal had to be interposed within ten days of the error, and immediately upon the sentence if asked orally, otherwise in writing within ten days.[6] The appellant was required to give fresh security for the appeal, whereupon he prayed and was granted apostles [the instance record], with a date set by which he had to retrocertify to the Judge the steps taken to prosecute the appeal, failing which the sentence would be executed.[7] With the transfer of appellate jurisdiction from the Court of Delegates to the Privy Council, the apostles were no longer sent to the Lord Chancellor for inscription and commissioning of delegates, as formerly.[8] The cause then proceeded summarily, with an inhibition of lower proceedings and a citation to the defence, an appellatory libel and answer, perusal of the apostles, hearing and sentence.[9] It should be noted

---

[1] Privy Council Appeals Act, 1832, §3.
[2] Judicial Committee Act, 1833, §§1, 2.
[3] See A. Browne, vol. 2, p. 29; Senior, p. 52.
[4] A. Browne, vol. 2, p. 435; also Admiralty Court Act, 1840, §17.
[5] See A. Browne, vol. 2, pp. 435–6.   [6] *Id.*, p. 436.
[7] *Id.*, pp. 437–8.   [8] *Id.*, pp. 438–9.   [9] *Id.*, pp. 439–41.

that appeals in Admiralty were and are technically trials *de novo*, in that new evidence may be received; but a decision based upon the legitimate discretion of the instance Judge will not generally be altered by the appellate court,[1] a rule preserved in the United States as well.[2]

Sir Christopher Robinson, and his successor, Sir John Nicholl, had equally short tenures as Admiralty Judge; because of the low ebb of business in the Court under Robinson, however, his judgeship is more difficult to evaluate. The inevitable impression is that his legal thought was dominated by Stowell, with whom he had been closely associated throughout the latter's judicial career; this is not to say that Robinson was not a skilled civilian, or incapable of original thought—his judgment in the case of *The Calypso*,[3] with its fine exposition of the history of salvage, shows the opposite. But Robinson never deviated from the pattern of Stowell's decision, nor did he establish any important new principles in Admiralty Law, though, ironically, his surrogate did establish the award of salvage to captors of royal fish.[4] In fairness, it must be added that Robinson was denied the vehicle which chiefly brought Stowell to greatness, in that there were no Prize causes before the Court during his judgeship; he is, nonetheless, perhaps best viewed as an adequate Admiralty Judge, unblessed with the brilliance of his predecessor.

Sir John Nicholl was born in 1759; he was educated at and became a Fellow of St John's College, Oxford, graduating D.C.L. in 1785, and was admitted to Doctors' Commons in the same year; he served in Parliament from 1802 to 1832, and was notable for his opposition to Roman Catholic emancipation; he succeeded Stowell as King's Advocate in 1798, becoming Admiralty Judge upon Robinson's death in 1833 and holding office until his own death in 1838; he was also the first Admiralty Judge of the nineteenth century to be Dean of the Arches Court, a post which he held from 1809 until 1834.[5]

---

[1] See *The Clarisse*, (1856) Swab. 129, 134 [P.C.]; but *cf. The Almizar*, [1970] 1 L1 Rep. 67 [App.].

[2] See *Yeaton v. United States*, 5 Cranch (9 U.S.) 281, 283 (1809); and, *cf. McAllister v. United States*, 348 U.S 19 (1954).

[3] (1828) 2 Hag. Adm. 209, esp. pp. 217–18.

[4] Dr Phillimore, in *Lord Warden of Cinque Ports v. The King in his Office of Admiralty &c.*, (1831) 2 Hag. Adm. 438.

[5] Holdsworth, *H.E.L.*, vol. 13, pp. 691–6; *D.N.B.*

One of Nicholl's first tasks as Admiralty Judge was to give testimony before a select committee of the House of Commons which had been appointed to evaluate the usefulness of the Admiralty Court and to make recommendations for its improvement. Other principal witnesses included Sir Herbert Jenner, Dr Lushington, and H. B. Swabey, the Deputy Admiralty Registrar. As might be expected, testimony by the civilians ran to complaints of the imperfections in the Court's jurisdiction and recommendations that the jurisdiction given to the Judge by his patent—*super altum mare*—and in all rivers up to the first bridge within the range of tidal flux—be realized, and that the Court be given cognizance of legal title, ship mortgages, charter-parties, average, etc.[1] More surprisingly, the testimony of common lawyers who appeared as witnesses was generally in support of that of the civilians, and Sir Nicholas Tindal, Lord Chief Justice of the Common Pleas, was among those who advocated an enlargement of the jurisdiction of the Admiralty Court.[2] The Committee's final recommendations were, concerning the Court's jurisdiction, a great triumph for the civilians; they were also most portentous for the future of the civil law in England, as will later be seen.

It may be fairly said that Nicholl was a stronger Judge than his immediate predecessor; though a close associate of Stowell's over an even longer period than Robinson, Nicholl seems to have been more inspired than dominated by that relationship. He had a sense of the prerogative power, particularly in pronouncing contempt,[3] and was never hesitant in exercising the Admiralty jurisdiction over maritime claims, though, as in *The Neptune*,[4] where he claimed the existence of a maritime lien for materialmen upon the proceeds of an action *in rem* despite the lack of such a lien on the *res*, he occasionally suffered reversal by the Judicial Committee.

It fell to Nicholl to render the classic and definitive judgments upon the Admiralty jurisdiction of droits; in the course of one incredibly complicated case, *R. v. Forty-Nine Casks of Brandy*,[5] he was required to make a determination upon each of the items according to its topographic position at recovery; his holding was

---

[1] See, *e.g.*, testimony of Wm. Fox, Proctor in Admiralty, in Parliamentary Paper [1833] (670) vii. (H.C. 15 August), p. 68.

[2] See Parl. Paper [1833] (670) vii. (H.C. 15 August), p. 135.

[3] See, *e.g.*, *Wyllie v. Mott & French*, (1827) 1 Hag. Ecc. 28 [Arches].

[4] (1834) 3 Hag. Adm. 129; *rev'd*, 3 Kn. P.C. 94.   [5] (1836) 3 Hag. Adm. 257.

that those casks picked up on the high seas, those found beyond low water, and those found floating on the ebb tide above the low-water mark—never having bottomed—were properly droits of Admiralty, whereas those bobbing on the ebb tide and occasionally striking bottom, and those grounded on the ebb tide, though not necessarily high-and-dry, were wreck within the right of the lord of the manor. But Nicholl himself effectively overruled this last proposition in the subsequent case of *R. v. Two Casks of Tallow*, where he said: 'I cannot agree . . . that things having once touched the ground thereby necessarily become the property of the lord of the manor'[1]—a decision which later enabled Dr Lushington to hold that in the case of a vessel stranded on the ebb tide and seized by the bailiff for the lord of the manor, but retaken on the flood tide and condemned as droits of Admiralty, the lord of the manor had no claim upon the proceeds of the sale of the vessel in Admiralty.[2]

Two of Nicholl's decisions were of particular importance to the later development of the substantive Law of Admiralty; in one of these cases he pioneered the right-of-way of sailing vessels over steamships,[3] a principle today enshrined in the International Rules of the Nautical Road[4] and applied by Admiralty Courts the world over. In the other case, Nicholl held for the first time that judgment in an action *in rem* might be decreed and enforced in excess of the value of the *res*;[5] the subsequent impact of this decision has been very considerable,[6] and it is greatly to be regretted that Nicholl neither cited authority nor gave reasoning in its support.

The death of Sir John Nicholl saw an end to the era of Lord Stowell's direct influence upon the development of the English Court of Admiralty; through Sir Christopher Robinson, whom he outlived, Stowell's personal influence was transmitted after the termination of his own service upon the bench; through Nicholl, though in lesser degree, Stowell's personal influence survived his own death.

The era of Stowell had seen the laying of a foundation—the next would see both construction and collapse.

---

[1] (1837) 3 Hag. Adm. 294, 298–9.   [2] *The Pauline*, (1845) 2 W. Rob. 358.
[3] *The Perth*, (1838) 3 Hag. Adm. 414.
[4] See 1960 International Rules, Rule 20(a).
[5] *The Triune*, (1834) 3 Hag. Adm. 114.   [6] See *infra*, pp. 171–2, 180.

CHAPTER 2

THE COURT RESURGENT

As the Admiralty Court in the era of Lord Stowell had awakened from a slumber of centuries, so it was that during the tenure of another eminent civilian, Dr Stephen Lushington, any lethargy of arousal gave way to a quick pulse of vitality.

Lushington, born in 1782, was educated at Eton and Oxford, where he attended Christ Church and became a Fellow of All Souls in 1802; he was called to the bar by the Inner Temple in 1806, and received his D.C.L. in 1808, becoming a member of Doctors' Commons in that same year. He was a Whig Member of Parliament from 1806 to 1808 and from 1820 to 1841, where his liberality in advocating the abolition of capital punishment, his opposition to the repression of Ireland and his vehemence against slavery earned for him a measure of notoriety. He succeeded Sir Christopher Robinson as Judge of the Consistory Court of London in 1828, succeeded Sir John Nicholl as Judge of the High Court of Admiralty in 1838, and became Dean of Arches and Master of the Faculties in 1858; he resigned as Admiralty Judge and Dean of Arches in 1867, but continued to hold the Mastership of the Faculties until his death in 1873.[1]

During the judgeship of Sir John Nicholl, the 1833 Report from the Select Parliamentary Committee lay unacted upon; but Lushington was determined to secure legislation which would implement the recommendations of 1833 for a wider Admiralty jurisdiction. As a Member of Parliament himself, Lushington was well-placed to spur the desired activity, and, in 1840, an Act was passed which effectively abolished the restrictions of the Acts of Richard II and confirmed and extended the Court's general jurisdiction, but which, despite the favourable and explicit recommendations of the select committee, did not restore to the Court the anciently profitable jurisdiction over all questions of contract, freight, and charter-party.[2] New jurisdiction conferred by the 1840 Act included cognizance of mortgages on ships

---

[1] Holdsworth, *H.E.L.*, vol. 16, pp. 140–6; *D.N.B.*
[2] Marsden, 'Six Centuries', p. 175.

incidental to actions *in rem*, questions of legal title and the division of proceeds of sale in suits of possession, and any 'claims in the nature of salvage' for services and necessaries[1]—all as recommended in the 1833 Report[2]—as well as claims for towage (a service reduced from the status of salvage by the advent of steam propulsion[3]) and such questions of 'Booty of War'[4] as might be submitted to the Admiralty Court by the Privy Council. It was made plain upon the face of the Act, however, that none of the jurisdiction thus conferred was exclusive, but concurrent with that of the courts of law and equity.[5]

One particularly curious provision of the 1840 Act was the inclusion of a discretionary power by which the Court might direct a jury trial of issues of fact to be held at common law, the power to grant a retrial of such issues if necessary—itself an appealable matter—and certification of the trial record up to the Admiralty Judge, together with any bill of exceptions.[6] This provision can only have been an attempt by the common lawyers to introduce the jury trial into Admiralty, and was probably taken from a recommendation in the 1833 Report[7] which, however, suggested a power of impanelling a jury of *merchants* [mercantile assessors, as are used in the continental civil law] at the discretion of the Judge or option of the parties. Such a trial would have taken place before some judge of assize or of a superior court,[8] but only one case has appeared in which such a jury was in fact impanelled,[9] and the function of the jury in that case is not known.

As fate would have it, the price paid by Dr Lushington to secure passage of the 1840 Act was both high and personal. In 1820 Lushington had appeared with Brougham, at the latter's request, as counsel for the defence of Queen Caroline in her trial upon a charge of adultery; the defence was eminently successful, the proceedings were halted, and the brilliant performance of Lushington, among others, marked him for future achievement.[10]

---

[1] Admiralty Court Act, 1840, §§3, 4, 6.
[2] Parl. Paper [1833] (670) vii (H.C. 15 August), p. 4.
[3] Roscoe, *Practice*, p. 187.
[4] Admiralty Court Act, 1840, §22.
[5] Admiralty Court Act, 1840, §23.   [6] Admiralty Court Act, 1840, §§11–16.
[7] Parl. Paper [1833] (670) vii (H.C. 15 August), p. 4.
[8] See Coote, 1st ed., p. 58.
[9] *Schroeder, Gebrüder & Co. v. Myers & Co.*, (1886) [unrep.], cited by Pritchard and Hannen, intro., p. vii.
[10] See Holdsworth, *H.E.L.*, vol. 16, pp. 140–6; *D.N.B.*

But by 1840 Lord Brougham, a rebellious Whig and a bitter political foe of the Whig Government of Lord Melbourne, had fallen out with Lushington, one of its strongest supporters in the Commons.[1] When the bill for the 1840 Act was introduced, Brougham vowed to kill it in the Lords unless a clause was inserted which would specifically disqualify the Admiralty Judge from sitting in Parliament.[2] Though a tremendous political hassle followed, Brougham was triumphant, and in a separate but simultaneous enactment it was provided that no person holding the office of Admiralty Judge should be eligible to be elected to or sit in any future Parliament;[3] this must have been a considerable blow to Lushington, for each of his predecessors as Judge in that century had been Members of Parliament, and Stowell held his seat during nearly all of his tenure, relinquishing it only upon his elevation to the peerage.

There was, however, some compensation for the loss of Lushington's seat in Parliament; the remuneration of the Admiralty Judge had hitherto been based upon fees collected by the Court, and despite the great decline in the Court's business, these fees had been adjusted only once since the conclusion of the Prize adjudications;[4] thus the same section of the 1840 Fees Act which disqualified the Judge from a Parliamentary seat also established a salary for the Judgeship of four thousand pounds *per annum*, to be paid out of the Consolidated Fund if not met by the Court fees, any surplus in fees thereafter being consigned to the Consolidated Fund in return.[5]

Aside from the clear extension of jurisdiction in §6 of the 1840 Act, it was unclear for some time following its passage what the effect of its other provisions would be. The language of §4, giving the Court jurisdiction of 'all questions' of salvage and damage was eventually held to apply to such causes arising in *any* locality, if involving a seagoing vessel,[6] but it was held that the same language applied to causes of title, also included in §4, would not permit the Court to entertain a suit for title to freight where no ancillary question was justiciable as well;[7] and it was said that

---

[1] See Merriman, P., *Address to the Canadian Bar Association*.
[2] See Campbell, pp. 503–4.   [3] High Court of Admiralty [Fees] Act,ˣ1840, §1.
[4] See Parl. Paper [1833] (670) vii (H.C. 15 August), p. 60.
[5] High Court of Admiralty [Fees] Act, ˣ1840, §1.
[6] See Edwards, pp. 151, 188–9.
[7] *The Fortitude*, (1843) 2 W. Rob. 217; 2 Not. Cas. 515.

only legal title was determinable under the same section,[1] though the Court had previously considered equitable titles, and even legal titles, to the extent of ensuring that such titles were not sham, and set up merely to defeat the Court's jurisdiction.[2] But the general rule-of-thumb for interpretation of the 1840 Act was laid down by Dr Lushington in *The Fortitude* as follows: '[The Act] was not, I apprehend, intended to confer any new separate and distinct powers on this Court, but merely to enable the Court to exercise its ordinary jurisdiction to the full extent.'[3]

There was not to be another direct statutory revision of the Admiralty jurisdiction for twenty-one years following the 1840 Act, but other enactments during that period did affect the Court's scope of activity in several ways. A segment of the Court's ancient jurisdiction disappeared in 1846 with the abolition of deodands,[4] but in the succeeding year the Court gained a new jurisdiction over all questions arising under an Act for the improvement of port facilities.[5] Jurisdiction to adjudge piracy for the purposes of awarding bounty and condemning pirates' goods was given in 1850,[6] and some almost incredible claims came before the Court in pursuance thereof.[7]

Throughout the history of the Admiralty Court there occur periods in which the position taken regarding a particular exercise of jurisdiction shifts rapidly across the judicial spectrum; one such perplexing matter was that of the jurisdiction of the Court to entertain a claim for the salvage [saving] of life in the absence of the salvage of property, as complicated by statutory enactments. Lord Stowell made the position clear in his judgeship, acknowledging that: 'The mere preservation of life, it is true, this Court has no power of remunerating . . .',[8] and this was the view taken by Dr Lushington in 1842.[9] In 1846, however, an Act was passed which, in the plainest language, appeared to authorize salvage recovery for the saving of life alone;[10] a leading textwriter then interpreted the Act as only prompting the Court's earnest consideration of a high award where life and property were saved,

---

[1] Edwards, p. 50.   [2] See *The Warrior*, (1818) 2 Dod. 288.
[3] Quoted by Edwards, at p. 49.   [4] [Abolition of] Deodands Act, ×1846.
[5] Harbours, Docks & Piers Clauses Act, 1847.   [6] Piracy Act, 1850, §§2, 5.
[7] See especially *The Magellan Pirates*, (1853) 1 Sp. 81.
[8] *The Aid*, (1822) 1 Hag. Adm. 83, 84.
[9] *The Zephyrus*, (1842) 1 W. Rob. 329, 331.
[10] Wreck and Salvage Act, ×1846, §19.

rather than giving a new recovery[1] for the salvage of life alone. In 1854 Dr Lushington awarded a substantial sum for life salvage under the Act of 1846 in a case in which very valuable property was also salved, but he observed that the 1846 Act was specifically worded to permit recovery for life salvage;[2] in the same year as that decision, another statute[3] gave a recovery for life salvage in much the same terms as the 1846 Act, which was thereupon repealed.[4] In 1865, however, Dr Lushington considered the history of life salvage awards in Admiralty and concluded that prior to 1854, there could have been no award for life salvage apart from the salvage of property.[5] It is therefore impossible to state with certainty that the Admiralty Court acquired jurisdiction to grant awards for the salvage of life alone under the Act of 1846, though the plain language of the statute would seem to have given that jurisdiction.

The Merchant Shipping Act of 1854 was the first comprehensive enactment concerning the Merchant Navy; its most important administrative feature was the transfer of superintendence of the Merchant Navy from the Admiralty to the Board of Trade,[6] and the Receiver General of Droits of Admiralty and all other receivers of droits were also placed under the control of the Board of Trade in the same year.[7]

One of the most pressing concerns of the day, reflected in the 1854 M.S.A., was the need for protection of the merchant seaman. He earned little enough to begin with, was expected to undergo the deprivations of long voyages, and was subject not only to the hazards of the elements, but also that of the Royal Navy press gangs—and the statutory penalty for merely cursing his fate could be two hours in the stocks.[8] Worse still, perhaps, was the degree of physical mistreatment, not only at the hands of their captors,[9] but by their own shipmasters.[10] Suits by mariners for such malicious personal injury occasionally came before the Admiralty Court,

[1] Edwards, pp. 195–6; see also pp. 193–4.
[2] [*Ten Bars of*] *Silver Bullion*, (1854) 2 Sp. 70.
[3] Merchant Shipping Act, 1854, Part 8.
[4] Merchant Shipping Repeal Act, 1854, §4.
[5] *The Fusilier*, (1865) Br. & Lush. 341, 344.
[6] Merchant Shipping Act, 1854, Part 1.
[7] Merchant Shipping Repeal Act, 1854, §§10, 11.
[8] See Maxwell, pp. 541–2.
[9] See, *e.g.*, *Die Fire Damer*, (1805) 5 C. Rob. 357.
[10] See, *e.g.*, *The Agincourt*, (1824) 1 Hag. Adm. 271.

and damages were occasionally awarded; but at that time any master might lawfully order a seaman to be flogged, needing only to show, upon complaint by the crew, that his order was reasonable under the circumstances.[1] It is a grave social commentary simply to note that in *The Lowther Castle* Lord Stowell held that a flogging of thirty-six lashes after five days in irons was a 'justified' punishment for a seaman whose sole offence was said to be 'laziness and disrespect'.[2]

It seems incredible in the present day that the civilized societies of Britain and America could for so long have remained indifferent to that wretched human condition; what eventually spurred authority to move against such brutalities was the public outcry raised in response to publication of the facts by such men as Dr Richard Henry Dana of Boston, an Admiralty lawyer who published both in the United States and England a narrative of his voyage around Cape Horn in 1834 as an ordinary seaman in the brig *Pilgrim*; the true account of the normal treatment of crewmen in Dana's *Two Years Before the Mast* surely must have made grim reading even in that day. But there was a touch of irony in this needed reform, for under the 1840 Act the Admiralty Court lost jurisdiction over claims for personal injury save in causes arising upon the high seas, inasmuch as §6 of the Act was interpreted to apply only to property damage.[3]

If the physical abuse of the merchant seaman was deplorable, the advantage taken of him in more insidious ways may have been worse yet. Seamen were considered fair game for cheating of the basest sort, and their chief defender, the Admiralty Court, was not always perfectly assiduous in the discharge of its duty to its 'wards'.[4] It can be said, however, that the Court was in general quite successful in exercising its equitable jurisdiction to uphold mariners' wage claims despite agreements which were designed to frustrate them in contravention of the general maritime law.[5] By comparison, the same claims fared very poorly at common law, and it was necessary to secure enactment in 1835 of provisions which guaranteed the inviolability of the seaman's wage claim in an action at law, and which encouraged mariners to bring their

[1] Abbott, p. 240.
[2] (1825) 1 Hag. Adm. 384.
[3] See Edwards, p. 155.
[4] See, *e.g.*, *William [Moakes's] Money*, (1827) 2 Hag. Adm. 136.
[5] See Edwards, pp. 138-9.

actions for wages in the common law courts rather than in Admiralty;[1] a re-enactment of the same basic provisions in 1844 provided more explicit guidelines for relief, and also transferred the great bulk of wage claims to the common law courts by establishing twenty pounds as the minimum limit of a claim for wages to be suable in Admiralty, unless the shipowner had been declared a bankrupt.[2] The 1854 M.S.A. sought to relieve even further the burden which these suits for wages placed upon the Admiralty Court by giving cognizance of such claims to any two Justices of the Peace, and raising the minimum claim limit for Admiralty jurisdiction to fifty pounds, though waiving the limit in cases of the owner's bankruptcy, or where the ship had been arrested and sold in Admiralty, or where neither the owner nor master resided within twenty miles of the place where the claimants were discharged or put ashore.[3]

Certain other miscellaneous provisions of the 1854 Merchant Shipping Act are worthy of note: masters were for the first time given the same remedies for wage recovery as seamen, but Admiralty was also given cognizance in such cases of defences including counterclaims and set-offs, as well as a statutory confirmation of the inherent jurisdiction to remove masters;[4] the Admiralty Court was given new jurisdiction in causes of salvage which involved arbitration,[5] and the Court's jurisdiction in salvage under the Act was extended to cover claims arising upon land as well as sea;[6] preferred ship mortgages were introduced[7] (similar to but not identical with those later introduced in the United States[8]); also all offences committed by British seamen in foreign ports were declared to be within the Admiralty jurisdiction,[9] and the Court was given the power to condemn vessels wrongfully masquerading false ownership or colours.[10]

At about this time, public attention came to be focused upon the administrative structure of the High Court of Admiralty; before discussing the particular incident responsible, however, it may be useful to look at some aspects of the two principal administrative offices of the Court.

---

[1] Merchant Seamen's Act, ×1835, §§5, 16.
[2] Merchant Seamen's Act, ×1844, §§5, 16.
[3] §§188, 189; *cf.* [U.S.] Act of July 20, 1790, c. 29, §6.   [4] §§191, 240.
[5] §§460, 464, 473; see also §§468, 492, 498.   [6] §476.
[7] Part 2, §§66–83.   [8] See Price, *L.M.L.*, p. 121.
[9] §268.   [10] §103.

Perhaps the Officer of the Court best known to the public in the present day—more so than the Judge or Registrar—is the Admiralty Marshal. And so it has been since the most ancient days of the Court's history, for in the execution of his duties as server of the Admiralty process, and in his appearances at official ceremonies witnessed by the public—whether pirate executions or splendid judicial processions—carrying upon his shoulder the great silver oar mace of the Court, he has been the figure to whom the romance of the Law and Court of Admiralty has attached. An interesting example of this symbolic personification of the jurisdiction and authority of Admiralty may yet be seen in a carved panel of the sarcophagus of the Elizabethan Admiralty Judge Dr David Lewes in the Church of St Mary, Abergavenny, Monmouthshire, depicting the Marshal of his day, Jasper Swift, carrying the silver oar.

Chief among the Marshal's duties is his responsibility for the service of process of the Admiralty Court. In modern times the Marshal has executed this duty, either personally or through his deputies, within the Port of London, service *in rem* elsewhere within the Court's jurisdiction being usually performed by officers of H.M. Customs acting as the Marshal's substitutes.[1] Confinement of the Marshal's exercise of his duties to the Port of London,[2] or 'within a circuit of five miles',[3] was certainly the rule in the nineteenth century with regard to service of process *in rem*, save in unusual circumstances,[4] but it is evident that at the time when commencement of the action *in personam* was by arrest of the person the Marshal himself executed such process within a circuit of twenty miles from London.[5]

In the nineteenth century, as today, the Marshal usually placed a member of his staff (known as a 'ship-keeper') aboard an arrested vessel of sufficient size, to prevent her from leaving the Court's jurisdiction and to protect her while in custody;[6] care of a vessel in the custody of the Court has always been the Marshal's direct responsibility, and Lord Stowell once gave a decree against the Marshal personally when property was lost from an arrested

---

[1] See *The Jarlinn*, [1965] 1 W.L.R. 1098, 1100.
[2] See *The Rendsburg*, (1805) 6 C. Rob. 142, 149.
[3] Coote, 1st ed., p. 136*aa*.   [4] See *id.*, p. 12.
[5] See A. Browne, vol. 2, p. 432.
[6] See R.G.M. Browne, p. 79; also *The Queen of the South*, [1968] 1 Ll. Rep. 182.

vessel, despite the Marshal's claim that his fees were not sufficient to provide a constant guard upon the ship in order to prevent waterfront predators from looting or tampering with her.[1] The Marshal's lot was later 'improved' considerably: he became salaried in 1840 at five hundred pounds *per annum*[2]—raised to seven hundred pounds by the end of Lushington's tenure as Judge;[3] moreover, the shipkeepers and others of the Marshal's staff also became salaried,[4] so that he was relieved of the burden of paying them out of his own fees; and as his duties included the appraisal and sale of vessels when decreed by the Court in actions *in rem*,[5] he was permitted to continue charging a nominal broker's fee upon such sales according to the established custom.[6]

The office of Admiralty Registrar is probably not of as great antiquity as that of the Marshal, but it has been in existence at least since 1539.[7] As the Court's chief administrative official, the Registrar's duties have been many and varied, including the control of use of the Seal of the Court,[8] the general supervision of the Admiralty Registry and matters pertaining thereto, and even, in former times, the preparation of Letters of Marque to be issued to privateers by the Lords Commissioners of the Admiralty.[9]

Perhaps the Registrar's most important duty, however, has been the exercise of his quasi-judicial function in matters referred to him by the Judge; this practice of 'reference' was well established at least by Lord Stowell's time,[10] and the basic mechanics of the reference procedure of the nineteenth century[11] have survived to the present day. Reference to the Registrar, who by custom has been assisted by two merchant assessors, might be had to determine any question of damages to be awarded to a successful suitor; such reference was usually directed following the decree of judgment as to liability,[12] though it might precede the decree in unusual cases.[13] Interestingly, some of the questions

---

[1] *The Hoop*, (1801) 4 C. Rob. 145.
[2] High Court of Admiralty [Fees] Act, *1840, §5.
[3] See Return to H.C. by Rothery, Adm. Reg'r., 8 May 1867, p. 3.
[4] *Ibid.*
[5] See Williams and Bruce, 1st ed., pp. 207, 233, also pp. 214–18.
[6] See Coote, 1st ed., p. 110.   [7] Thompson, pp. 8–9.
[8] See McGuffie, *Notes on Letter Books*, p. 90.
[9] *Id.*, p. 17.
[10] See, *e.g.*, *The Rendsburg*, (1805) 6 C. Rob. 142.
[11] See Coote, 1st ed., pp. 64–84.   [12] *Id.*, p. 64.
[13] *Id.*, p. 79.

to come before the 'Registrar and Merchants' were evidentiary as well as commercial—as in cases of collision, where a degree of fault must be applied to arrive at a quantum of damages—and this has special significance because of the jurisdiction of the referees to determine both actual and consequential damage.[1] The responsibility of the Registrar in virtually all causes heard in Admiralty has therefore been considerable, to say the least, and no less so because of the bar to attendance at references of counsel for the parties to the action.[2] It must be made clear that damages have never been *pronounced* by the Registrar and Merchants, for that is the exclusive province of the Admiralty Judge; but 'confirmation' by the Judge of the report given to him by the Registrar at the conclusion of a reference has been normal, though the Judge might modify any such report upon due objection by the adverse party with support of affidavits.[3] Such references were until 1959 conducted upon payment of a fee,[4] which in Dr Lushington's time was £5 5s., to each of the referees.[5]

The Registrar has also conducted—with the parties' lawyers in attendance—the taxation of the costs of each action, with a report given to the Judge as upon a reference, confirmed subject to objection.[6] In addition to these duties, the Registrar was at one time empowered to sit as surrogate for the Judge, and so was occasionally responsible for the entire function of the Admiralty Court.[7]

The Admiralty Registrar has been, almost without exception, a key figure in the Court's development; thus some holders of the office have made direct contributions to progress in addition to the dutiful execution of their responsibilities, taking the form of a zealous crusade for the reform of procedure,[8] the production of a better-informed Admiralty Bar through the publication of highly authoritative works on the Law and the jurisdiction and practice of the Court,[9] or the enrichment of scholarship through research into the history of the Admiralty Court and its personnel.[10] These positive contributions of Admiralty Registrars have

---

[1] See Coote, 1st ed., p. 71.
[2] See *id.*, p. 65. [3] *Id.*, pp. 84–5.
[4] McGuffie, *Notes on Letter Books*, p. 83. [5] Coote, 1st ed., p. 136*u*.
[6] *Id.*, p. 87. [7] See Thompson, pp. 8–9.
[8] *E.g.*, H.C. Rothery; see *infra*, p. 54.
[9] E.S. Roscoe and K.C. McGuffie; see Bibliography.
[10] E.S. Roscoe, G.H.M. Thomson, and K.C. McGuffie; see Bibliography.

had a telling effect upon the evolution of the court and the Law. It is unfortunately true, however, that negatives may be as effectual as positives in producing change—and historical objectivity demands that, amongst these positive efforts, there must by noted a rather intriguing negative.

When Charles George Perceval, Lord Arden, died in 1840 at the age of 84, he had been Admiralty Registrar for exactly fifty years—the longest known tenure of the office. Arden had received the appointment as a plum of Royal patronage, and he became a man of standing, influence (his younger brother, Spencer Perceval, was Prime Minister from 1809 to 1812) and considerable wealth. This last attribute is principally explained by the fact that Arden held the Registrarship during a period of great naval warfare, and at the peak of this his official remuneration from fees generated by Prize causes exceeded ten thousand pounds *per annum*; though the Registrar then had to bear the expense of maintaining the Registry and its staff, the years of Prize adjudication provided a very substantial balance.[1] Of course, not only the Registrar, but also the other Court officials were remunerated by fees; the Admiralty Marshal at this time was pocketing about £10,000 yearly,[2] and what Lord Stowell's income as Judge was may be imagined. In addition to fees, however, the Registrar also received as an emolument the interest derived from the investment of suitors' money paid into the fund of the Court.[3] Two rather feeble legislative attempts[4] to place some restrictions upon Arden's windfall proved wholly abortive, and it was not until a month after his death in 1840 that remuneration of Court officers by fee was abolished and salaries payable out of the Consolidated Fund substituted, providing a salary of £1,400 *per annum* for the Registrar.[5]

The reasons for the lack of success in controlling the Registrar's income during the period of Prize adjudication may probably be correctly described as political; but in all likelihood nothing was thereafter done until 1840 because the Prize business vanished, and the income from fees collected on the small volume of instance business was so insignificant as to eliminate controversy.

[1] Thompson, pp. 13, 14.
[2] *Id.*, p. 16.   [3] *Ibid.*
[4] Registrars of Admiralty and Prize Courts Act, ×1810.
Registrars of Admiralty and Prize Courts Act, ×1813.
[5] High Court of Admiralty [Fees] Act, ×1840, §2.

The man most affected by the substitution of a set salary for remuneration by fees was naturally Lord Arden's successor, one Henry Birchfield Swabey—who had been appointed a Deputy Registrar by Lord Stowell in 1810[1] and who drafted the 1840 Fees Act, under §2 of which he became Admiralty Registrar.[2] Swabey (not to be confused with Dr M. C. M. Swabey, Reporter of the Court from 1855 to 1859) performed his duties as Registrar with a degree of flamboyance which must have been somewhat unsettling to those accustomed to the aged Lord Arden, but the new Registrar seemed to be acceptable to Dr Lushington, who as a Member of the Commons could not have been much delighted that for two years as Judge his former Registrar had sat above him in the House of Lords.

All went well until the discovery in November, 1853, of large defalcations in the accounts of the Admiralty Registry.[3] Swabey thereupon executed a characteristically formal and elaborate 'proxy of resignation' which he arranged to have delivered to the Judge,[4] having meanwhile gone abroad—'address unknown'[5] (though South America has been rumoured)—which absence evidently became permanent, despite the interest in locating him shown by the Inspector General of Inland Revenue and others.[6] Though it came as a shocking revelation to the public by the Committee of the House of Commons appointed to investigate the 'Misappropriation of Monies entrusted to Mr. *H. Swabey*, late Registrar of the High Court of Admiralty' that Swabey took £26,700 from the Crown Fund, £29,516 from the Suitor's Fund,[7] and in all appeared to have embezzled in excess of £75,000,[8] there should have been some indications of matters amiss to those closely associated with the ex-Registrar. For (1) Swabey officially took the leases to the Registry premises in his own name, and for some time prior to his disappearance he had not paid the rent to Dr Addams, the landlord, who had threatened to sue for the arrears;[9] (2) Swabey had borrowed £1500 from a Junior Clerk in the Registry, which he had not repaid;[10] and (3), it must have been fairly general knowledge that for a good while Swabey had

[1] Thompson, pp. 16, 18.
[2] *Id.*, p. 18.
[3] McGuffie, *Notes on Letter Books*, p. 10.
[4] Thompson, p. 19.
[5] See McGuffie, *Notes on Letter Books*, p. 79.
[6] *Ibid.*
[7] See Parl. Paper [1854] (521) xlii (H.C., 6 July).
[8] See McGuffie, *Notes on Letter Books*, p. 71.
[9] *Id.*, p. 15.
[10] *Id.*, p. 71.

been conducting a proctor's business in the Admiralty Court under his son's name, collecting all the fees himself.[1]

However Swabey secured his appointment as Deputy Registrar in 1810, he came into that post at a time when the income of the Registrar, which Lord Arden evidently shared with his Deputies,[2] has never been greater—and the end of the Prize business, with the consequent drop-off in fees, must have come as a shock to him. How he survived the next twenty-five years is something of a mystery, but at Arden's death he was the sole Deputy,[3] and the post of Deputy Registrar was abolished by the 1840 Fees Act, which Swabey himself drafted.[4] From this, one may conjecture that, owing to Arden's advanced age, Swabey had for some time prior to his succession to the post been Registrar in fact if not in name, and that he was determined once he became Registrar not to share responsibility for financial matters, a suspicion strengthened by the fact that although an Assistant Registrarship was provided by the 1840 Fees Act, Swabey never requested the appointment of such an officer.[5]

In the end, only £2000 of the embezzled funds[6] were recovered, and a sum in compensation of the balance was voted by Parliament in 1855.[7] Perhaps the final irony of *l'affaire* Swabey, however, is that he himself drafted the statutory provision for the removal of an Admiralty Registrar,[8] a proceeding which he adroitly avoided by his 'proxy of resignation', and which in fact was never utilized.

Hardly a greater contrast can be imagined between Swabey and his successor, H. C. Rothery. Even under the burden of Swabey's 'shameful neglect of duty in every department of the Office',[9] Rothery was able to clean up matters in the Registry within a comparatively short time. The Court quickly emerged from the gloom of scandal—not only to the relief of the civilians, but also to that of the common lawyers, who had come to view the Admiralty jurisdiction as well established, and its Court as one of extreme competence.[10] An official reaction to Swabey's thievery was,

[1] McGuffie, *Notes on Letter Books*, pp. 75–6.
[2] Thompson, p. 14.   [3] *Id.*, p. 18.
[4] *Ibid.*   [5] *Id.*, pp. 18, 19.
[6] See McGuffie, *Notes on Letter Books*, p. 129.
[7] See *id.*, p. 74.
[8] High Court of Admiralty [Fees] Act, ×1840, §3.
[9] Rothery in McGuffie, *Notes on Letter Books*, p. 129.
[10] See *e.g.*, *Place v. Potts*, (1855) 5 H.L.Cas. 383.

however, quite inevitable; this took the form of a statute which, while its greater bulk dealt with needed reforms of evidentiary procedure and administration of oaths, nonetheless had as an avowed purpose the substitution of stamps in lieu of fees[1] in order to prevent the possibility of any future mismanagement. Two other notable features of the 1854 Court Act, in passing, were the introduction of a penalty for perjury identical to that at common law,[2] and the introduction of the proceeding by *monition*,[3] which will shortly be discussed as a separate matter.

The problem of unwieldy procedure now began to press upon the Admiralty Court. In America, Congress had renewed over a decade previously the power of the U.S. Supreme Court to make rules of procedure for causes in the District and Circuit Courts,[4] and that was followed, in 1845, by the promulgation of the first Admiralty Rules,[5] authored just prior to his death by Mr Justice Story.[6] While these rules were largely the codification of previously accumulated customs,[7] they did clarify important points such as the joinder of actions *in rem* and *in personam* in the same libel, expressly forbidding such dual actions against both ship and owner,[8] though later rules have reversed this position.[9] It ought here to be made clear that the libel in American Admiralty corresponded to the old Bill in Chancery in England[10] rather than to the English libel, which began to fall into disuse in the High Court of Admiralty with the growing tendency, after Lord Stowell's time, to utilize the truly summary procedure.[11] Basically, however, the Admiralty practice of the English and American Courts remained quite similar until 1855,[12] and on account of this similarity, Admiralty practitioners and textwriters in the United States kept (as they still keep[13]) a reasonably close eye upon the development of the Law and practice of Admiralty in England. Owing to this, and perhaps to a degree of smugness

---

[1] Admiralty Court Act, 1854, preamble.
[2] Admiralty Court Act, 1854, §9.
[3] Admiralty Court Act, 1854, §13.
[4] Act of August, 23, 1842, *c.* 188; see Wiswall, 'Procedural Unification,' p. 38.
[5] See Conkling, p. 785.   [6] Roberts, p. 64.
[7] Conkling, p. 353.   [8] Parsons, pp. 376, 378.
[9] See F.R.C.P. [1 July 1966], Adm. Rule C. (1) (b).
[10] See Conkling, p. 417.   [11] *Id.,* p. 564.
[12] See Dunlap, pp. 92–115.
[13] See *e.g.,* dissent of Frankfurter, A. J., in *Mitchell v. Trawler Racer, Inc.,* 362 U.S. 539, 551 (1960).

because of the recent codification of rules there, a leading American Admiralty textwriter of that day—viewing the situation in England —was moved to comment that:

Strange as it may seem, it appears . . . by the very latest Reports which have reached us, of the decisions of the High Court of Admiralty, that its practice, in many particulars, is still uncertain and fluctuating. Indeed, it may reasonably be inferred from the confused, obscure, and, in some respects, nonsensical statements rather ostentatiously introduced by **MR CHITTY** on the subject, in the second volume of his General Practice, that this knowledge is but little less inaccessible to an English lawyer habituated only to the practice of the common law courts.[1]

Whether this or similar observations were instrumental in provoking action in England, the needed reform was embarked upon shortly after Rothery's appointment as Registrar, and there seems little doubt that he was not merely, as has been stated by a contemporary, an 'associate' of Dr Lushington's in procedural reform,[2] but in reality was the *primum mobile*—Lushington having had the power since 1840 to initiate reform by making and/or repealing rules of procedure in the Court,[3] yet having done nothing at all in this regard until Rothery became Admiralty Registrar.

It has been said that the first formal Admiralty Rules were those of 1859,[4] but in fact the Rules of 1855 were the first attempt at a reform of practice, and even earlier Rules, dealing with extra Court days, had been promulgated in the previous year.[5] The 1855 instance Rules were divided into two parts, one dealing with fee procedures designed to implement the 1854 Court Act by substituting the sale of stamps for the receipt of cash, and the other dealing primarily with Court proceedings. In this latter section, certain procedures are worthy of particular note: (1) an instrument was designed to facilitate consideration of technical evidence by the Trinity Masters, and to prevent 'manufactured' defences,[6] to be given in prior to any pleadings, by each party, in any cause of collision; these 'Preliminary Acts' were to be sealed statements of all pertinent factual particulars surrounding the collision, such as time, place, courses, state of sea, etc., and were

[1] Conkling, at p. 381, n. (a).   [2] Coote, 1st ed., intro., pp. vi–vii.
[3] Admiralty Court Act, 1840, §18.   [4] Roscoe, *Studies*, pp. 3–4.
[5] Rules, Orders & Regulations, 1854 (O.-in-C. of 3 July).
[6] *Papers on 1855 Rules*, p. 12.

to remain sealed in the Registry until conclusion of the pleadings[1] [with minor modifications, the form of the Preliminary Act established in the 1855 Rules remains today the same[2]]; (2) secret examination of witnesses[3] was abolished in preference to examination with the parties' proctors in attendance,[4] though the questioning was still to be done by the Registrar or a commissioned examiner [the presence of parties themselves was still generally forbidden[5]]; (3) pleadings and proofs in all contested cases were required to be printed before the hearing,[6] an innovation of greater significance than might be supposed, and one which will be discussed in the next chapter. The balance of the 1855 instance Rules dealt with examination and transcription of evidence given at hearings or references, obviously designed mainly to expedite Court proceedings, thus continuing the progress toward a more summary procedure.[7] Oddly enough, two new points of Court procedure were also introduced in the section of the 1855 Rules dealing with instance fees, one establishing the use of the *caveat warrant book*, which will be dealt with at a later stage in this work, and the other requiring notice of any motion to be given in to the Registry at least two days prior to making the motion in Court.[8]

Portions of the 1855 Rules were obsolete even upon their promulgation; the primary reasons for this were a tremendous increase in the Court's instance business since the 1840 Act[9]— due not only to the Court's expanded jurisdiction but also to the new vitality of maritime commerce generated by steam navigation—and the breaking of the civilian monopoly of Admiralty practice by the common lawyers.[10] A fresh start was needed, replacing the ancient and now unworkable method of evidence by deposition with a better system; the answer, appropriately enough, was to permit the introduction of oral evidence as at common law—and so in 1859 the 1855 Rules were repealed and

---

[1] 1855 Instance Rules [Rules, Orders & Regulations, 1855 (O.-in-C. of 7 December)], r. 2.

[2] See McGuffie *et al.*, *Practice*, §672, p. 298; also *The Judith M.*, [1968] 2 Ll. Rep. 474, 485.

[3] See *Papers on 1855 Rules*, p. 12. [4] 1855 Instance Rules, r. 6.

[5] 1855 Instance Rules, r. 7. [6] 1855 Instance Rules, r. 10.

[7] 1855 Instance Rules, rr. 3–5, 8, 9.

[8] 1855 Instance Fee Rules [Rules, Orders & Regulations, 1855 (O.-in-C. of 11 December)], rr. 4, 15.

[9] See *infra*, pp. 57–8. [10] High Court of Admiralty Act,[x]1859.

replaced by a streamlined Court procedure which made oral examination of witnesses in open Court a principal feature.[1]

The outlines of the Admiralty procedure of Dr Browne's day were preserved by the 1859 Rules, but some innovations were: (1) the repeal of the old default proceeding, replacing it with a four-step procedure which gave a hearing and final decree within six days of a sale by the Court;[2] (2) a change in the form of the warrant of arrest *in rem*, permitting the Marshal to cite the interested parties wherever found, rather than at a specifically stated place;[3] (3) the introduction of a separate *citation in rem* for service upon vessels already under arrest, to replace subsequent warrants for subsequent actions *in rem*;[4] (4) the inclusion of the descriptive term 'vessel' in affidavits to lead warrants, in order to avoid bad warrants resulting from misdescription of the rig of the ship to be arrested;[5] (5) the introduction of the 'detainer' [order for detention] to restrain the *res* from leaving the Court's jurisdiction for up to three days pending arrest;[6] and (6) a new form of subpoena, directed to the subpoenant (to replace the old 'compulsory' which was directed to the Marshal)—which itself shows the increasing tendency to introduce common law procedures.[7] Indeed, it was observed by an Admiralty textwriter of the day that the 1859 Rules 'preserved those original peculiarities of the Court which were its excellences and its boast . . . , whilst approximating the practice in Admiralty to the more elastic procedure of Common Law . . .'[8]

Though new procedures had been devised to expedite business in the Court, the effect of custom proved difficult to shake off. Thus the proceeding by 'act on petition' came into being to replace that by 'plea and proof', which had become limited in use to causes of collision and bottomry;[9] but while an 'original act' in the proceeding by act on petition went beyond the old libel in requiring a statement of the plaintiff's entire case, and the new answer required inclusion of all defenses—at which stage the introduction of new matter was barred—the pleadings could still

---

[1] 1859 Rules [Rules, Orders & Regulations, 1859 (O.-in.-C of 29 November)], rr. 4(3), 78.

[2] 1859 Rules, rr. 18–26.   [3] 1859 Rules, form 5.

[4] 1859 Rules, form 10; Coote, 1st ed., p. 136*cc*.

[5] See Coote, 1st ed., p. 241.   [6] 1859 Rules, r. 15, form 8.

[7] 1859 Rules, form 42.   [8] Coote, 1st ed., intro., p. vii.

[9] *Id.*, p. 39.

drag on through a reply, rejoinder (in which the defendant had one final opportunity to state material facts), surrejoinder, rebutter and surrebutter.[1] It is also not clear whether in causes of collision the new 'Preliminary Act' immediately superseded the old 'protest'; here the new procedure was a clear improvement upon the old, for the protest, an ancient procedure[2] which made a statement of the factual circumstances surrounding the mishap given by the master after making port—based upon the log-book plus the recollections of officers and crew[3]—was admissible in evidence only when introduced by the opposing party to contradict the testimony of the owners or master,[4] admissible even if unsworn,[5] and introduceable at option rather than being required—though if not introduced, the Judge might properly infer that it would not have supported the allegation.[6] The protests of both vessels could be directed to be brought in upon application by either party, however, if the cause was to proceed by plea and proof rather than act on petition.[7] Protests made long after the collision or act of salvage[8] were also admissible, though given little weight unless supported by subsequent proofs.[9]

Despite the availability of oral testimony at the hearing upon application of either party or by independent order of the Court,[10] it seems that *viva voce* examination appeared even more unpalatable to many witnesses than examination by deposition and affidavit, and on occasion the 'threat' of issuance of a subpoena to testify orally in Court was used to persuade the prompt execution of an affidavit.[11] But the widening of opportunity for the use of oral testimony probably stands, in retrospect, as the most notable feature of the 1859 Rules, for in the following decade oral evidence became the general rule rather than the exception.[12]

The broader Admiralty jurisdiction granted by the 1840 Court Act was immediately effective in bringing a greater volume of

---

[1] Coote, 1st ed., p. 51.

[2] *The Belgenland*, 36 F. 504, 507 (S.D.N.Y. 1888).

[3] See Coote, 1st ed., p. 53 & n. (z); also Abbott, p. 575.

[4] *Ibid.*

[5] *The Mellona*, (1846) 10 *Jur.* 992, 994.

[6] Coote, 1st ed., p. 55.

[7] *Ibid.*   [8] *Ibid.* [see also 50 *L. Mag.* 57, 66–69 (1853)].

[9] *Id.*, pp. 54, 53.   [10] *Id.*, pp. 57–8.

[11] See, *e.g.*, *The Glory*, (1849) 7 Not. Cas. 263; 13 *Jur.* 991.

[12] See Williams and Bruce, 1st ed., p. 260; *cf. The Syracuse*, 23 Fed. Cas. 594 (No. 13718) (C.C.S.D.N.Y. 1868).

business before the Court, in which a total of 228 causes were instituted during 1841; but the number had so increased by 1860, in which year 562 causes were instituted,[1] that the case for an Admiralty jurisdiction truly comprehensive of maritime matters became undeniable. A bill, which was largely authored by Dr Lushington,[2] was introduced in 1861 to amend and generally enlarge the Admiralty jurisdiction, and after considerable debate the Admiralty Court Act, 1861, emerged as law. By this Act the Admiralty Court was finally constituted a Court of Record,[3] and the Court was given jurisdiction for the first time directly to entertain petitory as well as possessory suits involving vessels registered in England or Wales,[4] though the Court later came to give the territorial requirement a strict interpretation[5] more typical of the early nineteenth century.[6] Jurisdiction was given over claims for building, equipping or repairing a vessel if ancillary to an action *in rem*,[7] over masters' claims for disbursements,[8] over all claims upon mortgages of registered ships,[9] and, in partial vindication of Nicholl's judgment in *The Neptune*,[10] over all claims for necessaries supplied by materialmen to foreign ships, unless supplied in their home ports.[11] Admiralty was also finally given by this Act an original jurisdiction concurrent with that of Chancery regarding claims arising from the transfer of ownership of ships or shares therein, where of British registry,[12] and in limitation of liability, ancillary to actions *in rem*.[13] Jurisdiction to entertain life salvage claims was also extended to cases involving British vessels wherever occurring, and involving foreign vessels in British territorial waters.[14]

It is interesting to note that while causes of civil salvage sued upon in Admiralty following the sweeping grant of salvage jurisdiction in the 1840 Court Act[15] continued for a time to outnumber collision suits, the number of salvage suits did not generally increase in the years 1841–61, whereas the entered number of

---

[1] Return to H.C. by Rothery, Adm. Reg'r., 28 May 1867, No. 1.
[2] See Hansard, vol. 161 [H.L. Deb.], cols. 1394–97, 5 March 1861.
[3] §14. [4] §8.
[5] See *The Robinsons* and *The Satellite*, (1884) 5 Asp. 338.
[6] See *The Barbara*, (1801) 4 C. Rob. 1.
[7] §4. [8] §10. [9] §11.
[10] See *supra*, p. 38.
[11] §5. [12] §12. [13] §13.
[14] §9.
[15] Admiralty Court Act, 1840, §4.

collision causes (perhaps a by-product of the steamship era) rose consistently in that period, surpassing salvage suits in the years after 1852, and outnumbering them by more than half in 1860.[1] Since the Court by 1860 had jurisdiction to entertain any claim whatever for civil salvage,[2] there was a clear case for giving equally broad jurisdiction in an area of even greater activity, collision. The simple language of the 1861 Act therefore granted jurisdiction over any claim for damage done by any ship.[3] Even the sharp-eyed guardians of the interests of the common law, who objected vociferously to some features of the bill, could not have guessed the extent to which §7 would eventually enlarge the Admiralty jurisdiction—giving the Court cognizance, for example, of causes of collision arising within the body of a county,[4] of negligent damage to submarine cables,[5] and of damage done to a wharf located in a foreign country.[6] Without doubt, §7 has proven the most important and valuable grant in the 1861 Act.

The 1861 Act also gave decrees and orders of the Admiralty Court for the payment of money the same effect as a judgment at common law,[7] permitted the concurrent hearing of counterclaims,[8] permitted appeal upon the original bail and from interlocutory decrees,[9] gave power to the Judge to enforce discovery before trial as in any of the Superior Courts of common law,[10] extended service of subpoenas throughout the United Kingdom,[11] permitted the Judge to order a party evading service to proceed as if served,[12] and constituted the Registrar sole surrogate.[13]

As earlier indicated, passage of the 1861 Act was not secured without opposition from a faction which still viewed any extension of the Admiralty jurisdiction as a threat to the common law. Though not so blunt in stating their views as Mr Justice Johnson had been in the United States,[14] they were candid in their abhorrence of nautical assessors[15] and the absence of a lay jury; indeed, this latter factor was so rankling to them that one notable article

---

[1] Return to H.C. by Rothery, Adm. Reg'r., 28 May 1867, No. 1.
[2] Abbott, p. 998.   [3] Admiralty Court Act, 1861, §7.
[4] *The Malvina*, (1862) 6 L.T.R. 369.
[5] *The Clara Killam*, (1870) L.R. 3 A. & E. 161.
[6] *The Tolten*, [1946] P. 135.   [7] §15.
[8] §34.   [9] §§33, 32.   [10] §17.
[11] §21.   [12] §20.   [13] §25.
[14] See *Ramsay v. Allegre*, 12 Wheat. (25 U.S.) 611, 614 (1827).
[15] See, *e.g.*, 10 L. *Mag. & Rev.* (n.s.) 262, 267 (1861); also 50 L. *Mag.* 57, 70-1 (1853).

of the day, labelling the view of the non-jury school 'perverted',
went even so far as to advocate the extension of jurisdiction by the
bill, then under consideration by Parliament, *provided that* a
scheme of jury trials was introduced into Admiralty to replace
nautical assessors.[1] In effect, nothing less was sought by this faction
than a conversion of the Admiralty Court to a court of common
law. They could not have been much encouraged by Dr Lushington, whose views on the independence of the Admiralty Court were
well known,[2] and who was the author of most of the 1861 provisions; but it seems, from the account of the debate upon the bill
in the Lords,[3] that those who favoured retention of the proceeding
in Admiralty without jury trial, as well as an extension of jurisdiction, may have had to sacrifice some desired provisions such as
an unrestricted materialmen's lien and appeal of judgments
solely on the questions of law involved, in order to preserve that
portion of the *status quo*.

Though in general the tendency during Dr Lushington's period
of service as Admiralty Judge was towards a gradual expansion of
the jurisdiction of Admiralty, there were a few reverses. Some of
these were, in a sense, judicial frustration rather than retrogression.
Thus Dr Lushington felt that he could not entertain a suit for
general average, because historically the common law had retained
an exclusive jurisdiction over such questions,[4] though the common
law courts soon after came to recognize a limited ancillary Admiralty jurisdiction over questions of freight and average;[5] Lushington
also felt compelled to observe the pronouncements of common law
courts as to the territorial jurisdiction of Admiralty[6] where a
question of Admiralty jurisdiction conferred by statute was
involved.[7] There was, however, some actual retrogression written
into the 1861 Court Act to remove from Admiralty cognizance
any claims for cargo damage against English or Welsh shipowners;[8]
and with the increase in 1862 of the maximum jurisdictional
limit of salvage claims made cognizable in 1854 by Justices of the

[1] 'Prospects of the Admiralty Court', 10 *L. Mag. & Rev.* (n.s.) 262, 264, 267
(1861).
[2] See, *e.g., The Clarence*, (1854) 1 Sp. 206, 209.
[3] Hansard, vol. 161 [H.L. Deb.], cols. 1394–7, 5 March 1861.
[4] *The Constancia*, (1846) 2 W. Rob. 487.
[5] See *Place v. Potts*, (1855) 5 H.L.Cas. 383.
[6] See, *e.g., General Iron Screw Collier Co. v. Schurmanns*, (1860) 1 J. & H. 180,
193.
[7] See, *e.g., The Johannes*, (1860) Lush. 182.   [8] §6.

Peace from two hundred[1] to one thousand[2] pounds, and extension of this jurisdiction to claims arising outside the United Kingdom,[3] the Admiralty Court as a practical matter lost its jurisdiction (though perhaps willingly) in causes of salvage involving under £1000.

On balance, these restrictions of jurisdiction were more than compensated by other grants. The power of the High Court of Admiralty to issue letters patent appointing Judges, Registrars, Marshals and other officers of Vice-Admiralty Courts was statutorily affirmed in 1863[4]—not because of any difficulty in England, where the office of Vice-Admiral had become purely honorary by mid-nineteenth century[5]—but to put an end to the improper execution of certain offices in Vice-Admiralty Courts abroad, which had been filled without the correct authorization of the Lords Commissioners or patent from the High Court of Admiralty.[6] At the same time, jurisdiction was given to the Court to hear appeals of excessive charges by practitioners in Vice-Admiralty Courts.[7]

The Court's jurisdiction over cases of wilful disobedience of masters under naval convoy was made exclusive and new Prize jurisdiction was also given, by an Act of 1864,[8] and another statute of the same year conferred exclusive jurisdiction upon the Court over questions of distribution of Royal Navy salvage, bounty or prize monies, and an indirect jurisdiction to determine the apportionment of monies among Navy Ships' Agents;[9] in 1866 the Court gained jurisdiction over suits by merchants, shipowners or other interested parties against Officers of naval convoys for dereliction of duty and/or negligent damage,[10] bringing to a conclusion this series of enactments giving the Court naval business. Much of this legislation arose out of experiences and aftermaths of the Crimean War, which generated a good deal of diverse business in the Court, including applications by

---

[1] Merchant Shipping Act, 1854, §460.
[2] Merchant Shipping Act Amendment Act, 1862, §49; cf. Coote, 2nd ed., pp. 4–5.
[3] Merchant Shipping Act Amendment Act, 1862, §49.
[4] Vice-Admiralty Courts Act, 1863, §7.
[5] See McGuffie, *Notes on Letter Books*, p. 98.   [6] *Id.*, p. 96.
[7] Vice-Admiralty Courts Act, 1863, §19.
[8] Naval Prize Act, 1864, §§46, 52.
[9] Naval Agency and Distribution Act, 1864, §§22, 20.
[10] Naval Discipline Act, 1866, §30.

shipowners for compensation from the Royal Navy to cover the desertion of seamen, whom the owners alleged to have volunteered into the Navy.[1]

Other business came to the Court as a result of earlier statutory jurisdiction, such as that given by the 1840 Court Act over questions of distribution of booty captured on land[2] (a jurisdiction evidently exercised by the Admiralty Court during the eighteenth century[3]), the most notable exercise of which involved booty captured by the British Army at Banda and Kirwee, in India.[4] Equally, Dr Lushington lost no time in giving the fullest application to new statutes, and held collisions in foreign waters cognizable under §7 of the 1861 Court Act in the year following its passage;[5] it might be mentioned as well that in collisions within British territorial waters the Court since 1846 had enjoyed the advantage, in deciding fault, of a statutory application of the Trinity House collision rules.[6]

One provision of the 1861 Court Act which was of considerable practical importance permitted all of the jurisdiction conferred by the Act to be exercised either *in rem* or *in personam*.[7] And yet this seems at first a puzzling step, for the action *in personam* previously described by Browne (commencing with the arrest of the body of the defendant) had earlier been declared by Dr Lushington to be long obsolete—not having been employed, in fact, since the eighteenth century, to the best of his recollection,[8] though still technically capable of use even during Lushington's judgeship;[9] it is hardly surprising, however, that where its revival was mentioned as a possibility it was promptly condemned as a 'most offensive' suggestion, especially after the abolition at common law of arrest on mesne process.[10] At some time in the eighteenth century, prior to Stowell's judgeship, an answer to this seeming dilemma began to evolve; in the exercise of its prerogative power, and in the tradition of the civil law, the Court

---

[1] See McGuffie, *Notes on Letter Books*, p. 110.
[2] Admiralty Court Act, 1840, §22.
[3] See *LeCaux v. Eden*, (1781) 2 Doug. 594, 613.
[4] *The Banda & Kirwee Booty*, (1866) L.R. 1 A. & E. 109; *subs. proc.* (1875) L.R. 4 A. & E. 436.
[5] *The Diana*, (1862) Lush. 539.
[6] Steam Navigation Act, *1846.
[7] Admiralty Court Act, 1861, §35.   [8] *The Clara*, (1855) Swab. 1, 3.
[9] *The Alexander*, (1841) 1 W. Rob. 288, 294.
[10] Coote, 1st ed., p. 131.

began to *monish* [command] defendants to appear on pain of contempt, rather than to issue warrants *in personam* for their arrest.

The instrument for effecting such a command was known as a *monition*, a process exclusive to the civil law, which was addressed to the Marshal and commanded him to cite the defendant personally and admonish him to appear and answer.[1] While the original purpose of the monition was to command the performance of any act which could be ordered by the Court (somewhat in the fashion of a mandatory injunction in Equity), and while Browne makes no mention of the monition as an instrument for bringing defendants before the Admiralty Court, Lord Stowell certainly showed no hesitancy in issuing monitions to appear in cases where an action *in rem* was precluded; thus a monition was issued to recalcitrant shipowners to appear and show cause why salvage should not be decreed against them, where at their request the salvors had refrained from arresting the salved vessel;[2] and where an action *in rem* seemed possible, Stowell appears occasionally to have utilized the monition in preference to a warrant of arrest.[3] Actions brought upon claims against Crown vessels or wrongdoing vessels subsequently lost were evidently routinely commenced by monition,[4] though the process in the latter instance could only be employed where the owners were domestic residents.[5] Certainly by the time of Sir John Nicholl the procedure was very well established in cases of the absence of the *res obligata* from the Court's territorial jurisdiction.[6]

The appearance of the monition in the 1854 Court Act[7] as a mode of initiating Admiralty causes alternate to the warrant of arrest merely codified the pre-existing practice,[8] rather than offering a new action *in personam*. Indeed, it ought to be noted that though the monition was directed to a specifically described or named person, was personally served, and terminated in a personal judgment—assuming that the action thereby instituted enjoyed a successful prosecution—its use under the 1854 Court Act seems to have been confined to cases in which an action *in rem*

---

[1] *Black's Law Dictionary*, p. 1158.
[2] *The Trelawney*, (1801) 3 C. Rob. 216 *n*.
[3] E.g., *The Governor Raffles*, (1815) 2 Dod. 14, 15, 17.
[4] See Coote, 1st ed., p. 132.   [5] *The Carlyle*, (1858) 30 *L.T.* 278.
[6] See *The Meg Merrilies*, (1837) 3 Hag. Adm. 346.
[7] Admiralty Court Act, 1854, §13.   [8] Coote, 1st ed., p. 132.

might have been available,[1] and even in actions prior to that time which had been commenced by monition in the absence of the *res*, the form of an action *in rem*—even to the name of the ship in the title of the cause—seems to have been emulated.[2] Indeed, although very highly respected authorities have stated that the monition was used to commence actions *in personam*,[3] it appears that this is an incorrect observation because (1) there seems to be no authority to the effect that the monition was an alternative to a warrant for the arrest of the *corpus*, but authority has been shown to establish its use as an alternative to a warrant for the arrest of the *res*; and (2), disobedience of a monition could not result in default judgment, whereas disobedience of its eventual replacement, the *citation in personam*,[4] served in the same manner as a monition,[5] resulted in a personal default judgment,[6] rather than a contempt.[7]

While it is true that the monition was aimed at and had its effect upon the person, it was nonetheless an adjunct to the action *in rem*,[8] and so it seems better to speak of 'a personal action by way of monition', rather than 'an action *in personam* by monition'. However, it must then be said that the personal action by way of monition was probably the forerunner of the modern action *in personam*, for it bears more resemblance to the post-1859 action *in personam* by citation than to the pre-1859 action which commenced with personal arrest. In American Admiralty, the monition became in fact a personal summons,[9] and though it is said that the 1859 English *citation in personam* incorporated the old monition to appear and answer,[10] its penalty of default for disobedience shows it as a direct successor to the old warrant *in personam*. All personal actions after 1859 were commenced by the *citation in personam*, the contemplated process for the actions *in personam* specified in the 1861 Court Act.[11]

The 1859 Rules did not, however, put an end to the use of the monition in the Admiralty Court, for its original function was never lost, and at the time it was being used to institute personal

---

[1] See Admiralty Court Act, 1854, §13.
[2] See, *e.g.*, *The Meg Merrilies*, (1837) 3 Hag. Adm. 346.
[3] *I.e.*, Williams and Bruce, 3rd ed., p. 321; Roscoe, *Practice*, p. 184.
[4] 1859 Rules, r. 28.
[5] See Coote, 1st ed., p. 136*dd*. [6] See 1859 Rules, form 17.
[7] For further details, see *infra*, pp. 166–7, 198.
[8] See *supra*, pp. 62–3. [9] See Conkling, p. 486.
[10] Coote, 1st ed., p. 136*dd*.
[11] Admiralty Court Act, 1861, §35; see also §20.

actions, it was still being used as well to enforce orders of the Court upon pain of contempt. It was applicable to those who incited disobedience[1] in addition to those who actually disobeyed, and with reference to the former the Court was 'generally slow and reluctant to release the offenders until they have undergone some term of imprisonment.'[2] Prior to the 1861 Court Act, monitions for personal attachment [arrest] and/or committal were also the only available tool of the Court for obtaining the satisfaction of personal judgments.[3] The 1861 Act gave the Admiralty Court the power to issue writs for the execution of judgments as at common law,[4] but personal attachment under monition continued to be the chief mode of execution thereafter under §15 of the 1861 Act,[5] and this use of the monition survived Dr Lushington's tenure as Judge.

Other procedural provisions of the 1861 statute had a more immediate effect. The simultaneous hearing of counterclaims and cross-actions under §34 soon became a regular feature of Admiralty practice, and some cross-actions went on to the Privy Council as cross-appeals.[6] Pre-hearing discovery of documents, a practice which originated in the civil law,[7] was made easier by power given to the Judge in §17 of the 1861 Court Act, and Dr Lushington in at least one subsequent case even made an order under §17 for the production to him of documents claimed to be privileged, in order to enable him to decide an application by the opposing party for leave to inspect them prior to the close of pleading.[8]

Though the general outline of Admiralty procedure during Lushington's judgeship remained nearly identical to that of Lord Stowell's, there were a few features—apart from those already discussed—which seem to have emerged gradually; the majority of these were terminological changes, unworthy of specific mention; one, however, the *praecipe*[9] [authorization

---

[1] *The Bure*, (1850) 14 *Jur.* 1123.

[2] Coote, 1st ed., at p. 19.

[3] See Williams and Bruce, 3rd ed., p. 336.

[4] Admiralty Court Act, 1861, §22.

[5] See, *e.g.*, *The Zephyr*, (1864) 11 L.T.R. 351.

[6] See, *e.g.*, *The Saxonia* and *The Eclipse*, (1862) Lush. 410.

[7] See Williams and Bruce, 1st ed., p. 304.

[8] *The Macgregor Laird*, (1866) L. R. 1 A. & E. 307.

[9] *Cf. R. D. Wood Company v. Phoenix Steel Corporation*, 327 F. 2d 921, 923 (3 Cir. 1964).

form], seems to have been an innovation. It is most likely that the praecipe was an outgrowth of the changes in the procedures for the collection of Court fees, and its extensive use may ultimately have been a direct result of the Swabey affair, for each step in any proceeding thereafter required for its institution the filing of a praecipe upon which the proper fee stamp had been affixed; thus the method of instituting a suit in Admiralty changed from the 'entry of an action' in the 'action book',[1] to the filing of a 'praecipe to institute' the cause, and its entry in the 'cause book',[2] which, as all of these steps continued to take place in the Registry, may have been the 'action book' under a new name. In like manner, it was necessary to file a 'praecipe for a warrant' in addition to the affidavit to lead, a 'praecipe for service', a 'praecipe for notice of sale', etc.,[3] in order to enable the subsequent steps to be taken. Some praecipes also served an informative function as to the next step in the action; appearance, for example, was accomplished by filing a 'praecipe to enter an appearance', but if it was desired to appear under protest, it was necessary to file a praecipe which stated that desire before filing an act or petition setting forth the protest in specific terms.[4]

It may be of interest to note in passing that, in addition to the objection to the Court's jurisdiction by protest, it was also possible by that time to object to the plaintiff's 'right to sue'[5] even where the Court's jurisdiction was not in question;[6] this seems, however, to have been a 'judicial innovation' of Dr Lushington's, much as he established the right of intervention for bottomry bondholders who wished to assert claims in priority.[7]

In addition to filing the required praecipes, it was necessary as well to precede the filing of any documents in the Registry by payment of a fee, for which a 'minute of filing'[8] giving the nature of the document and the date of filing would be entered by a Registry Clerk in the 'minute book'.[9] It seems that this was the era of proliferation of paperwork in Admiralty practice, as witness the number of forms required upon a reference to the Registrar

---

[1] See *supra*, p. 12.   [2] See Williams and Bruce, 1st ed., p. 187.
[3] *Id.*, pp. 187, 190, 204.
[4] See *id.*, p. 202.   [5] Coote, 1st ed., p. 93.
[6] See *The John and Mary*, (1859) Swab. 471.
[7] *The Aline*, (1839) 1 W. Rob. 111.
[8] *Cf.*, *e.g.*, F.R.C.P. [1 July 1966], Adm. Rule E. (5) (b).
[9] See Williams and Bruce, 1st ed., p. 196.

and Merchants.[1] The partial insufficiency of these procedural safeguards and improvements is also demonstrated in that, at the conclusion of Lushington's service as Judge, it was still necessary for the successful plaintiff in a *contested* action *in rem* throughout which the *res* had remained under arrest to take the same steps to procure a judicial sale of the *res*—even after a decree in his favour—as he would have been forced to take in a default proceeding.[2]

If the evolution of more complex procedure and a far broader Admiralty jurisdiction were principal features of the Court's development during Lushington's judgeship, one cannot overlook an equally important feature—the complex judicial character of the Judge himself. And Dr Stephen Lushington ranks, beyond doubt, as the most enigmatic Admiralty Judge of all those within the scope of this work's consideration.

Despite Lushington's open criticism of Lord Stowell's reluctance to entertain the Admiralty claims of foreign parties[3] for fear of prohibition,[4] he was himself frequently troubled over the status of foreign suitors and defendants in the Admiralty Court. It must be admitted that in wage suits, where Stowell's hesitancy had been greatest, Lushington appeared to have few doubts as to the Court's jurisdiction; not only did he permit American masters—who did not then enjoy a maritime lien for wages in the United States[5]—to bring actions *in rem* for wage recovery under British law,[6] but he made orders for the payment of foreign mariners' wages out of balances of proceeds in the Registry *upon motion*, without any action for such recovery having been instituted at all.[7] Though he had first sanctioned this procedure only to satisfy the claims of materialmen (under §6 of the 1840 Court Act) for the supply of necessaries to foreign ships,[8] he later extended the advantage to foreign seamen and masters, and in one case where a shrewd Yankee skipper—one Henry Clay Dearborn—thus recovered his own wages and disbursements from the proceeds of a bottomry sale,[9] 'the Judge decreed a further

---

[1] See Williams and Bruce, 1st ed., p. 275.   [2] *Id.*, p. 224.
[3] See, *e.g.*, *The Courtney*, (1810) Edw. Adm. 239.
[4] *Id.*, at 241; see *The Milford*, (1858) Swab. 362, 366.
[5] See Price, *L.M.L.*, p. 127; see *supra*, p. 24.
[6] See, *e.g.*, *The Milford*, (1858) Swab. 362.
[7] See Coote, 2nd ed., p. 144.   [8] See Coote, 1st ed., p. 98.
[9] *The Henry Reed*, (1858) 32 L.T.R. 166.

sum to be paid to him on behalf of a seaman under age, for whose wages the master swore he was personally liable by the law of the [S]tate of Maine, to which the ship belonged.'[1]

On the question of the Court's discretion to refuse to exercise its jurisdiction over foreign suitors [*forum non conveniens*], though the 1859 Rules required notice to be given to the London Consul of the flag state of any foreign vessel against whom a suit was brought in Admiralty for the recovery of wages,[2] and though the Admiralty Law of other nations has historically considered the consent of the Consul as virtually an absolute condition to the entertainment of such a suit,[3] Dr Lushington held that the emphasis should be upon the Court's power to hear the suit rather than the Consul's consent to the exercise of that power, and that the protest of the Consul was not necessarily a bar to the Court's entertainment of the claim.[4] His tendency, in the main, seems to have been toward opening the doors of the Court to seamen suitors.

Where the suitors were foreign shipowners, Lushington found jurisdictional decisions more difficult to reach. Holding the Court unable to entertain a claim in one case,[5] he later found jurisdiction in a case with a very similar fact situation;[6] he would not entertain suit by a foreign shipowner for restraint pending security,[7] but he did exercise the Court's jurisdiction over the possessory claim of a foreign government (U.S.A.),[8] though in both cases the Court clearly had the *res* within its geographical jurisdiction; and in a suit between foreign shipowners he required bail from the defendant in the principal action *in rem*, but held that the Court had no power to require bail from the plaintiffs as defendants of a cross-action *in personam*, though the causes of action and equities of the parties were in both cases the same.[9]

Causes of action arising in foreign waters also proved troublesome for Dr Lushington; he entertained one cause of collision in an Indian river by reasoning that the jurisdiction of the High

---

[1] Coote, 1st ed., p. 99.   [2] 1859 Rules, r. 10.

[3] Parsons, p. 229, n. 2; *cf. Hay v. Brig Bloomer*, 11 Fed. Cas. 893 (No. 6255) (D. Mass. 1859).

[4] *The Golubchick*, (1840) 1 W. Rob. 143, 147; see also *The Nina*, (1867) L.R. 2 P.C. 38, 47; and 8 *B.D.I.L.* 390 *et seq.*

[5] *The Ida*, (1860) Lush. 6.   [6] *The Courier*, (1862) Lush. 541.

[7] *The Graf A. Bernstorff*, (1854) 2 Sp. 30.

[8] *The Beatrice*, (1866) 36 *L.J. Adm.* 9, 10.

[9] *The Carlyle*, (1858) 30 *L.T.* 278.

Court of Admiralty 'has always' been co-extensive with that of any Vice-Admiralty Court which might have taken the suit[1] (a patently incorrect statement[2]), yet, in the same year, he declared that the Admiralty Court would categorically refuse to exercise jurisdiction over cases of collision of foreign vessels in foreign rivers, on the somewhat unclear rationale that the prohibition by the statutes of Richard II of the exercise of Admiralty jurisdiction in English rivers was somehow applicable to foreign rivers as well;[3] these positions were ultimately reconciled under §7 of the 1861 Court Act, interpreted by Dr Lushington to permit cognizance of collisions upon foreign waters whether involving British[4] or foreign[5] vessels.

It may indeed have been the volume of legislation affecting the Admiralty Court during his judgeship which caused Lushington to adopt a view of its status that differed markedly from that of his predecessors. The earlier view, as stated by Lord Stowell[6] and Sir John Nicholl,[7] was that foreign parties could not enjoy the defences of municipal law because the Court of Admiralty in instance was a Court of International Law rather than a Court of Municipal Law; Dr Lushington's position was diametrically opposite, for in upholding the defence of a foreign shipowner—based upon municipal law—he remarked that: 'the Instance Court of Admiralty is a municipal court, and it is bound to obey the statutes of the realm in all matters.'[8]

Statutory interpretation frequently posed problems for Lushington; more difficult, no doubt, because the nature of most of the statutes affecting the Court was creative rather than amendatory. In some cases he evidently felt that a statutory provision was merely designed to emancipate a previously legitimate piece of the Admiralty jurisdiction from repression by prohibition,[9] but in others, where the applicable provision was one which clearly offered a totally novel extension of the jurisdiction, he often had a tendency to waver; this may be illustrated by two interpretations of §7 of the 1861 Court Act, one holding that 'damage done by any ship' included that done by a tug in negligently bringing her

---

[1] *The Peerless*, (1860) Lush. 30, 40; *aff'd*, 13 Moo. P.C. 484.
[2] See *infra*, p. 71.   [3] *The Ida*, (1860) Lush. 6.
[4] *The Diana*, (1862) Lush. 539.   [5] *The Courier*, (1862) Lush. 541.
[6] Nys, p. 137.   [7] *The Girolamo*, (1834) 3 Hag. Adm. 169, 184.
[8] *The Johannes*, (1860) Lush. 182, 188.
[9] See, *e.g.*, *The Ironsides*, (1862) Lush. 458, 466.

tow into collision with another vessel,[1] and the other, shortly thereafter, holding that the section did not cover the damage done by a tug in negligently bringing her tow aground,[2] his reasoning there being that this was a breach of contract actionable only at common law—because 'damage' meant only 'collision' (an historically unsound interpretation[3] which was later specifically overruled[4]).

In fairness it ought to be noted that interpretation of the 1861 Court Act is acknowledged to have 'given considerable difficulty' to later lawyers, and that because of this, many jurisdictional questions still remained unsettled at the end of the nineteenth century.[5] For some later doubts, however, Lushington is almost surely directly to blame; his decisional 'about-face' from the position that an action *in rem* could not be instituted unless an action *in personam* upon the same cause was also possible,[6] to the position that an action *in rem* could be brought where an action *in personam* was clearly impossible,[7] set in motion a judicial seesaw which has perhaps not yet come to rest.[8] Again, his shift from the award of costs which, together with the judgment, exceeded the bail in an action *in rem*[9] to a diametrically opposite position[10] and then, upon an interpretation of §19 of the 1861 Admiralty Court Act, returning to his previous holding,[11] has had interesting repercussions.[12] And in one decision, he neatly avoided the problem of apportioning costs by condemning a co-suitor with the Crown in the entire cost of the suit, rather than writing off the Crown's half of the costs to the fee fund.[13]

In general, the pattern of Lushington's decisions—barring occasional anomalies—tended toward an expansion of the Admiralty jurisdiction; and in this he was clearly influenced to a considerable extent by American decisions which had the same effect. He often quoted Mr Justice Story at length,[14] and would compare

---

[1] *The Nightwatch*, (1862) Lush. 542.
[2] *The Robert Pow*, (1863) Br. & Lush. 99.
[3] See *The Ruckers*, (1801) 4 C. Rob. 73; also A. Browne, vol. 2, p. 397, ¶2.
[4] *The Zeta*, [1893] A.C. 468, 485.
[5] See Marsden, 'Six Centuries', p. 176.
[6] *The Druid*, (1842) 1 W. Rob. 391.
[7] *The Ruby Queen*, (1861) Lush. 266. [8] See *infra*, pp. 148–9.
[9] *The John Dunn*, (1840) 1 W. Rob. 159.
[10] *The Mellona*, (1846) 10 Jur. 992. [11] *The Temiscouata*, (1855) 2 Sp. 208.
[12] See *infra*, pp. 174–5. [13] *The Leda*, (1863) Br. & Lush. 19.
[14] See, *e.g.*, *The Magellan Pirates*, (1853) 1 Sp. 81, 90–1.

or contrast Story's views with those of Stowell, Tenterden, and other English jurists.[1] Dr Lushington was fascinated by the evolutionary contrasts between his Court and those on the opposite side of the Atlantic, and in the course of one decision, he put forth this theory:

In the American Courts, probably, a wider jurisdiction is conceded [cit.]. And the Admiralty Courts in our North American provinces exercise a fuller jurisdiction than the High Court of Admiralty of England. The reason seems to be that, after the Revolution of 1640 broke out, there was a great jealousy against the Ecclesiastical Courts, and this was extended to the Court of Admiralty, and so in Lord Holt's time its jurisdiction was curtailed; whereas in our North American colonies, there were no Ecclesiastical Courts to excite any such jealousy, and the jurisdiction of the Admiralty remained on its ancient footing.[2]

He must have been fascinated by the peculiar statutory grant of a jury trial upon request in Admiralty causes arising upon the Great Lakes[3] (wondering, perhaps, what the influence of the 1840 Court Act, §11, might have been), and the great legal battle fought to the Supreme Court over that provision and the extension of Admiralty jurisdiction to the Lakes at all, culminating in the rejection of the ancient limitation of jurisdiction to tidal water.[4] Nor were such judicial extensions of jurisdiction as that encompassing wrongful conversion of a whale upon the high seas likely to have escaped his notice,[5] and it is perhaps little wonder that his decision establishing the discretion of the Court to apply the doctrine of *forum non conveniens*[6] bears a notable resemblance to a decision on the same point made a few years earlier by Judge Ware.[7] No Admiralty Judge before or since his time has had a better knowledge of the comparative features of the Admiralty Laws of the English-speaking world, and none put such knowledge to better use than Lushington.

In his view of the equitable nature of Admiralty, Lushington was consistently firmly assertive. In ordering the marshalling of

[1] See, *e.g.*, *The Constancia*, (1846) 2 W. Rob. 487, 490–1.
[2] *The Royal Arch*, (1857) Swab. 269, 277.
[3] Act of February 26, 1845, c. 20; see Conkling, pp. 3–8.
[4] See *The Genesee Chief v. Fitzhugh*, 12 How. (53 U.S.) 443 (1851); see also Parsons, pp. 163–5.
[5] *Taber v. Jenny*, 23 Fed. Cas. 605 (No. 13720) (D. Mass. 1856).
[6] *The Golubchick*, (1840) 1 W. Rob. 143.
[7] *The Bee*, 3 Fed. Cas. 41 (No. 1219) (D. Me. 1836).

assets for the payment of Admiralty claims, a practice which he made common in the Admiralty Court,[1] Dr Lushington declared that the Court 'sits as a Court of Equity';[2] and later: 'if a Court of Equity would relieve, and a Court of Law could not, . . . it would be my duty to afford . . . relief . . . The jurisdiction which I exercise is an equitable as well as a legal jurisdiction . . .'[3] Of course Admiralty jurisdiction has always exhibited an equitable character, particularly in rewarding salvage,[4] but Dr Lushington was the first Admiralty Judge consistently to claim an equitable jurisdiction *per se*, though he had some doubts that it was sufficient to permit him formally to try equitable titles;[5] but he had no hesitancy in applying the equitable doctrine of laches to bar the enforcement of stale maritime liens,[6] and his views as to the Court's equitable powers have served the Court well since it formally obtained the jurisdiction of Equity.[7]

Lushington, a complex personality, seems to have been at his best in coping with cases of great complexity—whether on the facts,[8] as in cases of possessory suits to determine the title to ships sold by the master abroad,[9] or on the law, as in considering the special status of passengers as salvors, involving a delicate balance of law and facts in determining whether the service was sufficiently extraordinary to merit reward.[10] Moreover, in reaching his decisions as Admiralty Judge, Dr Lushington showed a vigorous determination to preserve the independence of Admiralty, to the extent that he declared himself not bound by decisions at common law of the House of Lords,[11] and that, though he might attach great weight to such decisions, and felt bound to respect decisions of the Privy Council, and of the Courts of common law on the construction of statutes,[12] yet 'a verdict obtained in the same cause at Common Law, ought not to be cited' in the

---

[1] See Coote, 2nd ed., p. 143.
[2] *The Trident*, (1839) 1 W. Rob. 29, 35.
[3] *The Harriet*, (1841) 1 W. Rob. 182, 192.
[4] See Abbott, p. 999.
[5] *The Victoria*, (1858) Swab. 408, 410; *cf. supra*, pp. 11, 43.
[6] See, *e.g.*, *The Europa*, (1861) Br. & Lush. 89, 91, 97.
[7] See, *e.g.*, *The Tubantia*, [1924] P. 78.
[8] See, *e.g.*, *The Margaret Mitchell*, (1858) Swab. 382.
[9] See, *e.g.*, *The Bonita*, (1861) Lush. 252.
[10] See, *e.g.*, *The Vrede*, (1861) Lush. 323; *cf. Newman v. Walters*, (1804) 3 Bos. & Pul. 612.
[11] *The Actæon*, (1853) 1 Sp. 176, 177.
[12] See Coote, 1st ed., p. 16.

Admiralty Court, and any article in the pleadings which recited a prior action at common law was accordingly stricken.[1]

The final impression of Lushington as a Judge is an extremely mixed one; judicial inconsistency—a serious fault to bring to any bench—was surely his greatest and most obvious short-coming, and yet in some lines of decision traceable throughout his judgeship he clung tenaciously to the same principles;[2] he seemed sometimes to let an opportunity to extend the Court's jurisdiction slip from his grasp, and yet under his aegis it acquired jurisdiction never before possessed; and he made some totally unaccountable statements concerning the evolution of the Law and Court of Admiralty,[3] yet he was in general better versed in this small branch of history than any other holders of his office have been.

If in these ways Lushington was a man of contradictions, in others no doubts could gather. From the time of acting as advocate for the mistreated crewman of the *Lowther Castle*,[4] he was benevolent to the plight of the mariner. He was a lover of unpopular causes, and he made his foremost cause the strengthening and advancement of the Admiralty Court; he strove consistently for the modernization of the Admiralty Law, and his success in this was acknowledged.[5] And he had no fear of the common lawyers, at a time when they could have done much to upset the Court's progress had they so desired.

It is well to remember that a magnified view inevitably shows blemishes otherwise unnoticed. Dr Lushington was Judge of the High Court of Admiralty for one year less than the term of Lord Stowell, and yet in those twenty-nine years the Court grew more prodigiously than in any comparable period in its history; more importantly, the greatly increased volume of instance causes adjudicated during those years dealt heavily with both statutes granting new jurisdiction and exercises of that new jurisdiction to an extent which has never been equalled—and the overall result has been a body of decision which may still be relied upon to guide the Court's continuing development.[6]

---

[1] *The Clarence*, (1854) 1 Sp. 206, 209.   [2] See *infra*, p. 173.

[3] See, *e.g.*, *supra*, pp. 68–9; *infra*, p. 94.

[4] See (1825) 1 Hag. Adm. 384; *supra*, p. 45.

[5] See, *e.g.*, Roberts, p. 6.

[6] In the U.S. as well; see, *e.g.*, *The Nyland*, 164 F. Supp. 741, 743 (D. Md. 1958).

As to his ranking amongst Admiralty Judges, Dr Stephen Lushington can be considered second only to Lord Stowell—and in addition it must be granted that Lushington was Judge throughout the most difficult and challenging period in the history of the instance jurisdiction.

But that liberal quality which was Lushington's fame helped— quite unintentionally—to bring about the destruction of the civilians as an English institution, for it was during his judgeship, and partially as a result of his recommendations for Court reform, that the College of Advocates was dissolved.

CHAPTER 3

THE FALL OF DOCTORS' COMMONS

DOCTORS' COMMONS is situate in Great Knight-Rider-street, to the south of St Paul's Cathedral. It is the college of civilians, where the civil law is studied and practised, and derives its name from the civilians commoning together as in other colleges. Here are kept the courts which have cognizance of injuries of an *ecclesiastical, military,* and *maritime* nature.[1]

So commences a description of that bastion of the civil law in England, given at the dawn of the nineteenth century by the most elegant of London's pictorial surveys. But in modern London the few yards of Knightrider Street which run along behind the College of Arms bear no traces whatever of the College of Civilians, and the name of Doctors' Commons has itself lain ghostly for more than a century.

What this august body was, how it came to be, and, more significantly, how it came to be dissolved, is intricately bound up with and essential to an understanding of the subsequent evolution of the Law and Court of Admiralty, for it literally *was* the Admiralty Court for hundreds of years. Moreover, 'the part played by the doctors in ... the development of maritime law ... seems a topic of wider interest than anything they did as Canonists ...'[2]

As it is a natural concomitant of the existence of any profession that its practitioners associate themselves in some formal way, it is not surprising that those advocates in the courts of the civil law should have formed an association somewhat akin to the Inns of Court formed by their barrister counterparts at common law. The official title of this organization, the 'College of Doctors of Law, exercent in the Ecclesiastical and Admiralty Courts', was not acquired until its Royal Charter in 1768,[3] but the 'College of Civilians', 'College of Advocates', or, more popularly, 'Doctors' Commons' (taken from the physical premises of the College) had already been in existence for centuries. As for the practice of

---

[1] Ackermann, vol. I, p. 224.
[2] Senior, intro., p. v; but see Moore, p. 128; Nys, pp. 105–7.
[3] See Parl. Paper [1859] (19) xxii (H.C. 20 January), p. 2.

Admiralty, the Doctors were organized by 1430,[1] and records of the College itself run from its formal foundation in 1511 by Dr Richard Bodewell, then Dean of the Arches.[2]

The civilians were the descendants of the mediaeval canon lawyers, and retained that heritage by continuing their monopoly over Ecclesiastical as well as Admiralty practice;[3] it is said to have been the suppression of the canonists by Henry VIII—who abolished the Faculties of Canon Law at Cambridge and at Oxford—which turned them principally to the practice of the civil law,[4] and in this they must have established themselves without delay, for the Masters in Chancery during the Tudor era were evidently civilians.[5] Doctors' Commons seems to have been an 'offspring' of Trinity Hall, Cambridge, itself founded in 1350 as a college for study of the civil and canon laws,[6] and despite other schemes—such as that of Protector Somerset to found 'Edward's College' in the University of Cambridge for the sole study of the civil law[7]—Trinity Hall continued to act as 'parent' to Doctors' Commons until the latter received its own charter.

To become a Fellow of the College of Advocates, one must have earned a doctorate in civil law at either Oxford or Cambridge. This was a strict requirement; holders of doctorates from other universities were not eligible, nor would a 'Lambeth Degree' [by archiepiscopal mandamus] or doctorate *honoris causa* in one of the two ancient universities suffice.[8] Moreover, despite (or perhaps, because of) the ecclesiastical functions of the College and its concern with canon law, no person in holy orders was admissible —even if, as in the case of the unfortunate Dr Highmore, he had abandoned his clerical calling and taken a doctorate with the express intention of practising in Doctors' Commons.[9]

The candidate must then have been admitted as an advocate of the Arches, and elected by a majority of the Fellows of the College; admission as an advocate of the Arches was upon the completely discretionary fiat of the Archbishop of Canterbury directed to the Dean of the Arches, and this admission had to

[1] Senior, p. 33.
[2] *Id.* pp. 35, 72.
[3] See Roscoe, *H.C.A.*, p. 3.
[4] Senior, p. 65.
[5] *Id.*, pp. 70–1.
[6] *Id.*, pp. 75–6.
Reeve, pp. 32–3.
[7] Senior, pp. 69–70.
[8] *Id.*, pp. 77–8.
[9] *The King v. The Archbishop of Canterbury*, (1807) 8 East 213 [K.B.].

have been preceded by one year's Court attendance,[1] known as the 'Year of Silence', during which he was not allowed to plead.[2]

At Cambridge, where the doctorates of civil and canon law were conferred together in the LL.D., the course of study leading to the degree consumed a minimum of ten years for those not previously M.A. (otherwise eight years), and required both the attending and giving of lectures.[3] In addition to fulfilling these formal academic requirements, which were similar for the D.C.L. at Oxford, proceedings in the Courts of the two ancient Universities were also entrusted to the civilians.[4]

Because of the stringent course of qualification, the number of advocates was always small—and for this reason, perhaps, formal incorporation was delayed; but the body was large enough to require premises of its own. 'Wolsey is said to have planned the building of a fitting college in London for the doctors', most of whom were then lodged in Paternoster Row, by St Paul's.[5] But this scheme fell through, and so it was that in 1567 the Master of Trinity Hall, Dr Henry Hervey, obtained from the Dean and Chapter of St Paul's a lease (in the name of the Master and Fellows of Trinity Hall, Cambridge) in trust for the College of Advocates upon 'an ancient tenement, called Montjoy House' for the use of the civilians, and there the Admiralty Court soon began to sit,[6] having moved from the disused Church of St Margaret in Southwark.[7]

In 1665, the doctors fled the great plague, first sitting briefly in Winchester, and thence to Oxford, where the Court sat in the Hall of Jesus College[8] (of which the Admiralty Judge, Sir Leoline Jenkins, was the Principal). And then, with the civilians safe, the Fire of London in 1666 destroyed Montjoy House.[9] Evidently, while the new Doctors' Commons was being constructed upon the same site, the Admiralty Court sat at Exeter House in the Strand, returning in 1671 to the home of the doctors.[10]

Unfortunately, the Fire did nothing to resolve differences over

---

[1] See Holdsworth, *H.E.L.*, vol. 4, p. 236; vol. 12, p. 47; also Parl. Paper [1833] (670) vii (H.C. 15 August), p. 49.

[2] Nys, p. 118.

[3] See Holdsworth, *H.E.L.*, vol. 4, pp. 229–30 and n. 7.

[4] Senior, p. 11.   [5] *Id.*, p. 73, n. (2).

[6] See Parl. Paper [1859] (19) xxii (H.C. 20 January), p. 4.

[7] Senior, p. 27; also Roscoe, *Studies*, p. 9.   [8] *Id.*, p. 100.

[9] Parl. Paper [1859] (19) xxii, p. 5.

[10] See Roscoe, *Studies*, p. 3.

the lease, concerning which four great battles were fought with the Dean and Chapter; in the first three the doctors emerged victorious (though in the last of these only by a decree of the House of Lords), still paying in 1728 the same renewal fine negotiated by Dr Hervey—£20. The fourth battle, however, was won by the Dean and Chapter, and the existence of Doctors' Commons was quite precarious for a time, until the doctors decided to bargain with the Dean and Chapter without trustees, whereupon Trinity Hall lost its parental association with the doctors, and they, 'at a very considerable expense', obtained a Royal Charter in 1768. Whether this step was of much help may be doubted, for the best terms which the Doctors were able to secure amounted to a forty-year lease at a fine of £4,200 plus £105 *per annum* to the Dean and Chapter—which they could just meet by mortgaging the lease on hard terms. Only the success of a petition to the Crown averted financial disaster, and a Royal Bounty of £3,000 was granted from the droits of Admiralty in 1782, which enabled the purchase of the freehold.[1]

The number of Fellows of Doctors' Commons rose from seventeen at its incorporation to twenty-six by 1858[2]—still an incredibly small body to have had an absolute monopoly upon all the legal practice within its sphere. The monopoly was also physical, for in addition to the Admiralty Court, the Common [dining] Hall of Doctors' Commons was the sitting-place of the Court of Arches, the Court of Peculiars, the Prerogative Court of Canterbury, the Consistory Court of London, the Dean and Chapter of St Paul's Court, the Court of Rochester, the Court of Surrey,[3] the Archdeacons' Court, and the High Court of Delegates;[4] and it seems probable that, prior to the nineteenth century, it was occasionally host to other civil law courts such as the High Court of Chivalry [Court of Constable and Marshal].[5] Interestingly, maritime criminal proceedings were tried at Admiralty Sessions in the Old Bailey before two common law judges, with the Admiralty Judge presiding.[6]

Even granting the existence of a monopoly so comprehensive

[1] See Parl. Paper [1859] (19) xxii (H.C. 20 January), pp. 5–6; also Nys, p. 117.
[2] See Parl. Paper [1859] (19) xxii, pp. 2, 7.
[3] See Parl. Paper [1833] (670) vii (H.C. 15 August), pp. 9–27.
[4] See Ackermann, p. 225.
[5] *Id.*, p. 224 (note reference to *military* causes).
[6] See Parl. Paper [1833] (670) vii, p. 35.

that Sir John Nicholl—as Judge of the Admiralty, Dean of the Arches, Dean of Peculiars, and Judge of the Prerogative Court of Canterbury—heard virtually *all* Admiralty and probate matters in England, and both original and appellate ecclesiastical causes as well,[1] it must be admitted that the legal knowledge of the doctors was vast and unique, and acquired with a special view to the needs of the courts in which they practised. The instance side of the Admiralty Court was 'governed by the civil law, the laws of Oleron, and the customs of the Admiralty, modified by statute law';[2] and in addition to such technical legal knowledge, a grasp of the practicalities of the field was necessary, for 'the interrogator ... should possess some small knowledge of seamanship, otherwise his questions may excite ridicule'[3]—a point of particular importance with the advent of oral testimony—and he had to beware of witnesses who were brought up in the coal or coasting trade, particularly if in square-rigged ships, for their nautical acumen was alleged to be formidable.[4]

Not only was the doctors' knowledge of the law put to use in the civil law courts, but in those of common law as well, for Lord Mansfield established the practice of bringing the civilians into the King's Bench to give argument in causes involving maritime questions,[5] and a development of this custom can be seen in Dr Lushington's judgeship, where, in a case of murder on the high seas, Drs Dodson and Phillimore for the Crown, and Dr Addams for the defence, gave argument before thirteen Judges of the Court for Crown Cases Reserved in the Hall of Serjeants' Inn.[6]

In addition to their practice in Doctors' Commons and the academic work which many of the doctors retained, one of their chief occupations lay in their capacity as legal advisers to the Crown upon any questions of international law, and they were frequently appointed as official representatives of the realm in matters of legal diplomacy.[7]

The function of the doctors as surrogates, sitting temporarily for the judges of the courts of civil law, was fairly commonly

---

[1] See Parl. Paper [1833] (670) vii (H.C. 15 August), pp. 9–27.
[2] A. Browne, vol. 2, p. 29.   [3] Van Heythuysen, p. 8.
[4] See *id.*, p. 7.   [5] See Senior, p. 107.
[6] *R. v. Serva* (*The Felicidade*), (1845) 2 Car. & K. 54; *The Times*, 17 Nov. & 4 Dec.
[7] See Nys, ch., VII, pp. 123–38, 'Les Avis et les Consultations'; also 7 *B.D.I.L.* 243, 'Legal Advisers of the Crown'.

exercised until the mid-nineteenth century. And the custom must have arisen long before, for it is said that after Dr Lewes became Admiralty Judge in 1558 he continued to practise as an advocate (presumably in the other courts) for five or six years in order to make a living, and that he complained of his surrogates' withdrawal from the Court, which forced him to attend to all of his judicial duties.[1] Evidently all of the Fellows of Doctors' Commons were surrogates, or eligible to act as such, for the Judge of the Admiralty,[2] and occasionally a surrogate sitting for the Judge rendered a decision of importance, as in the case of *Lord Warden of the Cinque Ports v. the King in his office of Admiralty*[3] (this last being the proper form of address to the office of Lord High Admiral while in Commission[4]), where Dr Joseph Phillimore, sitting for Sir Christopher Robinson, established the principle of awarding a salvage recovery to the captors of royal fish. By the 1840 Court Act, only the Dean of the Arches was permitted to sit as surrogate for the Admiralty Judge, and then only in certain cases;[5] perhaps because of the uselessness of this provision after 1858, when Dr Lushington became Dean of Arches as well as Admiralty Judge, the 1861 Court Act allowed the Admiralty Registrar to sit as surrogate,[6] and from that time until the abolition of surrogates by the Judicature Acts the Registrar (and, in his place, the Deputy Registrar[7]) was the only surrogate. The last instance of the exercise of the Admiralty jurisdiction by a surrogate seems to have been in 1874, when the Registrar in that capacity pronounced a decree upon default in an action *in rem*.[8]

The attorneys and solicitors had their civilian counterparts as well; this other class of practitioners in Doctors' Commons was also of ancient origin, the title *proctor* being said to derive from the Roman *procurator*.[9] This body, though not subject to the rigorous process of selection which limited the number of advocates, was likewise a small one; there were only nineteen practising Proctors-in-Admiralty in 1833,[10] and the number had perhaps doubled by 1855.[11]

[1] Senior, p. 79.
[2] See *id.*, p. 78.
[3] (1831) 2 Hag. Adm. 438.
[4] A. Browne, vol. 2, p. 27.
[5] Admiralty Court Act, 1840, §1.
[6] Admiralty Court Act, 1861, §25.
[7] Thompson, p. 32.
[8] *The Vladimir*, [unrep.]; see Thompson, p. 32.
[9] Parsons, p. 358.
[10] See Parl. Paper [1833] (670) vii (H.C. 15 August), p. 62.
[11] See *Papers on 1855 Rules*, p. 16.

Not a great deal can be said concerning the life led by the proctors, save that they formed firms and had their offices in Doctors' Commons (though not members thereof), that they had a monopoly over their sphere of activity in the civil law, which corresponded to that of the advocates retained by them, and that, as will be seen, they were most conscious of any threat to their purses. The duties of the Proctor-in-Admiralty to the Court were the subject of comment by Lord Stowell, who evidently felt that not enough was done to secure settlement out of Court in appropriate cases—indeed, he accused one proctor of maintenance, and condemned him personally in the costs of the suit.[1] A similar action was taken by Dr Lushington on one occasion when in a suit commenced on behalf of the master, owners, and crew of a vessel, judgment having gone for the defendant, the plaintiffs' proctor confessed that he did not know who his clients were.[2] This situation may have arisen because the procedure whereby a proctor was required to exhibit a proxy by way of power of attorney to conduct the suit in order to institute it—though once a firm rule —had by Lushington's day become routinely ignored.[3]

Architecturally, Doctors' Commons was evidently quite splendid. The 'Great Quadrangle' (of which there is a drawing in the London Museum) was entered through an archway from Knightrider Street, and opposite was another archway leading into a second quadrangle and a garden. The buildings included the dwellings and chambers of the advocates and the offices of the proctors (which prior to 1770 were sublet by Trinity Hall), the Common Hall, and an informal dining room, over which was a 'spacious and well-stocked' library[4] (the catalogue of 1818 was 236 pages long[5]). The Admiralty Registry's address was 'Number 3 Paul's Bakehouse Court, Doctors' Commons', but it actually occupied numbers two and three, in the latter of which the Marshal also had his office. After 1770 the individual advocates became sublessors—it will be recalled that in 1853 the landlord of the Registry premises was Dr Addams.[6]

The Common Hall seems to have been used only infrequently for dining, and it is certainly better known as a courtroom. The hearing of ecclesiastical causes must have been both colourful

---

[1] *The Frederick*, (1823) 1 Hag. Adm. 211, 219–24, 225.
[2] *The Whilelmine*, (1842) 1 W. Rob. 335. [3] See Parsons, p. 358.
[4] Senior, p. 101. [5] Nys, p. 119 *et seq.*
[6] See McGuffie, *Notes on Letter Books*, pp. 14–15, 24.

and picturesque (see the plate, p. xxix), with the doctors resplendent in their scarlet robes, academic hoods and round black velvet doctors' bonnets, and the proctors in gowns of dark blue with the hoods of their degrees worn by those who were graduates of the Universities, and hoods lined with lamb's skin by those who were not; proceedings in Admiralty were slightly more sombre because the doctors wore their black academic gowns, but the gilt anchor remained fixed above the bench at all times, with the Judge and advocates seated upon a raised dais above the proctors, who were seated almost at floor level around a green-topped table, at one end of which was the bar of the Court.[1]

Charles Dickens, himself a freelance reporter in Doctors' Commons for about five years from 1828, later satirized the civilians in *David Copperfield*; Dickens had been office boy to the firm of Ellis & Blackmore, so his David became articled to the fictitious proctors' firm of Spenlow & Jorkins. He described[2] Doctors' Commons as 'a lazy old nook ... that has an ancient monopoly in ... disputes among ships and boats', the typical proctor as 'a sort of monkish attorney— ... a functionary whose existence, in the natural course of things, would have terminated about two hundred years ago', and the doctors, whose 'red gowns and grey wigs' he found noteworthy, were less curious to him than a certain Judge (possibly Sir Christopher Robinson), 'whom, if I had seen him in an aviary, I should certainly have taken for an owl.' The system of surrogates, complicated by a common courtroom for all of the various types of causes, evoked this vision:

... and you shall find the judge in the nautical case, the advocate in the clergyman's case, or contrariwise. They are like actors; now a man's a judge, and now he is not a judge ... but it's always a very pleasant, profitable little affair of private theatricals, presented to an uncommonly select audience.[3]

As to the whole of Doctors' Commons, Dickens concluded:

Altogether, I have never, on any occasion, made one at such a cosey, dosey, old-fashioned, time-forgotten, sleepy-headed little family party in all my life; and I felt it would be quite a soothing opiate to belong to it in any character—except perhaps as a suitor.[4]

[1] See Senior, p. 77; also Roscoe, *Studies*, pp. 6–7.
[2] See Holdsworth, *Dickens*, pp. 30–3.
[3] From *David Copperfield*, ch. 23; Holdsworth, *Dickens*, p. 31.
[4] *Ibid.; id.*, p. 33.

Judging by what evidence is available in the present, Dickens' satirical view is probably not far off the true mark of the outward appearance of Doctors' Commons in his day; but while allowing the accuracy of these external observations, 'let us not forget it was a talented little family . . . ; that some of its members . . . have left a permanent mark upon all those various branches of the law which once made up the sphere of the civilians' practice.'[1]

The tranquil atmosphere of Doctors' Commons was shattered in 1853 by the revelation of the Swabey affair, and it never was regained. In large part, this was due to the activities of the new Admiralty Registrar, H. C. Rothery, whose zeal for reform of the Admiralty Court often generated friction with the practitioners. Partly, this was a direct outgrowth of the Swabey matter itself, which soon resulted in the substitution of stamps for cash receipts by the Court Act of 1854; it appears that the collection of fees by stamps was first suggested by Rothery, in a letter written by him to the Treasury Secretary a few months prior to the passage of the 1854 Act.[2] This change was rather unwelcome to the proctors because they had earlier enjoyed the benefit of fee accounts kept in each name by a full-time fee clerk in the Registry. These accounts were rendered quarterly, so that the proctors might not have been billed until some months after the conclusion of a cause (and they were evidently slow to pay the accounts even once they had received them[3]). After the abolition of receipts for fees and the substitution of stamps, the proctors were naturally obliged to part with cash at each stage of an action which required a praecipe for its initiation—a grievous irritation to many of them. So thorough, indeed, was Rothery's fee reform, that the only fees to be collected without stamps after 1854 were those of the Seal Keeper (6d. to 1s. for each affixation) and the Court Crier (5s. upon each sentence or decree), who were the sole unsalaried officers.[4]

It was not Rothery's action in securing fees by stamp (which closely resembled the scheme already in use in Chancery[5]), however, which provoked the proctors into an attack upon him, but his proposals for effecting reform of the Court's procedure.

---

[1] Holdsworth, *H.E.L.*, vol. 12, p. 50.
[2] See *Papers on 1855 Rules*, p. 32, ¶5.
[3] *Id.*, ¶¶4, 5.   [4] *Id.*, p. 34, ¶3.
[5] See *id.*, p. 32, ¶5.

These he first put forth in a privately published pamphlet in 1853 entitled *Suggestions for an Improved Mode of Pleading*, and which, in itself, was by no means objectionable to the proctors though it emphasized particularly the need to modernize the rules governing oral testimony. It was later asserted that the adoption of Rothery's suggestions gave to the Admiralty Court a longevity not enjoyed by the other principal courts of Doctors' Commons,[1] and this may very well have been the case; but it is surely true that his successes in 1853 and 1854 put Rothery in a position of great strength regarding the introduction of other procedural reforms, some of which, in retrospect, are much more difficult to support. The suggestion upon which the ire of the proctors became focused was that advanced by Rothery in his 1855 rule proposals which called for the printing of each instance proceeding, including the pleadings and proofs for each party; in May 1855, a considerable number of firms and individual proctors signed a strong letter of protest addressed to Dr Lushington.

The proctors viewed Rothery's proposals 'with considerable alarm and anxiety', and they opened with the charge that 'these Rules have been kept from the body of Proctors, whilst some of the junior members of the profession have been consulted on the subject'.[2] While the letter then went on to complain that the proposed mode of examination of witnesses would, in their opinion, add to expense and delay, the great majority of the proctors' attention was directed to the printing proposal. There can be no doubt, despite other peripheral arguments, that the fear of the proctors was for their purses; they took pains to point out that Proctors-in-Admiralty traditionally advanced money out of their own pockets to carry on suits (a practice which sometimes developed to maintenance), and that the new practice of paying fees by stamps—which they viewed as 'excessive', and 'a great practical evil'—had already materially reduced their remuneration, so that the burden of cost of printing the proceedings—'a hazardous experiment'—would prove ruinous to them, as the printing of the bills in Chancery had to solicitors practising in that Court.[3]

Rothery offered a lengthy and reasoned reply to the complaints

---

[1] See 5 *L. Mag. & Rev.* (n.s.) 34, 35 (1858).
[2] *Papers on 1855 Rules*, p. 14, ¶1.   [3] *Id.*, pp. 14–15.

of the proctors, the crux of which was his calculation that 100 copies of a proceeding could be printed 'at little more than the price' of one manuscript copy, and this statement he supported by figures which he had prepared and circulated in 1854.[1] By itself, this impressive argument could probably have served Rothery's purpose, but, perhaps angered to the point of intemperance, he then ventured to suggest (1) that the proctors' clerks were abused by being forced to do 'constant routine copying, which ends by making them mere machines', (2) that the proctors' charges to clients in appellate causes were 'wholly unjustifiable', (3) that the situations in Chancery and Admiralty were not comparable, and (4), that 'the great majority' of the complaining proctors were 'not amongst the most competent to form a correct judgment', because their practice was largely in the Prerogative and Ecclesiastical Courts, and that many of the most active Proctors-in-Admiralty had not signed the letter.[2] Probably no answer could have been more calculated to infuriate the opposed proctors, and to Rothery's last assertion must be compared two names in particular amongst those who did sign the letter, Dr Edwin Edwards and Henry C. Coote, both of whom authored leading texts on Admiralty jurisdiction and practice.

Prior to the Registrar's answer, Dr Lushington released his draft of the Order-in-Council for the 1855 Rules, and from a comparison of it with the letter written by the proctors[3] it can be seen that several of Rothery's proposals were dropped from the eventual 1855 Rules, and these were, specifically, seven rules which would have forced the proctors to use the Admiralty Registry as an agent for the printing of the proceedings, at a fixed fee.[4] But the provision for compulsory printing of the proceedings, Rule 10, was secured nonetheless, and the 1855 Rules therefore embodied the proctors' major objection, which evidently continued to be voiced, for in the following year Rothery said of the 1855 Rules: 'They give me a great deal of occupation and some anxiety from the continued opposition of the Proctors.'[5] It was during this unrest that the last crisis of the existence of Doctors' Commons began.

Three Judges of the High Court of Admiralty (Sir Charles

---

[1] See *Papers on 1855 Rules*, pp. 19, 25–30. [2] *Id.*, pp. 20–4.
[3] *Id.* pp. 3–5, 14, 15. [4] *Id.*, p. 21.
[5] McGuffie, *Notes on Letter Books*, p. 128.

Hedges, Sir George Hay, Sir John Nicholl) had in addition held the Judgeship of the Prerogative Court of Canterbury, which tried nearly all testamentary causes in England; despite virtually unanimous testimony, including that of Sir John Nicholl, in opposition to a consolidation of the two judgeships, the 1833 Report of the Select Parliamentary Committee on the Admiralty Court recommended not only a single Judge for the Admiralty and Prerogative Courts, but the merger of the latter with the Court of Arches, and the abolition of all other ecclesiastical courts.[1] Why nearly a quarter of a century passed before any action was taken upon that recommendation is not clear, but by Act of Parliament in 1857 a Court of Probate was established, the testamentary jurisdiction of the ecclesiastical courts was abolished and an exclusive jurisdiction conferred upon the new Court, a Judge of Probate was provided for, and it was also provided that the Judgeships of Admiralty and Probate might be merged upon the next vacancy in either office.[2]

Alone, this move was no threat to the security of the civilians; their *judicial* monopoly was still preserved. But probate matters had always been the mainstay of Doctors' Commons, and it was the monopoly over this *practice* which provided the great majority of the civilians' financial support. What would be the consequence of breaking this monopoly was made clear by several witnesses in the 1833 Report, including the Lord Chief Justice; and the most succinct expression of this common opinion came from one later proven highly qualified in matters involving the finances of the courts of civil law—the then Deputy Registrar of the Admiralty Court, H. B. Swabey—in response to a question from Henry Labouchere, M.P.:

Q.: If the jurisdiction in matters testamentary were transferred from the Spiritual Courts to the Courts of Equity, could a bar and a set of practitioners be maintained for the Admiralty jurisdiction and the matrimonial only?—

A.: Certainly not.[3]

Despite that clear warning, the Court of Probate Act in 1857 broke the civilians' monopoly and admitted the common lawyers

[1] Parl. Paper [1833] (670) vii (H.C. 15 August), pp. 4–5.
[2] Court of Probate Act, 1857, §§3–10.
[3] Parl. Paper [1833] (670) vii, p. 62.

to probate practice, though reciprocally admitting the civilians to the practice of the common law.[1] And at the same time, another Act ended the monopoly over matrimonial causes, abolished the ecclesiastical matrimonial jurisdiction, conferred it upon a new Court for Divorce and Matrimonial Causes, and constituted as its Judge Ordinary the Admiralty Judge.[2]

Unaccountably, there have arisen complete misconceptions about the effect of the Court of Probate Act upon Doctors' Commons and its Admiralty practice; two statements in particular deserve attention, that 'by it [the Act] the College of Advocates ... was dissolved',[3] and that the Act 'abolished' the 'special privilege' of the civilians alone to practise in Admiralty;[4] these statements are unfortunately quite incorrect, and the truth is considerably more complex. What the 1857 Court of Probate Act did contain was a means of self-destruction for Doctors' Commons, in two sections which enabled the College of Advocates to buy and sell real and personal estates belonging to it, and to surrender its charter and dissolve itself.[5]

The Parliamentary debates of both Houses upon the bill were heavily concerned with proper compensation to the proctors for the loss of their monopoly, as the cost of entering that branch of the profession of the civil law had been so notoriously great—principally because of the tremendous premiums involved in securing articles and partnerships. Only once, however, does the plight of the doctors appear to have entered consideration—an M.P. asked briefly whether the College of Advocates, whose 'business ... would be at an end', ought not to be given the power to dispose of its assets—and in an equally brief reply the Attorney-General stated his opinion that legislative permission was not necessary, but that he would nonetheless welcome the inclusion of covering provisions in the Act.[6] At least this exchange serves to prove that the Act was not passed without the effect having been considered, and, indeed, it was clearly passed in anticipation of the doctors' loss of business.

One's impression must be that this was the final triumph of the

[1] Court of Probate Act, 1857, §§40, 42, 43, 45.
[2] Matrimonial Causes Act, 1857, §§2, 6, 11, 15.
[3] Roscoe, *H.C.A.*, pp. 3–4; *Studies*, p. 2.
[4] P.R.O., *Guide*, vol. 1, p. 157.
[5] Court of Probate Act, 1857, §§116, 117.
[6] Hansard, vol. 146 [H.C. Deb.], cols. 1307–8, 10 July 1857.

common lawyers—that they condemned the civilians and then handed them a razor with which to cut their own throats—and while this is essentially the case, such an assertion must be modified by two considerations: first, that it was done seemingly without a trace of malice, and in the sincere quest for betterment of the legal system, and, secondly, that the civilians need not have executed themselves, but might have continued to live, if not to prosper as before. These considerations, and the actual circumstances of the dissolution of Doctors' Commons seem wholly to have escaped subsequent exposure, and even the sole published work professing to deal specifically with the fall of the College places the onus upon the 1857 Act, *viz.*: 'thus encouraged, the doctors at last put an end to their corporate existence.'[1]

Again, the truth is somewhat more complicated; there in fact was a bitter and hard-fought battle within the College of Advocates. A faction of some size, headed by John Lee, LL.D., desired the preservation of the College as an institution for the promotion of the study of civil and canon law, and objected to any move to sell the property or surrender the charter of the College, which they felt might be 'handed down to a race of successors for as many years as it has by the prudence and wisdom of our predecessors already existed'.[2] The opposition to Dr Lee seems not to have been led by any one of the Fellows in particular, but there is every indication that Dr Lushington, at whose suggestion the merger of the Judgeships of Admiralty and Probate was provided for in the 1857 Act,[3] was willing to accept dissolution of the College as the inevitable price. It is not possible, however, to ascribe the highest motives to all of those who desired the surrender of the College charter, for it was also provided in the Act that upon surrender, all of the real and personal property of the College— amounting in value to many thousands of pounds—would be distributed in equal shares among the then Fellows of the College 'for their own use and benefit'.[4] Sadly, the main motive of the majority of the doctors in desiring the dissolution of the College appears to have been nothing more than simple avarice.

The Court of Probate Act came into operation on 11 January 1858, and on the 15th the Fellows first met to make their decisions;

---

[1] Senior, p. 110.   [2] Parl. Paper [1859] (19) xxii (H.C. 20 January), p. 9.
[3] Hansard, vol. 145 [H.L. Deb.], col. 390, 18 May 1857.
[4] Court of Probate Act, 1857, §117.

by 4 February, a majority of the Fellows had voted the immediate distribution of the College's personal property—£600. in consols to each—and Dr Lee had resolved to fight to the bitter end.[1] Lee's case was set forth in a memorial to the Visitors of the College, including the Archbishop of Canterbury and the Lord Chancellor, by which he argued that dissolution would be a breach of trust under the charter and contrary to the intent of the founders of the College, that the true intent of Parliament was to permit a reorganization of the college to enable it to continue its functions under the new circumstances, that dissolution would be a breach of faith with a public which looked to the College for inducement to those wishing to undertake study of the civil or canon law, that Parliament had not given any authorization for release of trusts set up under the charter, and that the resolution of the majority of the Fellows purporting to compel the compliance of Dr Lee and those who stood with him was an act *ultra vires* and void; and he concluded by praying that the Visitors would exercise their powers under the charter to institute an inquiry.[2]

An eminent legal historian has said of Dr Lee's argument, 'But, seeing that the College had never performed any educational functions, and that the property had been purchased by its members for purposes which could now no longer be carried out, it is impossible to support this contention.'[3] What could have induced such a fatuous statement is difficult to say, for even a superficial reading of the Court of Probate Act reveals (1) that the exclusive practice of the civilians was preserved in all non-contentious cases,[4] (2) that the civilians were as easily empowered to buy new property as to sell old property, and to apply income from property to the maintenance of their corporate body,[5] and (3) that nothing contained in the Court of Probate or Matrimonial Causes Acts affected in any way the monopoly still enjoyed by the civilians in practice before the Admiralty and Prize Courts and the yet-extant Ecclesiastical Courts. No one could argue that the doctors might have continued to practise law in the manner enjoyed under the probate and divorce monopolies, but it is

[1] Parl. Paper [1859] (19) xxii (H.C. 20 January), p. 11.
[2] Parl. Paper [1859] (19) xxii, pp. 6–16.
[3] Holdsworth, *H.E.L.*, vol. 12, p. 49.
[4] See Court of Probate Act, 1857, §40.
[5] Court of Probate Act, 1857, §116.

equally fallacious to assume that the purposes for which the College was established could no longer have been carried out. The statement that 'property had been purchased by its members' is incompatible with the fact of a corporate existence, confirmed in the statement that 'the *College* had never performed any educational functions', which in turn places a very narrow interpretation upon the function of the College in sustaining a body of learned civilians, many of whom were also great teachers and scholars, for upwards of three hundred years.

Dr Lee's plea to the Visitors was of no avail, and on 18 March 1858, the Fellows met for the reading of the engrossment of a deed constituting five of them trustees for the liquidation and distribution of the entire assets of the College. Both Dr Lee and Dr Tristam attempted to delay the adoption of the deed, but they were outvoted, and the seal of the College was affixed.[1] Still determined to avert extinction of the College, Dr Lee petitioned the new Home Secretary—the Government having changed since passage of the 1857 Acts—to initiate legislation to repeal §§116 & 117 of the Court of Probate Act and replace those sections with provisions which would have made Doctors' Commons Hall the probate courthouse, have re-vested the property covered by the deed in the College, and have amended the charter so as to open membership in the College to Doctors of Law of any Universities of the United Kingdom.[2] In this too, Dr Lee was unsuccessful, and after June 1858 he appears to have given up the fight.

Dr Lushington had in 1833 advocated opening the bar of Doctors' Commons to the common lawyers, a move which he felt would stimulate competition;[3] as it became apparent that the civilians were doomed to extinction, there was no point in further maintaining their monopoly over Admiralty practice, and so, with the passage of an act in 1859 which enabled Serjeants, Barristers, Attorneys and Solicitors to practise before the Admiralty Court,[4] the civilians became completely open to competition save in the Ecclesiastical Courts, where their peculiar expertise in the canon law was itself a sufficient barrier to competition.

It was the admission of the common lawyers to practise in

---

[1] Parl. Paper [1859] (19) xxii (H.C. 20 January), p. 17.
[2] *Id.*, pp. 1–18, and esp. pp. 17–18.
[3] Parl. Paper [1833] (670) vii (H.C. 15 August), p. 49.
[4] High Court of Admiralty Act,ˣ1859.

Admiralty that necessitated the 1859 Rules, which attempted to lay a complete procedural scheme before the new members of the Admiralty bar. This recodification, it might be added, gave to Rothery and Dr Lushington an opportunity to extend the printing requirements, over which controversy had died with the events of 1857–8, and thereafter it was necessary for each party to cause one hundred and fifty copies of the proceedings to be printed, of which seventy were filed and forty delivered to the opposing party.[1] This almost unbelievable requirement was rather belatedly condemned as a 'needless extravagance' by the Evershed Committee in 1951,[2] which perhaps served to placate a few restless proctorial ghosts in Knightrider Street.

So Doctors' Commons died by its own hand, with the shadow of mammon casting its pall over an otherwise glorious existence. Upon the doctors' vote to surrender, 'it is said that . . . the rooks, which some held to embody the spirits of departed civilians, forthwith forsook the trees in the College garden.'[3] As for the Admiralty Court, it continued to sit in the Hall of Doctors' Commons until early in 1860, when by Order-in-Council it was moved to Westminster Hall.[4] The Admiralty Registry is said to have moved to Somerset House in 1859,[5] but since it was still in 1867 giving its 'return address' as Doctors' Commons,[6] there is considerable doubt as to its complete removal until the termination of Dr Lushington's judgeship. The Common Hall of Doctors' Commons was, at any rate, demolished in 1861,[7] and the splendid library was dispersed, many of the volumes remaining today in the Admiralty Registry or in the storage basement of the Royal Courts of Justice.

Viewing the wreckage of this great institution of the civil law, one is struck by a final irony. The Doctors, in doing so excellent a job of exterminating themselves, probably helped to do likewise for their ancient rivals the Serjeants-at-Law. For, following the pattern almost exactly, the Order of the Coif was dissolved in 1877, Serjeants' Inn was sold along with other property of the guild, and the proceeds were distributed to the membership.

[1] 1859 Rules, r. 101; see Coote, 1st ed., p. 136s.
[2] Sup. Ct. Practice Comm., *Second Report*, Cmd. No. 8176, at 13–14, ¶¶30, 31 (1951). [3] Senior, p. 110.
[4] See Roscoe, *Studies*, p. 3. [5] *Id.*, p. 7.
[6] See Return to H.C. by Rothery, Adm. Reg'r., 28 May 1867, p. 1.
[7] Roscoe, *Studies*, p. 3.

The finest monument to Dr Lee's argument was probably the notable success achieved in practice and scholarship by a number of civilians following the dissolution of Doctors' Commons, and the somewhat chaotic upheavals in the civil and canon law following the civilians' final extinction.[1] The latter will be dealt with at a later stage, but of the former a word deserves now to be said.

The Proctors-in-Admiralty, who were paid as compensation for the loss of their livelihood a relatively insignificant sum equal to half of the yearly average of their income from probate work over the five years preceding the 1857 Act,[2] were able to recover themselves and continue to practise in the Admiralty Court, as did several of the doctors.[3] The new practitioners from the common law were given the benefit of a new treatise on Admiralty jurisdiction and practice written specifically for them by a proctor, Henry Coote,[4] continuing in the tradition of scholarly civilians such as Browne, Holt, and Van Heythuysen—whose works appear to have been overlooked by the Court's most eminent historian[5]—and Edwards. Scholars of the Court's early history were given a most valuable work by Dr Travers Twiss,[6] who edited Rolls series of the *Black Book of the Admiralty* in four volumes during the 1870s; Twiss also became the leading advocate at the Admiralty bar after the fall of Doctors' Commons, and was the last Queen's Advocate.[7] Such achievements effectively counter the assertion that the civilians had become 'superfluous', and the Doctors' Commons had 'outlived by many years its *raison d'etre*',[8] for as a body of learned specialists, so deferred to that scholars of legal systems ruled by the civil law felt it necessary to apologize to the doctors for presumptuousness in publishing treatises on maritime and international law,[9] it has since been unequalled in its eminence and unreplaced in its sphere.

In case it might be thought that the necessity for a college of civilians has been belied by the success of a system of Admiralty Law in nations such as the United States, which have never possessed such an organized body, certain contrasts ought to be illustrated. In the case of the United States, where a system of

[1] See Moore, pp. 128–9.   [2] Court of Probate Act, 1857, §105.
[3] See Roscoe, *Studies*, pp. 8–11.   [4] See Coote, 1st ed., intro., p. vii.
[5] See Marsden, 'Six Centuries', p. 176.
[6] See Fifoot, *Letters of F. W. Maitland*, Nos. 14, 100, 186.
[7] Roscoe, *Studies*, p. 8; H.C.A., p. 6.
[8] Senior, p. 111.   [9] See, *e.g.*, Reddie, intro., p. xxv.

ecclesiastical jurisdiction could never have developed owing to the absence of an established church, there was no need for canonists, and the civil law was restricted in application to matrimonial and Admiralty matters; as the former of these was reserved exclusively to the jurisdiction of the States, and the latter exclusively to the Federal jurisdiction, a bar which unified both was also an impossibility.

Despite the unpopularity of the Vice-Admiralty Courts as instruments of the British Exchequer, and resentment of the lack of trial by jury,[1] both the substantive[2] and procedural[3] aspects of the civil law survived into the Admiralty Law of the United States, with a clear recognition of both its European origin and its British transmission.[4] Owing, however, to the decentralization of both the Colonial Vice-Admiralty and Federal Admiralty Courts, and the practice of civil law in those Courts being restricted solely to Admiralty matters, it is manifest that during the eighteenth and early nineteenth centuries no lawyer could have sustained himself by limiting his practice to the civil law; therefore, though the legal profession was then divided in America as it was then and is today in England, Proctors-in-Admiralty were also Attorneys and Solicitors-at-Law, and Advocates in Admiralty were also Counselors at Law.[5] Fusion of the Admiralty branch of the profession was underway early in the latter half of the nineteenth century,[6] but even in the present day, with a completely integrated bar, it is necessary for an American lawyer to be first admitted to practise as a Solicitor, Attorney and Counselor before he may qualify as a Proctor and Advocate in Admiralty.

Without an organized body of civilians of its own, the American Admiralty bar came to rely for practical guidance upon the examples set by Doctors' Commons in England,[7] and it was necessary as well—as indeed it yet is—for Admiralty lawyers in the United States to supplement their training in the common law by making 'the civil law the subject of closest study'.[8]

The evolution of the American legal system thus produced a

[1] See Ubbelohde, pp. 143, 199.
[2] U.S. Constitution, Article III, §2, cl. 1.
[3] Judiciary Act of September 24, 1789, ch. 20, §2.
[4] See, e.g., Dunlap, p. 85.
[5] See Betts, pp. 9–14.
[6] See Parsons, p. 358.
[7] See Conkling, p. 409, n. (a).
[8] Betts, intro., pp. vii–ix.

bar which was less expert in the civil and international law than was Doctors' Commons, yet in general more educated in those fields than the common lawyers in England; this fact was noted early in the nineteenth century by a member of the College of Advocates,[1] and again after the fall of Doctors' Commons by the author of an English text on maritime legislation,[2] both observations being put forth in the course of arguments establishing the importance of Doctors' Commons as an English national institution.

While some Americans mastered the civil law—Judge Ware is a notable example[3]—there was an unevenness of quality in this regard which does not appear to have afflicted Doctors' Commons. A few eminent American civilians of the early nineteenth century, such as Dr Henry Wheaton (whose *Elements of International Law* survived not only many editions but many translations as well), were accused of mixing 'national bias' with scholarship,[4] and others, though competent to treat of the Admiralty Law of their day, made historically inaccurate assertions concerning the civil law and its application in England.[5] This must not be taken to intimate that the knowledge of the English civilians was perfect —indeed, Dr Lushington's holding that Admiralty could not take cognizance of general average because it was based upon a common law lien[6] (rather than stating simply that this exercise of the Admiralty jurisdiction had been repeatedly prohibited by the courts of common law) demonstrates an ignorance of the *Lex Rhodia* and its adoption into the Roman Law,[7] to say nothing of the references made thereto by such jurists as Selden,[8] which may seem remarkable in view of the extensive training of the civilians in the Digests.

Such an isolated example, however, does not disprove the value to the English legal system of the College of Advocates, nor can it offset the uneasiness of some who, observing the usefulness of the civilians in matters such as *R. v. Serva*,[9] wondered what

---

[1] Parl. Paper [1833] (670) vii (H.C. 15 August), p. 68
[2] Wendt, intro., p. xxiv.
[3] See, *e.g.*, *The Bee*, 3 Fed. Cas. 41 (No. 1219) (D.Me. 1836).
[4] See, *e.g.*, Reddie, intro., p. xxiv.
[5] See, *e.g.*, Parsons, p. 159, n. 1.
[6] *The Constancia*, (1846) 2 W. Rob. 487.   [7] Digest 14.2.1.
[8] See Senior, pp. 15–16.
[9] [*The Felicidade*], (1845) 2 Car. & K. 54; *The Times*, 17 Nov. & 4 Dec.

portent the fall of Doctors' Commons held for the future of English justice:

The great importance of this point [the lack of expertise in the civil law by the common lawyers] ought not to be lost sight of, as in case, by certain positive enactments, the Judgeship in the Admiralty Court, and a seat in the Appeal Court, should not be reserved for learned civilians, it is difficult to see, not only how these courts can be efficiently administered, but where the Foreign Office and the Lords of the Admiralty, as well as the general public, are in future to choose their advisers in matters of international and general Maritime Law, whom, for centuries, they have been accustomed to look for amongst the civilians.[1]

Whether or not such apprehension was well founded is a question which it is as well not to attempt to answer at this point, for at the time it was voiced Doctor's Commons was still fresh in memory and several of the civilians were still active in the practice of Admiralty.

Thus the civilians as an English institution were destroyed with Doctors' Commons; but like the branches of an ancient tree newly uprooted, a few of the doctors continued to live and to blossom, employing their resources as before. What they managed to accomplish while in that state is important to the development of Admiralty Law, for it was under their care that the Admiralty Court underwent, in terms of its organization, its great transition from the civil to the common law—and it was under their care that the Court retained its civilian character despite that transition.

[1] Wendt, intro., p. xxiv.

CHAPTER 4

THE GREAT TRANSITION

UPON Dr Lushington's retirement as Admiralty Judge in 1867, the volume of the Court's instance business had almost exactly trebled since his first years on the bench;[1] the direct cause of this increase was of course the expansion of Admiralty jurisdiction by statute—principally the Acts of 1840 and 1861. Much of the new business was also due, however, to Lushington's own dynamism in the discharge of his office, effecting, in the words of one of his admirers, 'a fresh creation of law'.[2] And while opinion might be reserved for the moment as to the wisdom of some of his ideas for Court reform, it is plain that Lushington handed to his successor a Court of far greater strength and vitality than he had himself inherited twenty-nine years previously.

Dr Lushington's successor, Sir Robert Phillimore, was a man whose background and training ensured his fitness for the office. Born in 1810, he was the son of Dr Joseph Phillimore, Regius Professor of Civil Law at Oxford and the Admiralty Advocate; he attended Westminster School and Christ Church, Oxford, graduating D.C.L. in 1838, and was elected a Fellow of Doctors' Commons in the following year. He was called to the bar by the Middle Temple in 1841, and, like his predecessors, was a Member of Parliament, serving from 1852-7. He followed in his father's footsteps by becoming Admiralty Advocate in 1855, and became Queen's Advocate in 1862 and Judge Advocate General 1871-2, holding the latter post while Admiralty Judge and Dean of Arches, as both of which he succeeded Dr Lushington in 1867; he had earlier served as Judge of the Admiralty Court of the Cinque Ports, a position to which he was appointed in 1855—an experience which particularly suited him to the Admiralty Judgeship. A scholar of international law, he was the author of a great treatise in the field; upon Lushington's death in 1873 he became Master of the Faculties, but resigned that office and the Deanship of the Arches in 1875; he survived the creation of the Admiralty Division

[1] See Return to H.C. by Rothery, Adm. Reg'r., 28 May 1867, p. 1.
[2] Coote, 1st ed., preface, p. vi.

to remain as Admiralty Judge until his retirement in 1883, and died in 1885.[1]

There were no major extensions of the Admiralty jurisdiction during the first half of Phillimore's judgeship, but several miscellaneous statutes are worthy of note, as are a few interpretative decisions. Statutorily, the Court acquired jurisdiction over seamen's claims in the nature of wages for expenses of food and treatment ['maintenance and cure'] during illness under conditions defined by statute,[2] exclusive jurisdiction in certain cases to pronounce condemnation and forfeiture of British vessels enlisted in the services of foreign belligerents during hostilities to which Britain remained neutral,[3] concurrent jurisdiction to pronounce forfeiture of cargoes of statutorily defined 'dangerous goods' (chiefly explosives),[4] and concurrent jurisdiction over any questions arising under the Slave Trade Acts, as well as exclusive jurisdiction over claims for bounty under the Slave Trade Act of 1873[5] (theoretically, slaves may even today be sued as a *res* under the 1873 Act and condemned *in rem* as forfeit to the Crown, by whom they are then released to freedom[6]).

In addition to the jurisdiction conferred by these new statutes, Phillimore's interpretation of some older enactments enabled the Court to assume a jurisdiction which was not contemplated in the statutes themselves, such as questions of damage to submarine cables.[7] And decisions of other courts, such as that of the Court for Crown Cases Reserved, which held that foreign subjects serving aboard British ships were British seamen under the law regardless of the ship's location,[8] provided a basis for interpretation of earlier enactments such as the Merchant Shipping Act, 1854, §268, to which applied the Admiralty jurisdiction over 'British seamen'.

It was early in Phillimore's judgeship that—despite considerable opposition[9]—a limited instance jurisdiction in Admiralty was conferred upon the County Courts in England and Wales. Under this statute, appellate jurisdiction was given to the High

---

[1] Holdsworth, *H.E.L.*, vol. 16, pp. 146–50; *D.N.B.*

[2] Merchant Shipping Act, 1867, §7.   [3] Foreign Enlistment Act, 1870, §19.

[4] Merchant Shipping Act, 1873, §§27, 23.

[5] Slave Trade (Consolidation) Act, 1873, §§5, 19.

[6] See McGuffie, *Practice*, p. 33, ¶69.

[7] *The Clara Killam*, (1870) L.R. 3 A. & E. 161.

[8] *R. v. Anderson*, (1868) L.R. 1 C.C.R. 161.   [9] See, *e.g.*, Wendt, p. 624.

Court of Admiralty in all cases, together with the power to transfer proceedings to the High Court of Admiralty from the County Courts at the discretion of the Admiralty Judge, upon motion or appeal.[1] It ought here to be noted that, besides the County Courts, the Admiralty Court of the Cinque Ports, the Mayor's Court of the City of London, and the Court of Passage of the Borough of Liverpool each possessed some form of instance jurisdiction at that time. These courts are still functioning, though it seems that only the Liverpool Court of Passage ever entertained actions *in rem* with any frequency;[2] appeal now lies from the Court of Passage to the Court of Appeal rather than to the Admiralty Court,[3] though appeal was to the High Court of Admiralty in Sir Robert Phillimore's day.[4]

An interesting question arose following the grant in 1869 of jurisdiction to the County Courts to entertain actions *in rem* for breach of charterparty[5]—a jurisdiction not possessed at that time by the Admiralty Court itself; upon a motion for transfer of such an action from a County Court to the Admiralty Court, the question arose whether the latter could take cognizance by transfer of a matter not within its original jurisdiction. Phillimore's decision that the Admiralty Court could accept such an action by transfer[6] has been upheld in the present century;[7] and the result is not really surprising in view of the similar problems which arose in the eighteenth century with regard to appeals from Colonial Vice-Admiralty Courts which exercised a wider instance jurisdiction than the High Court of Admiralty,[8] which were nonetheless heard by the latter until the Judicial Committee of the Privy Council came into existence.[9]

While the procedure for bringing cases on appeal to the Admiralty Court from inferior courts is properly a subject which is linked to the procedure of those courts and hence without the scope of this work, there existed a notable anomaly in appeals from one particular body, the Salvage Commissioners of the

---

[1] County Courts Admiralty Jurisdiction Act, 1868, §§6, 32.
[2] See Williams and Bruce, 2nd ed., p. 271.
[3] Liverpool Corporation Act, 1921, §260.
[4] See, *e.g.*, *The Alexandria*, (1872) L.R. 3 A. & E. 574.
[5] County Cts. Adm. Jurisdiction Amendment Act, 1869, §§1–3.
[6] *The Swan*, (1870) L.R. 3 A & E. 314.
[7] *The Montrosa*, [1917] P. 1.
[8] See *The Royal Arch*, (1857) Swab. 269, 277.
[9] Judicial Committee Act, 1833, §2.

Cinque Ports. The oddity was that, procedurally, causes coming up from the Commissioners were introduced into the Admiralty Court as if instance rather than appellate matters, and appeals in such cases were actually commenced by issuance of a *citation in personam* in original form,[1] though the Court's jurisdiction was clearly appellate.[2]

A few minor changes in instance procedure were made in 1871, but aside from a confirmation of the Marshal's authority within the Port of London and an extension of his authority elsewhere throughout England and Wales to serve warrants *in rem* either personally, or, in the latter venue, as well by the Collector of Customs nearest the *res* acting as his substitute, there were no actual additions to procedure. The 1859 Rules regarding default were amended, however, permitting filing of the summary petition in the absence of appearance within twelve days of service of the warrant or citation, setting of the cause for hearing after a further twelve days of non-appearance, decree for the plaintiff upon the hearing without any reference and report, order for appraisement and sale without previous notice, and order for direct payment of the proceeds of sale without payment first into Court.[3] It is probable that these changes were prompted not only by a desire to render the Court's procedure more summary, but also to bring procedure more into line with that of the common law for the benefit of practitioners whose lack of civilian training must have made the old procedure difficult to understand.

A more fundamental change in the Court's post-hearing procedure for the enforcement of money judgments came in 1874. The English-speaking world—influenced to some degree, no doubt, by the writings of Charles Dickens—had begun in the early days of the latter half of the nineteenth century to recognize both the cruelty and futility of the practice of imprisoning judgment-proof debtors. The practice was abandoned at an early date in the Federal jurisdiction of the United States, and the Admiralty Rules of the Supreme Court were amended in 1850, 1851, and 1854 to effect the abolition of imprisonment for debt in Admiralty causes.[4] In England, a bill of general application was passed in

---

[1] Williams and Bruce, 3rd ed., pp. 512–14.
[2] Cinque Ports Act, 1821, §4.
[3] Additional Rules for the H.C.A., 1871 (O.-in-C. of 24 March), rr. 2 & 3, 4 & 5.   [4] See Parsons, pp. 747 *et seq.*

1869 providing that, with a few specific exceptions for defaults in payment, no person should thereafter be arrested or imprisoned for failure to discharge a debt, and that in none of the excepted cases might imprisonment exceed one year.[1] The effect upon the Admiralty Court's procedure was of course considerable, as the sole method used to obtain satisfaction of money judgments in Admiralty was attachment and/or committal of the person of the defendant; under the terms of the Debtors Act, this procedure at once became almost wholly obsolete, and after 1869 it was necessary in each instance of an application for an order for attachment to establish in some informal way whether the Act would permit the order to issue—even provisionally—under the particular circumstances of the case. After five years of such informal inquiries, new rules were adopted to ensure compliance with the Act by requiring prior notice of any motion for an order for attachment to be given to the Judge and served, where practicable, upon the debtor, and requiring also an affidavit on behalf of the plaintiff, attesting and offering proof of the debtor's ability to pay.[2]

The most important event of Sir Robert Phillimore's judgeship was of course the passage of the Judicature Acts, which consolidated the central superior courts of the realm into a unified system. In this process Phillimore had at least some direct involvement, as he was appointed a member of a Royal Commission to inquire into the court structure and to make recommendations for its improvement. The First Report of the Judicature Commission appeared in 1869, and contained recommendations specifically pertinent to the Admiralty Court. The Report opened with a number of noteworthy observations, one of which was that the Admiralty jurisdiction as expanded by the Acts of 1840 and 1861—and enjoying exclusively the advantage of the proceeding *in rem*—would probably continue to extend its cognizance into areas where the jurisdiction of common law was concurrent but its procedure less convenient, analogous in some ways to the manner in which the jurisdiction of Chancery had already extended to cover 'a large class of cases properly cognizable in Courts of Common Law . . .'.[3] Surprisingly, in light of the events of the previous decade, the Commission identified as the root cause of

---

[1] Debtors Act, 1869, §4.
[2] Additional Rules for the H.C.A., 1874 (O.-in-C. of 12 May), rr. 1–3.
[3] Parl. Paper [1869] (1) xxv (R.C. 25 March), p. 7.

the extension of Admiralty jurisdiction 'the imperfection of the Common Law system, and the consequent necessity of seeking for a more complete remedy elsewhere'.[1] But the inability of the Admiralty Court to afford a complete remedy in every case was also recognized, and the Report cited the common but distressing situation in which a claim might be instituted against a foreign shipowner in Admiralty for damage to cargo, while the shipowner, having a cross-claim for freight, was obliged to proceed against the cargo-owner at common law; one of the major advantages of a unified court system would therefore be the elimination of jurisdictional conflicts, with the added benefit that 'no suitor could be defeated because he commenced his suit in the wrong Court. . .'.[2]

Happily—and perhaps due to the presence of Phillimore—the Commission, in recommending a system which would unite the principal courts of the realm in one structure, also recognized the advantages to be gained by encompassing together the courts of civil law, and the Report stated that 'as regards the Courts of Admiralty, Divorce and Probate, we think it would be convenient that those Courts should be consolidated, and form one Chamber or Division of the Supreme Court.'[3]

The wisdom of the Commission's Report was, in general, quite unquestionable; with the obvious need for widespread court reform which existed at that time, there was surely no plausible reason why advantage should not have been taken of the opportunity to make a great collective improvement rather than a host of individual ones. Some specific recommendations, however, were never acted upon, while others were considerably mutilated by the machinery of legislation; but there were, in retrospect, a few recommendations which would if enacted have proven most unwise, such as the abolition of the Admiralty Court's Prize and other special jurisdiction. The credit for preventing the confusion which might have very well proven disastrous in subsequent times of both war and peace must go directly to Sir Robert Phillimore, who, in the course of signing the Report and commending most of its suggestions, nonetheless made specific reservations concerning the abolition of any of the Admiralty jurisdiction as recommended by the Commission.[4]

Four years after the Report of the Royal Commission, most of

[1] Parl. Paper [1869] (1) xxv (R.C. 25 March), p. 7.   [2] *Id.*, pp. 8, 9.
[3] *Id.*, p. 9.   [4] *Id.*, p. 25.

its recommendations were enacted by Parliament in the first of the Judicature Acts. By this Act of 1873, the High Court of Chancery, the Court of Queen's Bench, the Court of Common Pleas at Westminster, the Court of Exchequer, the High Court of Admiralty, the Court of Probate, the Court for Divorce and Matrimonial Causes, and the London Court of Bankruptcy were consolidated as the 'Supreme Court of Judicature'.[1] Because of the confusion which would have resulted if appeals from the courts of civil law continued to go to the Judicial Committee of the Privy Council while appeals from the common law courts went to the Exchequer Chamber and on to the House of Lords, the Judicature Commission recommended the substitution of a 'Common Court of Appeal',[2] and so in the Act of 1873 the Supreme Court of Judicature was further divided into two hemispheres— one, comprising the courts of original jurisdiction, to be known as 'Her Majesty's High Court of Justice', and the other, created to exercise all appellate jurisdiction, was to be called 'Her Majesty's Court of Appeal'.[3] The 1873 Act also denied any appeals from the Supreme Court of Judicature to either the Privy Council or the House of Lords, and made provision for the transfer of the jurisdiction of the Judicial Committee of the Privy Council to the Court of Appeal.[4]

Within the new High Court of Justice, five Divisions were created: Queen's Bench, Common Pleas, Exchequer, Chancery, and Probate, Divorce and Admiralty (hereinafter referred to as 'P.D.A.'[5] or Admiralty Division), and to these Divisions was assigned the respective jurisdiction of the previously existing courts.[6] Rules of law in force in Admiralty, such as half-damages under the both-to-blame rule in collision causes,[7] were specifically preserved by the 1873 Act[8]—in response to the anticipation of problems of conflict between the Admiralty rule and the rule of contributory negligence at common law, as raised in the 1869 Report[9]—and the Admiralty Division thereby became bound to

---

[1] Supreme Court of Judicature Act, 1873, §3.
[2] Parl. Paper, [1869] (1) xxv (R.C. 25 March), p. 8.
[3] Supreme Court of Judicature Act, 1873, §§4, 18, 19.
[4] Supreme Court of Judicature Act, 1873, §§20, 21 [never effective; see Appellate Jurisdiction Act, 1876, §24].
[5] Humorously called 'wills, wives & wrecks'.   [6] §§31, 31(5), 16.
[7] See *The Milan*, (1861) Lush. 388.   [8] §25(9).
[9] Parl. Paper [1869] (1) xxv, pp. 7–8.

apply them.[1] Miscellaneous provisions included the necessary merger of law and equity, 'Divisional Courts' of a number of judges to hear certain matters within a given Division (including Admiralty), power to transfer causes between Divisions, and a rule-making power for the Supreme Court.[2] Though it was specifically provided that the rules of procedure prevailing in the High Court of Admiralty should govern Admiralty proceedings in the P.D.A. Division,[3] the rulemaking power was utilized to create several rules of basic application to the High Court of Justice, including the Admiralty Division, and actions in Admiralty were thereafter commenced by writ of summons[4] rather than by praecipe to institute. It might be noted here that although the 1873 Act introduced the common law terminology of 'action' to cover all forms of proceedings in the High Court,[5] custom has preserved the jurisprudential term for a proceeding in Admiralty as 'suit', in the same manner as it is customary to speak of a 'suit in equity' as opposed to an 'action at law'.

The 1873 Act was scheduled to come into operation late in 1874,[6] but in mid-1874 it was recognized that there were many flaws of omission and effect that would have to be corrected prior to putting the judicial reformation into operation; an Act was therefore passed which had as its sole object the delay of operation of the 1873 Act until 1875,[7] by which time the necessary amendments would have been decided upon. These amendments appeared in an Act of 1875. While the basic structure set up in the 1873 Act remained unchanged, the 1875 Act served to fill in some neglected details; thus specific provisions were made for the salary, pension and precedence of the Admiralty Judge and Admiralty Registrar,[8] provision was made for appeals to Divisions of the High Court from inferior courts,[9] and the Rules of the High Court of Admiralty were again declared to remain in force in the Admiralty Division,[10] save as altered under new rulemaking powers.[11] The greatest amendment of the 1873 Act, however, was

---

[1] *The Drumlanrig*, [1911] A.C. 16.
[2] Supreme Court of Judicature Act, 1873, §§24, 37–41, 44, 36, 23.
[3] Supreme Court of Judicature Act, 1873, §70.
[4] R.S.C. [Rules of the Supreme Court], 1873, r. 2.
[5] R.S.C., 1873, r. 1.
[6] Supreme Court of Judicature Act, 1873, §2.
[7] Supreme Court of Judicature (Commencement) Act, 1874.
[8] Supreme Court of Judicature (Amendment) Act, 1875, §8.
[9] §15.   [10] §18.   [11] §24; see also §§16, 17, 25.

in the Schedule of Rules; the 1875 Act completely re-ordered and re-constituted the 1873 Rules, with many elaborations and additions. With specific reference to Admiralty, there was introduced a special form of writ of summons *in rem*,[1] the affidavit to lead was preserved, but was used to lead the writ rather than the warrant, and the statement of claim was required to be indorsed upon the writ before issue,[2] the default procedure *in rem* was preserved with no substantial alteration,[3] the demurrer and the writ of delivery were for the first time introduced into Admiralty practice,[4] and enforcement of judgments by *fieri facias* or *elegit*, though probably technically possible since 1861,[5] was first specifically permitted by the 1875 Act;[6] the writ of *audita querela*, long obsolete, was finally abolished.[7]

The new uniform mode of pleading introduced by the Judicature Acts—by statements of claim and defence[8]—did not depart in structure from the existing plea by petition and answer,[9] which had been substituted for the ancient modes of Admiralty pleading in 1859[10] and was itself modelled upon common law procedure; the proceeding by libel then also became obsolete, though it had earlier fallen into disuse. In balance, the convenience of joinder of multiple parties, which had been for so long of peculiar advantage to Admiralty suitors, was made applicable in all Divisions of the High Court.[11]

While there was no direct expansion of Admiralty jurisdiction contained in the Judicature Acts, one immediate effect was to make the Admiralty jurisdiction exclusive in claims for limitation of liability.[12] Earlier, even after the 1861 Admiralty Court Act, the jurisdiction had primarily been Chancery's, with Admiralty having jurisdiction only ancillary to other actions *in rem*;[13] under the provisions of the 1873 Act providing for the assignment of business between the Admiralty and Chancery Divisions,[14] and later rules governing transfer of causes between Divisions, all

---

[1] R.S.C., 1875, form A., I, 4.
[2] R.S.C., 1875, O. 5, r. 11; O. 3, r. 1; see p. 117, *infra*.
[3] R.S.C., 1875, O. 13, r. 10 (a)–(h).   [4] R.S.C., 1875, OO. 23, 49.
[5] See Admiralty Court Act, 1861, §§15, 22.
[6] R.S.C., 1875, O. 42, r. 15.   [7] R.S.C., 1875, O. 42, r. 22.
[8] R.S.C., 1875, O. 19, esp. rr. 2, 3, 30; O. 21, r. 3.
[9] See Williams and Bruce, 3rd ed., p. 341.   [10] 1859 Rules, r. 55.
[11] R.S.C., 1875, O. 17.   [12] See Roscoe, *Practice*, p. 242.
[13] See, *e.g.*, *The Northumbria*, (1869) L.R. 3 A. & E. 24.
[14] Supreme Court of Judicature Act, 1873, §42.

limitation cases were simply directed or transferred to the Admiralty Division.

Interestingly, the grant to the new High Court of the collective jurisdiction of the previous individual courts[1] meant that each of the High Court Judges possessed the same jurisdiction (though exercising it according to the business before his Division); this not only permitted transfers of cases between Divisions, but it also prevented any Judge from issuing a prohibition to any of his brethren. And thus the courts of common law at last lost the power to prohibit the exercise of jurisdiction by the Admiralty Court—a power which, despite the vanquishment of Doctors' Commons, the triumph of the common lawyers and the impending unification of the court system, continued to be exercised virtually on the eve of the Judicature Acts.[2]

One provision of the Judicature Acts which immediately aroused great controversy was that which abolished the appellate jurisdiction of the House of Lords.[3] Perhaps foreseeing that the Judicature Commission's recommendation for a 'Common Court of Appeal'[4] would, if implemented, mean at least a dilution of its jurisdiction, the House of Lords appointed a Select Committee of its own to examine the question of its appellate jurisdiction. This Committee, reporting in 1872, proposed establishment of 'The Queen's Great Council of Appeal', to consist of the Lord Chancellor and five salaried judges, which would hear all appeals formerly directed to either the Lords or the Privy Council.[5] The recommendation was never implemented, and in the 1873 Act, as previously noted, the appellate jurisdiction of the House of Lords was abolished in common law cases, and that of the Privy Council severely restricted in civil law cases; but in 1876 a bill was introduced to restore the Lords' appellate jurisdiction. Though technically establishing a new jurisdiction to hear causes coming up from the new Court of Appeal,[6] the clear intent of the Act was the restoration of the jurisdiction formerly enjoyed; the wholly new jurisdiction conferred by the Act in appeals from Chancery and the courts of civil law appears to have been a

---

[1] Supreme Court of Judicature Act, 1873, §16.
[2] See, *e.g., Smith v. Brown*, (1871) L.R. 6 Q.B. 729.
[3] Supreme Court of Judicature Act, 1873, §20.
[4] Parl. Paper [1869] (1) xxv (R.C. 25 March), p. 8.
[5] Parl. Paper [1872] (1) 149 (H.L. 9 July).
[6] Appellate Jurisdiction Act, 1876, §§3–9, 24.

'fringe benefit'. As soon as the bill had been published, an enormous clamour arose from the mercantile interests, and a great many letters were written by insurers, steamship brokers, chambers of commerce, etc., to the Board of Trade and to the Lord Chancellor, protesting the addition of another appellate rung in Admiralty procedure and objecting to the innovation as unnecessary, wasteful, and time-consuming.[1] Despite this powerful opposition the bill became law,[2] but at least the safeguard of nautical assessors was adopted on Admiralty appeals to the Lords,[3] and the addition of a third appellate stage does not appear to have proven a particular drawback to the proper functioning and exercise of jurisdiction by the Admiralty Court, nor does it seem to have been prejudicial to maritime interests, as had been feared.[4]

Altogether, the effect of the Judicature Acts themselves upon the Admiralty Court was not great; jurisdiction remained largely unaltered in scope, and the Acts did not change the exercise of the jurisdiction with regard, for example, to suits between foreign parties.[5] Within the prior scope of Admiralty jurisdiction, however, the Court did gain a more complete cognizance of matters such as ship mortgages.[6] Procedurally, the situation was similar; previous practices such as appearances under protest could still be utilized[7] under the clause saving prior procedure,[8] but confusion was generated by conflicting wording of statutes in some minor matters such as appeal from the Admiralty Division to the Court of Appeal of causes which came to the Admiralty Division on appeal from the Salvage Commissioners of the Cinque Ports, because it was not clear whether the Salvage Commissioners were an 'inferior court' within the provisions of the Judicature Acts.[9]

The best illustration that the pattern of business in the Admiralty Court was undisturbed by the Judicature Acts is provided by the figures for the issuance of process: 395 citations in 1874, 416 writs of summons in 1876;[10] there was a drop in business during 1875 to 285 citations/writs, which might be ascribed to confusion as to the effect of the Acts on the Court's jurisdiction

[1] Parl. Paper [1877] (1) 69 (H.C. 14 June).
[2] Appellate Jurisdiction Act, 1876.   [3] See *The Nautilus*, [1927] A.C. 145.
[4] See, *e.g.*, Wendt, p. 681.   [5] *The Evangelistria*, (1876) 2 P.D. 241.
[6] See Boyd, p. 76, n.   [7] See *The Vivar*, (1876) 2 P.D. 29.
[8] Supreme Court of Judicature (Amendment) Act, 1875, §18.
[9] See Williams and Bruce, 3rd ed., pp. 515–16.
[10] Figures supplied by Admiralty Registry, 1966.

in rem, inasmuch as the drop was in actions *in rem* rather than in actions *in personam*, but in the following year business regained the previous level, which it maintained over the next five years, with 410 writs issuing in 1881.[1]

If the Court's operation remained smooth throughout its transition from an independent to a consolidated body, its organization was chaotic. Despite his seniority and his civilian training, Sir Robert Phillimore never became head of the Admiralty Division—yet he remained sole Admiralty Judge, and acted quite independently. The first President of the Division administering the civil law was in fact a common lawyer, Sir James Hannen. Hannen was born in 1821, attended St Paul's School and Heidelberg University, was called to the bar by the Middle Temple in 1848, became a Justice of the Queen's Bench and was made Serjeant in 1868, and was appointed Judge of the Probate and Divorce Courts in 1872, from which position, by operation of the Judicature Acts, he became President of the Probate, Divorce and Admiralty Division of the High Court in 1875. He served as president of the Parnell Inquiry Commission in 1888, and was, appropriately, given an Hon. D.C.L. (Oxon.) in the same year; he became a Lord of Appeal in Ordinary in 1891, served as an arbitrator in the Bering Sea Dispute in 1892, and died in 1894.[2]

It was undoubtedly because of the greater volume of probate and divorce business as compared to the number of causes tried annually in Admiralty that Sir James Hannen became President of the new Division. Sir Robert Phillimore, however, was senior to Hannen not only in tenure as Admiralty Judge, but as a member of the Judicial Committee of the Privy Council, to which Phillimore had been appointed in 1867, and to which Hannen was not appointed until more than five years thereafter.[3] This seniority, and Phillimore's civilian character, manifested themselves in the Admiralty Division, for while all other Judges of the High Court of Justice were addressed as they are today, Phillimore continued to be known both in public and in the reports of Admiralty cases as 'Sir Robert', and was never addressed as 'The Rt Hon. Mr Justice Phillimore'; moreover, though §84 of the Judicature Act of 1875 specifically provided that officers of the Division should be appointed by the President, Phillimore

---

[1] Figures supplied by Admiralty Registry, 1966.
[2] Holdsworth, *H.E.L.*, vol. 16, pp. 156–8; *D.N.B.*   [3] *D.N.B.*

in fact appointed both a new Admiralty Registrar and Assistant Registrar in 1878, with Hannen only adding a note of confirmation to the appointments signed by Phillimore—and, quite remarkably, the appointments were then submitted by Phillimore to the Lords Commissioners for their assent, though the Court had in 1875 become completely dissociated from and independent of the Admiralty.[1]

If Phillimore's status as Admiralty Judge seems unusual, so too was his (best-remembered) status as an Ecclesiastical Judge, though in quite a different way. It will be recalled that, although Phillimore succeeded Dr Lushington not only as Admiralty Judge but as Dean of Arches in 1867, Lushington retained the Mastership of the Faculties; this was because the Mastership carried with it all of the emoluments which made the Deanship tenable, so that Lushington was thereby permitted to continue to collect the emoluments without performing most of the services which they had been designed to compensate, while Phillimore's salary as Dean did not alone suffice to meet even the expenses of the Office. This situation prevailed until Lushington's death in 1873, whereupon Phillimore succeeded to the Mastership; but because the framers of the Judicature Acts felt that no Judge of the new High Court ought to hold any judicial office outside the Supreme Court for fear of conflicts of duty and interest, it was provided in the Acts that no salary should attach to the Office of Admiralty Judge for so long as he should continue to hold the Office of Dean of the Arches[2]—and so Phillimore had no sooner secured a just remuneration for his services as Dean than he was coerced to resign the Office,[3] in which, however, he remained active until the Judicature Acts became effective.[4]

With the fall of Doctors' Commons, the Admiralty Court had been moved to Westminster. Here the scene was far removed from the splendour of the doctors' Common Hall, for the new courtroom was a mean and dingy little garret known as 'The Cockloft', situated high up under the eaves of the Law Courts which had themselves 'grown up as excrescences on Westminster Hall'.[5] How this move must have affected Dr Lushington can

---

[1] Thompson, p. 20.
[2] Supreme Court of Judicature (Amendment) Act, 1875, §8.
[3] See Holdsworth, *H.E.L.*, vol. 16, pp. 146–50.
[4] See, *e.g.*, *Durst v. Masters*, (1876) 1 P.D. 373 [P.C. App.].
[5] Roscoe, *Studies*, p. 7.

only be imagined, for though he endured the new surroundings for seven years, he seems to have done so in silent suffering; it is possible that Sir Robert Phillimore may have taken an affectionate view of The Cockloft, for it was his courtroom during the whole of his tenure as Admiralty Judge.

Thanks to the reminiscences of E. S. Roscoe, one may get an intriguing picture of the Admiralty Court during Phillimore's judgeship; it is plain that no-one 'danced . . . like a semi-despondent fury'[1] in The Cockloft, but that its seclusion, which freed it from spectators, and its business, which freed it from any large professional attendance, gave it 'the atmosphere of a select social club.'[2] Sir Robert is described as 'a courteous elderly gentleman, with a rosy complexion and a quiet voice'—a great contrast to the 'flamboyant' William Baliol Brett (later Lord Esher, M.R.), a common lawyer who succeeded Sir Travers Twiss as the Court's leading counsel when Twiss began to retire from active practice. Twiss, who was Professor of Civil Law at Oxford, 1855-70, was the last Queen's Advocate[3]—a post which, together with Queen's Proctor and Procurator-General, is now combined with that of Treasury Solicitor.[4] A new bar of common lawyers, such as Charles Butt, Gainsford Bruce, and, despite civilian training, Sir Robert's son Dr Walter (later Lord) Phillimore, became predominant over survivors of Doctors' Commons such as Twiss and Dr Deane, Q.C., who sat in the front row with a 'smiling countenance' and black mittens upon his hands, and old proctors—even such as Mr Jemmett:

[who,] with unkempt beard, generally untidy and cross-eyed, was steeped in Admiralty lore, and the main object of his life appeared to be to preserve the old Admiralty practice against the attacks of the Common Law. For this purpose he had always some precedent or point which he pressed on counsel, hoping to keep the court in its ancient ways.[5]

Through the Judicature Acts, the Court preserved its identity, with the same Judge and practitioners applying the same law in the same manner, and with the same officers. The officers of the High Court of Admiralty were in fact transferred to the Admiralty

---

[1] Gilbert, *Trial by Jury*, 'When I, good friends . . .'.
[2] Roscoe, *Studies*, p. 11.
[3] *Id.*, pp. 8-9.
[4] Holdsworth, *H.E.L.*, vol. 16, p. 139.
[5] Roscoe, *Studies*, pp. 9-10; *H.C.A.*, pp. 12-13.

Division by the Judicature Acts, and their powers and duties remained the same except for the Registrar,[1] who, though he could no longer sit as surrogate for the Admiralty Judge, retained the power—as did his Assistant—to entertain and dispose, while sitting for the Judge, of all applications which could have been dealt with by the Judge in chambers.[2] The last judicial decision by a Registrar as surrogate was given in 1874.[3]

At this juncture, it might be mentioned that H. C. Rothery retired as Registrar in 1878 to become Wreck Commissioner of the United Kingdom, and that he was succeeded by H. A. Bathurst, who had been appointed Assistant Registrar in 1858, and who was in turn succeeded as Assistant Registrar in 1878 by one J. G. Smith.[4] Rothery closed his career as Registrar in giving, quite typically, testimony as to needed reform in the Registry organization to the Judicature Acts (Legal Offices) Committee, which recommended that the Registry staff be centralized, in order to ease the conditions of overwork described by Rothery, who favoured centralization, and further recommended that the Admiralty Registrar become a Master of the Supreme Court not specifically attached to the Admiralty Division.[5] These proposals were fortunately shelved, and the value of a separate Registry and Registrar has since been both proven and recognized.[6]

The period of Sir Robert Phillimore's tenure which followed the Judicature Acts did not see any major developments in Admiralty Law or procedure, though a few miscellaneous points deserve mention. The Court acquired in 1875 a jurisdiction concurrent with Vice-Admiralty Courts abroad to condemn, forfeit or restore vessels or goods seized under the Pacific Islanders Protection Acts, and to award damages for unlawful seizure.[7] The bounds of the territorial waters of the United Kingdom were declared by statute in 1878, and jurisdiction over offences within territorial waters was given to 'the admiral', *i.e.*, to the nearest court with applicable Admiralty jurisdiction;[8] and, significantly, the first of the statutes of Richard II, the Admiralty Jurisdiction

---

[1] R.S.C., 1875, O. 60, r. 1; O. 54.   [2] Williams and Bruce, 2nd ed., p. 511.
[3] *The Vladimir*, (March, 1874) [unrep.] see Williams and Bruce, 2nd ed., p. 511, n. (*y*).   [4] Thompson, p. 20.
[5] Parl. Paper [1878] (5) 25 (H.C. March).
[6] See (1934) 177 *L.T.* 54, 55.
[7] Pacific Islanders' Protection Act, 1875, §§4, 5.
[8] Territorial Waters Jurisdiction Act, 1878, §§2, 7.

Act, ×1389, was wholly repealed in 1879.[1] Somewhat curiously, the power of the Admiralty to issue appointments of Vice-Admiralty Judges, Registrars and Marshals was confirmed by statute in 1876, and the power to issue patents for those offices was not passed from the High Court of Admiralty to the Admiralty Division.[2]

The most important procedural development resulted from a series of enactments which provided for the investigation of shipping accidents; one of these gave power to the Lord Chancellor to make rules for the appeals from findings of courts of inquiry into shipping mishaps;[3] this power was reaffirmed and broadened by a statute of 1879, which also conferred appellate jurisdiction upon the Admiralty Court in cases wherein the Board of Trade refused to order a rehearing following the cancellation of the licence ['ticket'] of any Officer of the Merchant Navy.[4] The Rules governing such appeals were promulgated in the following year, and were made applicable to appeals to the Admiralty Division from any investigations into shipping casualties, whether by the Board of Trade, the Wreck Commissioner, or other authorities;[5] the procedure on such appeals was to be, generally, the same as that in any cause normally brought before the Admiralty Court, save that without special permission of the Judge there should be no formal pleadings;[6] the Admiralty Judge might add parties to the appeal at his discretion, subject to objection, and might receive new evidence in any form and make any order as to costs.[7] It was also made a specific requirement that the Judge hear the appeal with two assessors, and that he send a 'report of the case' to the Board of Trade at the conclusion of the proceedings.[8] To make the Admiralty Court's jurisdiction in such cases truly comprehensive, any appeals from refusals to order rehearings by colonial courts or tribunals convened under an Act of 1882 were also directed to the Admiralty Division.[9]

The post-Judicature Acts procedure of the Court was, as

---

[1] Civil Procedure Acts Repeal Act, 1879.

[2] Appellate Jurisdiction Act, 1876, §23.   [3] Merchant Shipping Act, 1876, §30.

[4] Shipping Casualties Investigations Act, 1879, §§3(1), 2(2).

[5] Shipping Casualties (Appeal & Rehearing) Rules [S.C.R.], 1880 (by order of the Ld. Chancellor, 17 April), r. 3.

[6] S.C.R., 1880, r. 6(j).   [7] S.C.R., 1880, rr. 6(e)–(i).

[8] S.C.R., 1880, rr. 6(d), 6(k).

[9] Merchant Shipping (Colonial Inquiries) Act, 1882, §6.

earlier indicated, largely unaltered during the balance of Sir Robert Phillimore's judgeship; the 'preservation clause' of the Acts saved not only the formal but the customary procedure of the High Court of Admiralty, so that practices such as the requirement of proof of or agreement upon the value of a salved vessel prior to its release from arrest continued in force in the Admiralty Division.[1] In the continuing effort to render proceedings more summary, one new provision permitted the Judge upon motion to accelerate the trial at any stage[2] (akin to a motion for summary judgment), but it is not known how frequently this procedure was employed.

In January of 1883 the construction of the new Royal Courts of Justice in the Strand was completed and all of the civil courts were transferred there, Admiralty and common law from Westminster, and Chancery from Lincoln's Inn.[3] This must have seemed to Phillimore, then aged seventy-two, the proper time to retire—which he did in March 1883, two years before his death.

As a scholar, Sir Robert Phillimore was better known as an international lawyer, and as a Judge better recognized as a canonist, than he was in either of these capacities as an Admiralty jurist;[4] and yet he was admirably suited to the Admiralty Judgeship, and discharged his Office with a wisdom and diligence which by no means suffers in comparison with the erratic brilliance of his predecessor. If in the ordering of greatness in the list of Judges of the High Court of Admiralty he must be placed below Lushington, it is because his term of office was too brief and the Court's business too mundane to have afforded him the necessary opportunity.

Some idea of Phillimore's quality as Admiralty Judge may nonetheless be gleaned from a few of his decisions. He used his knowledge of the international law to the best advantage in a difficult case of collision involving a vessel of the Khedive of Egypt; the Khedive sought to invoke the principle of sovereign immunity to protect his ship—which flew the flag of the Royal Ottoman Navy—from arrest in an English action *in rem*; Phillimore, noting that the vessel was actually engaged in commerce, decided

---

[1] Haynes, ¶161, p. 49.
[2] R.S.C., 1875, O. 62, r. 7; see Haynes, ¶175, p. 54.
[3] See Roscoe, *Studies*, p. 4.
[4] Holdsworth, *H.E.L.*, vol. 16, pp. 146–50; *D.N.B.*

that, as the true sovereign of the Ottoman Empire was its ruler the Sultan of Constantinople, the Khedive—a mere Prince without the powers of a sovereign—was not entitled to confer the protection of sovereign immunity upon his ship.[1] The qualities of rationality, lucidity, diplomacy and legal expertise which abound in this decision make it illustrative of Phillimore's contribution to the jurisprudence of Admiralty. He was conscious as well of the equitable powers of the Court, especially as reinforced by the Judicature Acts' consolidation of jurisdiction, and he used them in a notable case to set aside an unconscionable contract for life salvage.[2] He was as well versed in the customary Law of Admiralty (as for example the evidentiary problem of a sufficiently contemporaneous log entry[3]) as he was in the legal powers conferred upon the Court by statute, and he established the implied power of the Court to compel a master judicially removed to deliver up to the Court the ship's papers and certificate of registry.[4]

Phillimore did upon occasion show a reluctance to exercise jurisdiction; this was sometimes understandable, as in declaring the Court a *forum non conveniens* following a protest to jurisdiction by a foreign consul,[5] and sometimes unfathomable, as in his application of a statutory immunity from suits for negligence in navigation by Trinity House Pilots to a Liverpool Pilot, who clearly did not enter the purview of the enactment.[6] But in general Phillimore possessed great judicial acumen, and he was both inventive and independent; to expedite more summary procedure, he abandoned as soon as he came to the bench the practice of summing up the evidence in open Court for the nautical assessors and instead retired from the courtroom with them to consider the evidence[7]—a practice followed ever since.[8] Such was his wisdom and fairness that, like Lord Stowell before him,[9] he was several times called upon to serve as arbitrator of collision and salvage claims against the vessels of foreign sovereigns immune to suits in Admiralty.[10]

[1] *The Charkieh*, (1873) L.R. 4 A. & E. 59.
[2] *The Medina*, (1876) 2 P.D. 5 [App.].
[3] *The Henry Coxon*, (1878) 3 P.D. 156.   [4] *The St. Olaf*, (1877) 2 P.D. 113.
[5] *The Leon XIII*, (1883) 8 P.D. 121; cf. *supra*, p. 68, n. 4.
[6] *The Alexandria*, (1872) L.R. 3 A. & E. 574.
[7] *The Hannibal*, (1867) L.R. 2 A. & E. 53, 56 (n.).
[8] See Roscoe, *Practice*, p. 4.
[9] E.g., *The Prins Frederick*, (1820) 2 Dod. 451, 481.
[10] See *The Constitution*, (1879) 4 P.D. 39, 45.

Sir Robert Phillimore was the last civilian Judge of the Admiralty Court. His feelings upon resigning the Judgeship must have been intense, for he had served the Court as counsel, Admiralty and Queen's Advocates, and finally Judge, for over forty-four years—and he knew that there was no civilian to succeed him. He had been appointed in 1867 as the Deputy of the Queen in her Office of Admiralty, and not simply by the Queen upon the advice of the Lord Chancellor, as with the common law judges.[1] And at the instant that his 1867 appointment ceased effect in 1875 it was replaced by another—vesting him with new powers, but no longer unique in form and constituting him no more as the Admiral's Deputy but as one of Her Majesty's Judges.

Yet the business of the Admiralty Court remained quite constant throughout the hurricane winds of change that altered its form, if not its substance. The Court continued to sit for not more than four days each week,[2] though the trained eye would surely have detected the slow transition from the learning and scholarship of the civilians to the businesslike attitude of the less formally educated but more commercially aware common lawyers. The change, so rude for most other courts and fatal to the ancient Exchequer and Common Pleas, was almost imperceptible in Admiralty—but by 1883 it had been wrought. If the Judicature Acts produced a hurricane, then The Cockloft was surely the hurricane's 'eye', and Phillimore, having weathered the fury, must have known with the instinct of a wise old mariner that the time had come to hand the wheel to a new watch.

With sentiment and misgivings, many beheld the change as disastrous:

. . . I viewed with alarm the merging of the High Court of Admiralty by the Judicature Acts into a branch of one of the Divisions of the Supreme Court of Judicature . . . ; I did not expect that the old and venerable Admiralty Court would be changed.
I felt at once that many and great difficulties would arise.[3]

There were indeed difficulties, and perhaps they were in fair measure the legacy of the civilians to their common law successors.

---

[1] Marsden, 'Six Centuries', p. 86; cf. A. Browne, vol. 2, p. 28.
[2] Roscoe, *Studies*, p. 10.
[3] Wendt, p. 624.

But to examine some of those difficulties and their solutions it is necessary to open a new chapter in the history of English Admiralty, for the retirement of Sir Robert Phillimore marked the great turning point for the Court, from which it has emerged out of the past and into the present.

CHAPTER 5

THE COURT UNDER COMMON LAWYERS

BARELY six months after Sir Robert Phillimore's retirement as Admiralty Judge, a sweeping reform of procedure was put into effect. It is doubtful that it was anything more than mere coincidence that the reform should have awaited the departure of the last civilian Judge, for it was applicable to the entire High Court and not limited in effect to the Admiralty Division, but many changes of detail, though few of substance, nonetheless altered procedures in the Admiralty Court.

Of chief importance were the changes regarding the appearance of defendants: while they might yet appear at any time prior to the actual giving of judgment, they did not—if they appeared after the date specified in the writ for appearance—continue to enjoy the benefit of an unrestricted defence, but were denied, save by order of the Judge in exceptional cases, any extensions of time.[1] It is also of interest to note a specific requirement that notices of appearances entered in Admiralty actions should thenceforward be given by the Central Office to the Admiralty Registry,[2] indicating perhaps that this had not always been done in the past, to the possible detriment of proceedings in the Admiralty Court. In specifically preserving the earlier summary procedure in collision causes by which the Judge might open the Preliminary Acts and hear evidence without the filing of any pleadings, it was required that any party intending to offer the defence of compulsory pilotage thereafter give notice to that effect at least two days prior to the opening of the Acts.[3] Other new provisions gave an absolute right of removal of actions *in rem*, in certain circumstances, from County Courts to the Admiralty Division,[4] and abolished the use in Admiralty of the demurrer,[5] which had been introduced only eight years previously.[6]

Of greater significance than any of these changes, it would seem, was the emphasis which the 1883 Rules placed upon the preserva-

---

[1] R.S.C., 1883, O. 12, r. 22.   [2] R.S.C., 1883, O. 12, r. 3.
[3] R.S.C., 1883, O. 19, r. 28.   [4] R.S.C., 1883, O. 35.
[5] R.S.C., 1883, O. 25, r. 1.   [6] R.S.C., 1875, O. 23.

tion of pre-Judicature Acts procedure in Admiralty. Aside from new rules which re-enacted earlier procedures without identifying them as such, as in restoration of the affidavit to lead the *warrant in rem*,[1] and payment into Court in lieu of bail to secure release of a previously arrested *res*,[2] there were rules which incorporated procedures in use in the High Court of Admiralty by specific reference to them as such, as with intervention of third parties in actions *in rem*.[3] In addition to these particular provisions, a 'preservation clause' similar to those contained in the 1873 and 1875 Rules was included in the 1883 Rules to retain pre-existing practices and procedures where no replacement or alteration had been specified.[4] There was an oddity to this, however, in that the 1859 and 1871 Rules, which had been declared by the Judicature Acts to 'remain in force' save where they conflicted with the Rules in the 1873 and 1875 schedules, were annulled by the 1883 Rules;[5] thereafter, such pre-Judicature Acts procedures as the appearance under protest could be utilized only by performance of the 'judicial miracle' of resurrecting the pertinent sections of the completely defunct pre-Judicature Acts Rules, as, in the case of the appearance under protest, 1859 Rules 30 and 70–7.[6]

Some of the old procedures sought to be saved by the 1883 Rules died nonetheless, as, for example, the *monition*. It was provided in 1883 that money judgments in Admiralty might be recovered by any method which would have been available to the Admiralty Court prior to the Judicature Act of 1875,[7] and it may be recalled that the usual mode of obtaining satisfaction of personal judgments in both contested[8] and uncontested[9] cases was by decree of a monition for attachment and/or committal of the person, despite the availability of execution as at common law after 1861.[10] Following the passage of the Debtors Act in 1869, and prior to the Judicature Acts, it was considered necessary to separate the monition to pay from the decree of attachment, and to serve the monition immediately after judgment, allowing an

[1] R.S.C., 1883, O. 5, rr. 16, 17; *cf.* R.S.C., 1875, O. 5, r. 11.
[2] R.S.C., 1883, O. 29, r. 3. [3] R.S.C., 1883, O. 12, r. 24.
[4] R.S.C., 1883, O. 72, r. 2 (1044).
[5] See Williams and Bruce, 2nd ed., intro., p. vii; 3rd ed., p. 276.
[6] See, *e.g.*, *The Vera Cruz (No. 1)*, (1884) 9 P.D. 88.
[7] R.S.C., 1883, O. 42, r. 3.
[8] See Williams and Bruce, 3rd ed., p. 336.
[9] 1859 Rules, rr. 33, 34.
[10] Admiralty Court Act, 1861, §§15, 22; see *supra*, pp. 64–5.

interval for compliance before attachment;[1] the 1883 Rules, while not specifically annulling that practice, nonetheless did specify that no prior demand for the payment of a judgment should be necessary,[2] so that the monition to pay became obsolete. Attachment and/or committal might still have been resorted to,[3] but it was quickly found more convenient to employ the common law methods of execution, and after 1883 money judgments in Admiralty were enforced by *fieri facias* or *elegit*,[4] though the latter fell into disuse in the very early years of the present century.[5] The monition, in use as a process in Admiralty since the ancient days of the Court, fell into complete disuse once deprived of its most usual employment, and was replaced by injunction[6] and mandamus, either of which the Admiralty Judge had power to issue by order or judgment.[7] Attachment itself survived, however, as the Court's mode of punishing contempt for (1) arrest-breaking *in rem* (discussed in detail later), (2) attempted levying upon an arrested *res*, (3) defiance by a master or part-owner of a decree of possession, (4) wilful disobedience by any person of an order of the Court,[8] and (5) noncompliance by a solicitor with his undertaking to appear and answer in lieu of arrest *in rem* (discussed in detail later).[9]

Post-1883 arrest in actions *in rem* was effected separately for each cause where a number of claims were brought against the same vessel,[10] in contrast with the procedure earlier outlined[11] in which pre-Judicature Acts *citations in rem* were served upon the Registrar in such instances; after 1883, however, consolidation came to be utilized to prevent a multiplicity of suits—hence, multiple *arrests* are rare.[12] 'Arrest' of a vessel by telegram from the Marshal to his substitute began to be employed in particularly urgent cases,[13] though in form this 'arrest' is really a detention upon pain of contempt until regular service of the warrant effects the actual arrest. In actions during which the *res* remained under arrest, and in which an order issued commissioning the Marshal

---

[1] See R. G. M. Browne, p. 252.   [2] R.S.C., 1883, O. 42, r. 1.
[3] R.S.C., 1883, O. 42, r. 3(581); see Williams and Bruce, 2nd ed., p. 495.
[4] Williams and Bruce, 2nd ed., p. 486.   [5] *Id.*, 3rd ed., p. 338.
[6] *Id.*, 2nd ed., p. 486; R.S.C., 1883, O. 42, rr. 7, 24 (585, 602).
[7] Williams and Bruce, 2nd ed., p. 491.
[8] See R. G. M. Browne, p. 250.   [9] See *infra*, pp. 186–8, 192.
[10] R. G. M. Browne, pp. 34–5.   [11] See *supra*, p. 56.
[12] See Williams and Bruce, 3rd ed., p. 392.
[13] R. G. M. Browne, p. 102.

to appraise and sell, the advertisement of sale required by the 1883 Rules was carried by *The Times*, the *Shipping and Mercantile Gazette*, and some newspaper local to the interested parties specified in the order;[1] the auction of the vessel then took place in Lloyd's Captains' Room at the Royal Exchange.[2]

The 1883 Rules also permitted the parties to a dispute to stipulate agreement as to facts and then to bring the matter before the Admiralty Judge as a 'special case' for his opinion solely on the questions of law involved (*i.e.*, a declaratory judgment not having the force and effect of a judgment rendered in an ordinary case).[3] This was not a new procedure, however, having been informally utilized by the Admiralty Court for some years.[4] And though the Court had historically entertained the suits of indigent mariners,[5] the 1883 Rules made the first provision for suits in *forma pauperis* as at common law.[6] Hearings proceeded as before, with Trinity Masters appearing as nautical assessors at the request of either party—in answer to a praecipe in collision and salvage causes, otherwise by summons[7]—and their task remained simply to give advice to the Admiralty Judge based on the admissible evidence alone.[8] The Registrar, assisted by two Merchants appointed with the approval of the President of the P.D.A. Division, continued to preside at references, though in cases of default he had come to be assisted by only one mercantile assessor,[9] and in causes of salvage the Court was said to become reluctant (for no discernible reason) to direct inquiries to the Registrar and Merchants.[10]

Interpretation of the 1883 Rules, somewhat surprisingly, frequently had the effect of preserving rather than abolishing the old procedure. By the procedural 'preservation clause'—despite the clear requirement that all matters should be commenced in the Court by 'action'—the old method of institution by *praecipe* was retained for special matters involving (1) pirate goods and bounty money, (2) removal and appointment of masters, (3) sale of the ship or share of an unqualified (non-British) owner, (4)

---

[1] R. G. M. Browne, p. 157; see also Williams and Bruce, 2nd ed., p. 379.
[2] *Ibid.*
[3] Williams and Bruce, 2nd ed., p. 360; 3rd ed., p. 361.
[4] *E.g., The Zeta*, (1875) L.R. 4 A. & E. 460.
[5] See *supra*, p. 16.   [6] R.S.C., 1883, O. 16, r. 22.
[7] Williams and Bruce, 3rd ed., p. 443.   [8] Pritchard and Hannen, p. 1467.
[9] Williams and Bruce, 2nd ed., p. 450.   [10] *Id.*, 3rd ed., p. 454.

questions of security for salvage, title to wreck, or enforcement of salvage bonds, and (5) decisions respecting certificates for repayment of excess wages paid to substitutes of seamen leaving merchant ships and entering the Royal Navy (arising under §§214-220, M.S.A., 1854).[1] And in spite of the clear wording of the 1833 Rules that an order for sale could only be made upon the hearing of the cause,[2] the Judge continued with some frequency to make orders for sale prior to the hearing where in his opinion it was desirable so to do,[3] which retained the effect, if not the form, of the procedure in Dr Browne's day.[4]

The forms appended to the 1883 Rules soon proved most troublesome. Designed to bring the pleadings and practice in the Admiralty Court into closer conformity with the system prevailing in the common law courts, the 1883 forms tended to demand too much information from the parties, as with the requirement of a statement of particulars of loss and damages in the claim in collision causes[5]—the question of loss and damages of course being for the Registrar and Merchants only after a finding of liability by the Court, which ordinarily does not consider the issue of damages and therefore has no need of such information—or else to demand too little information, as with the 1883 form of claim in causes of salvage, which proved insufficient to permit the Court to reach a decision in a case arising in that year.[6] The inadequacy of the 1883 forms posed a ticklish problem, for they could not be relied upon and yet could not very well be completely rewritten so soon after promulgation; the solution came with a judicial declaration by Sir James Hannen that the forms were 'not to be slavishly adhered to',[7] whereupon practitioners began to employ forms very similar indeed to those in use before 1883, and as this move met no official resistance or objection, there was soon, for all practical purposes, a complete reversion to the pre-1883 Admiralty forms.[8]

Another problem arising after the 1883 Rules involved the service of Admiralty process *in rem*; it will be recalled that the pre-Judicature Acts warrant of arrest *in rem* contained a citation to the interested parties to appear and defend the *res*,[9] and that the

[1] R. G. M. Browne, p. 219.
[2] R.S.C., 1883, O. 13, r. 13 (113).
[3] Williams and Bruce, 2nd ed., p. 275.
[4] A. Browne, vol. 2, pp. 403-4.
[5] Williams and Bruce, 2nd ed., pp. 343-4.
[6] *The Isis*, (1883) 8 P.D. 227.
[7] (1883) 8 P.D. 227, 228.
[8] See Williams and Bruce, 2nd ed., pp. 342-3.
[9] See 1859 Rules, form 5.

Admiralty Marshal or his substitute alone had the right to board the offending vessel and serve the warrant, affixing a copy to the mainmast.[1] The Judicature Acts, however, removed the citation from the warrant of arrest and placed it in a new writ of summons *in rem* which was a separate instrument;[2] while the Marshal continued exclusively to serve the warrant of arrest, considerations of economy and convenience gave rise to the practice of service of the writ of summons *in rem* by the clerks of plaintiffs' solicitors,[3] who had in any case been accustomed since before the Judicature Acts to serving Admiralty process *in personam*.[4] Inevitably, one of these lay servers of a writ *in rem* was forcibly resisted in his attempt to board and serve a vessel, and the question arose as to the right of such individuals to serve such process; it was ruled that only the Admiralty Marshal had the *right* to board a ship and nail a writ to the mast,[5] which doubtless explains the customary modern practice whereby the Marshal serves both warrant and writ simultaneously,[6] though lay service of writs is occasional.

After 1883, the impact of the common lawyers' domination of the Court began to manifest itself in Admiralty practice as well as procedure. The informal motion practice before the Judge in Chambers which had prevailed under the civilians gave way to the more conventional practice of the common law whereby motions were generally made only in open Court,[7] and the wording of the 1883 Rules with respect to written evidence illustrates the totality of the change in emphasis from written to oral testimony,[8] a change which, though it had begun more than half a century previously, was undertaken in open imitation of the procedure at common law. Moreover, the beginnings of the great confusion of the common lawyers by the specialized jurisprudence of Admiralty were also manifested in the 1883 Rules, which, in oblivious repetition of a misconception introduced in the Judicature Acts,[9] classed an action for *distribution* of a recovery for salvage previously awarded as an action *in rem*;[10] since the object of a suit for distribution of salvage was and is the recovery of money paid as an

---

[1] 1859 Rules, r. 14.
[2] R.S.C., 1875, form A., I, 4.
[3] See *The Solis*, (1885) 10 P.D. 62.
[4] See 1859 Rules, r. 32.
[5] *The Solis*, (1885) 10 P.D. 62.
[6] See R. G. M. Browne, p. 70.
[7] See Williams and Bruce, 3rd ed., p. 500.
[8] R.S.C., 1883, O. 38, r. 2.
[9] R.S.C., 1875, O. 5, r. 11(d.).
[10] R.S.C., 1883, O. 5, r. 16(38)(d.).

award to a salvor, which money, upon payment, loses its identification with the salved *res*, and since that salvor—and not in any way the salved *res*—becomes the defendant in an action for distribution of salvage, the action is properly *in personam* (against the salvor) and not *in rem* (against the *res*). The pre-Judicature Acts suit for distribution of salvage was clearly *in personam*, and it seems plain that the post-Judicature Acts misconception of its nature was the result of confusion by the common lawyers concerning the jurisprudential distinction which must be drawn in Admiralty between actions *in rem* and actions *in personam*.[1]

Sir Robert Phillimore's successor as Admiralty Judge was Sir Charles Butt, who had been called to the bar by Lincoln's Inn in 1854, after which he was for some years the correspondent of *The Times* in Constantinople, where he also carried on a sizeable maritime law practice in the Consular Court; upon his return to London he entered into practice in the Admiralty Court, and though said to have been 'by no means a consummate lawyer', he was acknowledged to be a skilful advocate at the bar, and took silk in 1868.[2] Butt was described during his years at the Admiralty bar as 'bearded and worn-looking from hard work and the climate of Constantinople'[3] (his caricature by 'Ape' from *Vanity Fair* is wondrous), and while it is true that he lacked the academic training and 'ecclesiastical erudition' of the advocates of Doctors' Commons,[4] his knowledge of Admiralty Law and its practice, together with his purposive nature, undoubtedly made him the worthiest of the candidates for the Admiralty Judgeship.

Unfortunately, though Butt was appointed specifically because of his ability to discharge the Office left vacant by Sir Robert Phillimore's retirement, it became the policy of the President, Sir James Hannen, to sit alternately with Butt in Admiralty matters. Resentment grew against this on the part of the bar and of the maritime interests which had a natural concern over the Court's viability, and the eventual result was a published criticism of Hannen for keeping Butt away on circuit and substituting himself, the reason given being that the Court ought to have a full-time Judge in the tradition of the civilians.[5] A more compelling—but unstated—reason for discontent may have been that

---

[1] See Williams and Bruce, 2nd ed., p. 246, n. (*u*).
[2] *D.N.B.*   [3] Roscoe, *Studies*, p. 9.
[4] *Id.*, p. 5; *H.C.A.*, pp. 6-7.   [5] (1884) 76 *L.T.* 286.

Hannen, though his name appeared as co-author of a large digest of Admiralty practice and procedure, was in truth not an Admiralty Lawyer and had no 'experience of shipping law',[1] and the fear may have been not so much of Butt's absence as of Hannen's presence. In any event, Butt seems after 1884 to have sat more consistently in Admiralty matters, while Sir James concentrated on probate and divorce.

If the urgent problem had been solved, Hannen's action in sitting as an alternate had nonetheless broken the ancient succession of single Judges in the Admiralty Court, and never since has the Admiralty Judge had the opportunity enjoyed by his civilian predecessors both to personify the Court of Admiralty and to exert almost a sole influence upon its development; indeed, the formal title of Admiralty Judge lapsed with Sir Robert Phillimore's retirement, and the dignity of the ancient Office has become vested in the President of the P.D.A. Division, in whose Court the gilt anchor hangs and before whom, upon the formal hearing of causes in Admiralty, is displayed the great silver oar mace of the High Court of Admiralty. Sir Charles Butt, then, as the first 'Admiralty Judge' from the ranks of the common lawyers, is also the first to whom that title is applied solely as a description of his function, and the term 'Admiralty Judge' as applied to Butt and to his successors down to the present is used hereafter purely to designate those Judges of the Admiralty Division who sat predominantly in Admiralty matters, and who have either made a significant contribution to Admiralty Law or jurisprudence, or have played a significant part in the Court's later development.

As Admiralty Judge, Sir Charles Butt left no great impression upon the Law of Admiralty, though his decision in *The Vera Cruz (No. 1)*[2] indicating the possibility of finding negligence *per se* ['statutory fault'] on the basis of *non*-contributory violation of a safety regulation,[3] may, if recent American experience is any guide,[4] become significant in the future of Admiralty tort litigation in England. There was no notable judicial extension of the Admiralty jurisdiction ascribable directly to Butt; his reluctance to order a stay of action at common law *pendente lite* despite what

---

[1] Roscoe, *H.C.A.*, pp. 6–7; *Studies*, p. 5.
[2] (1884) 9 P.D. 88.
[3] *Contra, The Fanny M. Carvill*, (1875) L.R. 4 A. & E. 417, 422, 430.
[4] See *Kernan v. American Dredging Co.*, 355 U.S. 426, 78 S.Ct. 394 (1958).

appears to have been a clear statutory power so to do[1] seems to typify his rather unadventuresome judicial outlook. However, if Butt's contribution to Admiralty jurisprudence was not scintillantly affirmative, there were those in other judicial positions whose overall contributions may have been almost negative—two of these in particular being Sir Gainsford Bruce and William Brett, Lord Esher. Born in 1815, Esher attended Westminster School and Gonville and Caius College, Cambridge, taking his M.A. in 1845; he was called to the bar by Lincoln's Inn in 1846, took silk in 1861, and became a leading practitioner at the Admiralty bar; he was made a Justice of the Common Pleas in 1868, Lord Justice of Appeal in 1876, Master of the Rolls in 1883, and died in 1899.[2] He delivered a judgment in the celebrated Crown Case Reserved of *R. v. Keyn*,[3] which established criminal jurisdiction over ships passing through territorial waters, and his judgment in *The Gas Float Whitton (No. 2)*,[4] which settled the non-vessel status of waterborne aids to navigation, thus exempting them from salvage claims, is also notable for its discussion of the historical development of Admiralty jurisdiction in salvage.

Despite these admirable achievements, Lord Esher was notorious for a lack of judicial discretion,[5] and it was said that 'his judgments . . . , even within his own special domain of mercantile and marine law, [were] by no means unimpeachable.'[6] That this was a reasonable statement is illustrated in two cases on appeal from the Admiralty Division concerning recovery for wrongful death under Lord Campbell's Act, which will be discussed later, and particularly in the case of *R. v. Judge of City of London Court*,[7] which was an appeal from refusal of a Divisional Court of the Queen's Bench Division to issue a mandamus compelling the Judge of the City of London Court to exercise that Court's Admiralty jurisdiction *in personam* under the County Courts Admiralty Jurisdiction Act to entertain a suit against the negligent pilot of a Thames barge. The argument recited and relied upon, in part, Mr Justice Story's opinion in *DeLovio v. Boit*,[8] which had earlier been accepted and approved by the Privy Council;[9]

---

[1] *The Nereid*, (1889) 14 P.D. 78.   [2] *D.N.B.*
[3] (1876) 2 Ex. D. 63 [C.C.R.].   [4] [1896] P. 42, 47–53 [App.].
[5] See *D.N.B.*   [6] 22 *D.N.B.* 265.
[7] [1892] 1 Q.B. 273.   [8] 7 Fed. Cas. 418 (No. 3776) (C. C. Mass., 1815).
[9] *The Bold Buccleugh*, (1850–1) 7 Moo. P.C. 267, 284 [*via The Nestor;* see *infra*, p. 157].

Esher, ignoring the principle that a decision of the Privy Council when the final court of appeal in Admiralty is as 'formally and technically' binding upon the Court of Appeal as is a post-Judicature Acts Admiralty decision of the House of Lords,[1] proceeded to discount completely the effectiveness in England of Mr Justice Story's reasoning,[2] and, making it plain that he viewed the proceeding below as an ill-clothed attempt to procure an extension of Admiralty jurisdiction, said: 'I for one will not reopen the floodgates of Admiralty Jurisdiction upon the people of this country.'[3] This statement should demonstrate that the Judicature Acts did not smother the ancient feud between the common law and Admiralty, a fact which retains importance in the present day. Esher was not alone in scorning *DeLovio*, for Kay, L.J., remarked that Story, if literally read, would include even slander within the Admiralty jurisdiction;[4] slander, of course, was within the ancient jurisdiction of Admiralty when committed at sea, as was any tort,[5] and damages for oral defamation were once regularly awarded by the Court[6] without interference by the courts of common law.[7] The unduly restrictive decision in *R. v. Judge of City of London Court* is worthy of a more expert criticism than may be offered here,[8] but it is plain that by this time the common lawyers' ignorance of precedents established by the civilians had become a very material factor in Admiralty decisions both in and out of the Admiralty Court.

As opposed to the real damage done by Lord Esher out of incomplete knowledge and fundamental hostility, the smudges left upon the Admiralty Law by Sir Gainsford Bruce might well be termed 'friendly blunders'. An active Admiralty barrister and author of the leading text for many years on Admiralty jurisdiction and practice, Bruce was described as 'a sensible and pleasant north countryman, with a somewhat horse-face', which gave rise to the cruel pun that, when a nautical chart was placed before him for examination, it was a case of 'putting the chart before the horse.'[9] In spite of his agreeable attributes, Bruce was never

---

[1] *English & Empire Digest*, vol. 1, p. 117; *The Cayo Bonito*, [1903] P. 203, 215, 220.   [2] [1892] 1 Q.B. 273, 293–4.
[3] [1892] 1 Q.B. 273, 299.   [4] [1892] 1 Q.B. 273, 310.
[5] See *The Plymouth*, 3 Wall. (70 U.S.) 20, 36 (1866).
[6] See, *e.g.*, *Raynes c. Osborne*, (1579) 2 *Sel. Pl. Adm.* 156.
[7] Marsden, 10 *L.Q. R.* 113 (1894).
[8] *Ibid.*   [9] Roscoe, *Studies*, p. 10.

considered to possess a legal intellect of the highest order, and his appointment in 1892 as a High Court Judge in the Queen's Bench Division has been called 'dubious', and 'it was not welcomed by the Press at the time';[1] more significantly, it was not welcomed by Lord Chief Justice Coleridge, who took exception to it in a letter to the Lord Chancellor (Halsbury),[2] and the 'justification' which it 'would seem to require'[3] has never been supplied. Bruce retired in 1904 and died in 1912, but prior to his retirement he occasionally sat as an alternate in the Admiralty Division, exercising that jurisdiction as a result of the vesting in each Judge of the entire jurisdiction of the High Court by the Judicature Acts. In that capacity he rendered no decisions contributing significantly to the development of Admiralty jurisdiction, though in one case, *The Theta*,[4] he surely had a great opportunity of doing so; the issue in that case revolved around the meaning of the word 'damage' in §7 of the 1861 Court Act, and the specific question was whether 'damage' included negligent personal injury suffered aboard a ship in dock. A previous case had established that the meaning of 'damage' was not restricted to collision,[5] and Bruce very reasonably accepted that 'damage' might include personal injury, but despite the firm holding that the 'damage done by any ship' clause gave jurisdiction within the body of a county,[6] he refused to extend §7 to cover injuries suffered in dock. Bruce did, however, render one decision which has had a fundamental impact upon Admiralty procedure and jurisprudence in the present century: *The Nautik*,[7] which will be discussed in detail in the following chapter—and which alone provides sufficient justification for the many reservations over Bruce's appointment to the bench.

At the outset of the common lawyers' dominion over the Admiralty Court, the Admiralty jurisdiction remained essentially that of the twilight of the civilian age, and the 1883 Rules even established this more firmly by providing that any cases which would have come before the Court prior to the Judicature Acts should be assigned automatically to the Admiralty Division.[8] Powers

---

[1] Heuston, pp. 46–8.   [2] *Ibid.*
[3] *Id.*, pp. 40–1.   [4] [1894] P. 280.
[5] *The Guldfaxe*, (1868) L.R. 2 A. & E. 325; *The Zeta*, [1893] A.C. 468.
[6] *The Malvina*, (1862) 6 L.T.R. 369.
[7] [1895] P. 121.
[8] R.S.C., 1883, O. 5, r. 5.

possessed by the Court under the civilians, such as that to stay Admiralty actions in inferior courts, remained basically unaltered,[1] though there seems for a time to have been some question whether the Judicature Acts[2] restricted the hearing on appeal from inferior courts of causes which could not have been brought before the Court at instance;[3] that jurisdiction was judicially affirmed, however, early in the present century.[4] Appellate jurisdiction in salvage causes comprehended cases originally brought before Justices of the Peace or their Umpires, Stipendiary Magistrates, or County Court Judges, where the sum in dispute exceeded fifty pounds.[5]

The ancient and inherent jurisdiction of the High Court of Admiralty remained vested in the Admiralty Division, including that of matters of international comity as a court of civil law.[6] But by the same token the ancient restrictions placed upon the Court by the common law and not removed by statute were also passed on, so that 'mixed' [land-sea] contracts, such as charterparties, were actionable only in the Queen's Bench Division[7] unless Admiralty had ancillary jurisdiction in a particular case. The Court's ancillary jurisdiction was in fact broadened by the acquisition under the Judicature Acts of common law jurisdiction, which, like the Admiralty jurisdiction, was thereafter technically shared by all Divisions of the High Court; the result was that causes *in rem* and *in personam* arising out of a single incident, such as a suit for collision brought against an offending vessel in Admiralty and an action for negligence brought against her pilot at common law, which previously had to be tried in separate courts, could after the Judicature Acts and the 1883 Rules be tried together in the Admiralty Division.[8]

During these first years under the common lawyers, a few miscellaneous pieces of jurisdiction were conferred upon the Court by statute. An Act of 1883 regulating fishing vessels placed legal proceedings thereunder upon the same basis as those under the M.S.A., 1854, thus giving the relevant jurisdiction to the

---

[1] See Roscoe, *Practice*, p. 245.
[2] Supreme Court of Judicature (Amendment) Act, 1875, §15(3).
[3] See R. G. M. Browne, p. 20.   [4] *The Montrosa*, [1917] P. 1.
[5] See Williams and Bruce, 2nd ed., p. 515.
[6] Pritchard and Hannen, p. 639.   [7] Smith, p. 9.
[8] *E.g., The Altyre*, (1885) (Feb. 27) S.G.S. 150; see Williams and Bruce, 3rd ed., p. 107, n. (*f*).

Admiralty Division when read with the Judicature Acts and 1883 Rules, and in any suits for wages under the Act jurisdiction was specifically given to consider its forfeiture provisions.[1] Concurrent jurisdiction to try offences involving submarine telegraph cables was given in 1885,[2] and an Act of 1891 affected the Court's jurisdiction in that it forbade detention or arrest of vessels of any nationality defined as 'exempted mail ships' by international convention.[3]

A few aspects of the Court's procedure were likewise affected by statute in this period. Under an Act of 1883, power was given to the Lord Chancellor to transfer jurisdiction under the 1869 Debtors Act to the Queen's Bench Division, and this was done early in 1884;[4] thereafter, satisfaction of any Admiralty Court judgment or order for the payment of money by attachment and/or committal could be effected only upon application to a Judge of the Queen's Bench Division. The Admiralty Judge was given power in 1885 to name persons to conduct examinations or take depositions beyond the Court's geographical jurisdiction.[5] Appeal upon motion to the Admiralty Division from County Courts was facilitated in 1888,[6] and the appellate jurisdiction of the Privy Council in cases coming from Vice-Admiralty Courts[7] survived the replacement in 1890 of the Vice-Admiralty Court system by Colonial Admiralty Courts, which were vested with a jurisdiction and power modelled upon that of the Admiralty Division.[8]

It is of extreme interest to observe that the Admiralty jurisdiction was as readily extended by judicial fiat under the common lawyers as it had been when in the hands of the civilians. This was most frequently accomplished by transfer of actions into the Admiralty Division from the Queen's Bench Division, as upon applications stating as grounds that the matters, e.g., salvage,[9] were not triable at common law, or by retaining suits in Admiralty on matters such as mixed contracts, which ought technically to

---

[1] Merchant Shipping (Fishing Boats) Act, 1883, §§51, 29.
[2] Submarine Telegraph Act, 1885, §6(5).
[3] Mail Ships Act, 1891, §5.
[4] See Bankruptcy Act, 1883, §103.
[5] Evidence by Commission Act, 1885, §2.
[6] County Courts Act, 1888, §120.
[7] See, e.g., The Thomas Allen, (1886) 12 App. Cas. 118 [P.C.].
[8] Colonial Courts of Admiralty Act, 1890.
[9] See, e.g., Game Cock Towing Co. v. Grey, (1887) (Hilary Term) Q.B.D. [unrep.]; Williams and Bruce, 3rd ed., p. 396.

have been transferred to the Queen's Bench Division, and which, upon application, were done so only with the greatest reluctance;[1] indeed, it was in this latter manner that the Admiralty Court during the last quarter of the nineteenth century acquired cognizance of suits upon policies of marine insurance.[2]

But the most significant jurisdictional struggle of these first years of the Court under the common lawyers was one which in fact had its genesis in the first half of the nineteenth century, for it involved the application in Admiralty of one of the most significant pieces of legislation in English history, the Fatal Accidents Act, 1846—better known by the name of its author as Lord Campbell's Act. By permitting actions for infliction of death to be maintained by the survivors of the deceased, this statute in effect created the modern tort of wrongful death; but because the Act made no mention of or specific provision for suits in Admiralty, there was no immediate attempt to apply it in the Admiralty Court. In 1868, however, Sir Robert Phillimore came to grips with the really crucial issue—the ability to sue a *vessel* in Admiralty under Lord Campbell's Act—and held that since a suit could be maintained *in rem* for 'damage done by any ship',[3] and that since 'damage' must reasonably include personal injury or death, there was no jurisdictional bar to a recovery upon suit *in rem* under Lord Campbell's Act.[4] This view was subsequently adopted by the Judicial Committee of the Privy Council in affirming another judgment of Phillimore's on the same grounds.[5] Remarkably, despite the clear position of the Privy Council, the Queen's Bench in 1871 issued a prohibition against an Admiralty suit *in rem* seeking recovery for wrongful death, making it plain in the process that the common lawyers' real objection to such a recovery was that it would, in Admiralty, be awarded without a jury trial.[6] The two views came into head-on collision in a post-Judicature Acts appeal from another recovery *in rem* awarded under Lord Campbell's Act by Sir Robert Phillimore; the Court of Appeal upheld Phillimore in a split decision, Baggallay and James, L.JJ., relying upon the Privy Council's decision in *The Beta*, and Brett [Esher]

---

[1] See, *e.g.*, *Price v. Sea Insurance Co.*, (1889) (12 January) P.D. [unrep.]; Williams and Bruce, 3rd ed., p. 397, n. (*n*).

[2] *Ibid.*   [3] Admiralty Court Act, 1861, §7.

[4] The *Guldfaxe*, (1868) L.R. 2 A. & E. 325.

[5] *The Beta*, (1869) L.R. 2 P.C. 447.

[6] *Smith v. Brown*, (1871) L.R. 6 Q.B. 729.

and Bramwell, L.JJ., ignoring *The Beta* completely in favour of the Queen's Bench in *Smith v. Brown*. After this decision, *The Franconia*,[1] Sir Robert Phillimore completed his years as Admiralty Judge confirmed in the reasoning which he had given in the first year of his tenure. In the year following Phillimore's retirement, Sir Charles Butt awarded a recovery *in rem* for wrongful death under Lord Campbell's Act,[2] and an appeal was taken from that decision to the Court of Appeal; Brett, newly appointed Master of the Rolls, at last prevailed, and the decision below was reversed.[3] Brett's judgment in *The Vera Cruz (No. 2)* is worthy of some dissection; he based his decision upon the narrow equation of the word 'damage' in the 1861 Admiralty Court Act with 'collision', excluding such interpretations as that made by Sir Robert Phillimore in *The Guldfaxe*. Brett was not alone in this reading of 'damage', for the same position had been taken by Dr Lushington in interpreting the same clause;[4] but since Lord Stowell had earlier defined 'damage', used in the same sense, as inclusive of personal injury,[5] the validity of Lushington and Brett's position is very doubtful. More significantly, Brett and his associates' holding against Admiralty jurisdiction *in rem* under Lord Campbell's Act in *The Vera Cruz (No. 2)* again ignored the Privy Council's holding in *The Beta*, and did so despite the citation of that case in argument, and despite the reliance upon it in the decision in *The Franconia*, which Brett took pains to distinguish from the case at bar. On all points, there is clearly very little justification for the refusal of Brett and his colleagues to acknowledge *The Beta*, and its status as a decision of the highest appellate court in Admiralty ought to have produced a different result in *The Vera Cruz (No. 2)*.[6] Though the wrongful death jurisdiction was not judicially restored to Admiralty, at least the restrictive interpretation of 'damage' was soon overruled by Lord Herschell, L.C., in *The Zeta (Mersey Docks and Harbour Board v. Turner)*,[7] and Lord Stowell's view was thereafter restored to favour.[8]

---

[1] (1877) 2 P.D. 163 [App.].   [2] *The Vera Cruz (No. 1)*, (1884) 9 P.D. 88.
[3] *The Vera Cruz (No. 2)*, (1884) 9 P.D. 96 [App.].
[4] *The Robert Pow*, (1863) Br. & Lush. 99.
[5] *The Ruckers*, (1801) 4 C. Rob. 73.
[6] See *supra*, p. 125; *cf. The Cayo Bonito*, [1903] P. 203, 215, 220.
[7] [1892] P. 285; [1893] A.C. 468, 483–7 [H.L.].
[8] See, *e.g.*, *The Theta*, [1894] P. 280.

When Sir James Hannen retired as President of the Admiralty Division in 1891, he was succeeded by Sir Charles Butt; Butt, however, was in poor health at the time, and was President only a few months until his own retirement, which was followed shortly by his death.[1] The new President of the Division was Sir Francis Henry Jeune, who had been appointed Judge of the Division only a few months previously (for the purpose, if seems, of taking over the bulk of the probate and divorce work from Hannen). Jeune was born in 1843, attended Harrow School and Balliol College, Oxford, was called to the bar by the Inner Temple in 1868, took silk in 1888, and became Judge of the P.D.A. Division in 1891. After his appointment in 1892, Jeune served as President for thirteen years, and in addition served without compensation as Judge-Advocate-General from 1892 until 1904.[2] Owing to the previous uncertainty of the status and precedence of the Presidency, legislation was enacted to settle the matter,[3] and in consequence Jeune was the first President to enjoy precedence equal to that of a Lord Justice of Appeal. He retired in 1905 and was given an hereditary peerage as Baron St Helier, and his career upon the bench has been described as 'successful', though personally considered as 'not in the very first rank of English Judges.'[4]

The illness and untimely death of Sir Charles Butt thrust Admiralty matters upon Jeune very soon after he came to the bench. This was unfortunate, for 'of admiralty he had little or no special knowledge at the time of his appointment as a judge . . .',[5] and Jeune's lack of expertise in this admittedly esoteric field did not restrain him, even in the first months of his judgeship, from rendering decisions based upon his personal concepts of the historical development of Admiralty jurisdiction and procedure.

In following the reasoning and precedents of the civilians he was generally on firm ground, as with his exposition of the action *in rem* as the ancient foundation of the suit for salvage, given soon after coming to the bench,[6] which found him in agreement with Dr Lushington.[7] But Jeune is best remembered as a pioneer of new doctrines in Admiralty, and in a decision given just after his appointment as President, *The Dictator*, he departed from the

[1] *D.N.B.*
[2] *Ibid.*
[3] Supreme Court of Judicature Act, 1891, §2.
[4] Heuston, p. 46.
[5] 1901–11 *D.N.B. Supplement*, p. 374.
[6] *The Elton*, [1891] P. 265.
[7] See *The Fusilier*, (1865) Br. & Lush. 341, 344.

precedent and reasoning of the civilian Admiralty Judges of the ninteenth century to establish the concept of personal liability in actions *in rem*;[1] and near the end of his judicial career he expanded this view to hold charterers for the first time personally liable to pay salvage claims.[2] *The Dictator* is perhaps, jurisprudentially, the most important single case within the period covered by this work, and that decision, together with the issues raised by it, is discussed at length in the succeeding chapter. For better or for worse, it is fair to say that Sir Francis Henry Jeune had a greater influence upon the development of the Law of Admiralty than any single common lawyer since Coke.

One procedural development of importance during Jeune's Presidency was the introduction by statute of a right of appeal from interlocutory orders in the Admiralty Division which had the effect of a determination of liability, without permission of the judge making the order;[3] this constituted the first fundamental departure from the doctrine, which had prevailed in Admiralty since the days of Dr Browne and before, that interlocutory decrees were not generally appealable.[4]

A jurisdictional development of more curiosity than importance came with the enactment of legislation giving to local authorities the right to recover, 'in the same manner as salvage', expenses incurred by the disposal of animals washed ashore from wrecks.[5] Though recently repealed, this provision at one time involved the Admiralty Court in determinations such as the applicability of the statute to the disposal of frozen mutton washed ashore from a wrecked refrigerator ship.[6]

By far the most significant enactment of this era, however, was the Merchant Shipping Act, 1894, a consolidation and rewriting of all of the earlier Merchant Shipping Acts, including one which only five years previously had statutorily confirmed the jurisdiction of the Admiralty Court over claims or questions concerning masters' disbursements.[7] It repealed, wholly or in part, several sections of the 1861 Admiralty Court Act and all previous Merchant

---

[1] [1892] P. 64, 304.
[2] *The Cargo ex Port Victor*, (1901) 84 L.T.R. 363.
[3] Supreme Court of Judicature (Procedure) Act, 1894, §1.
[4] See A. Browne, vol. 2, pp. 435–6.
[5] Diseases of Animals Act, 1894, §46.
[6] *The Suevic*, [1908] P. 292 [App. to Adm. Div.].
[7] Merchant Shipping Act, 1889, §1.

Shipping and Shipping Casualties Investigations Acts,[1] and reissued all of the pertinent provisions in a single vast body of legislation.

The 1894 M.S.A., while too large to examine here in great detail, covered the registry and established the priority of ship mortgages,[2] dealt with seamen's rights of wage recovery, discharge compensation, and liens for wages (immune to forfeiture) and salvage (may be forfeited),[3] defined the power of the Admiralty Court to rescind maritime contracts[4] and to remove and appoint shipmasters,[5] dealt with legal proceedings for forfeiture and/or fine under other provisions of the Act,[6] set forth the procedures and powers of tribunals investigating shipping casualties[7] (including the power of the Minister of Transport to order a re-hearing by the Admiralty Division[8]), gave a statutory lien for freight enforceable in Admiralty,[9] established the liabilities of registered and beneficial shipowners,[10] gave to the Admiralty Court the power to consolidate, upon application, claims against foreign and domestic shipowners,[11] established a concurrent jurisdiction for the Admiralty Court over claims relating to recovery or apportionment in salvage and wreck,[12] and defined the geographic limits of jurisdiction under the Act, giving a right of detention of foreign ships within British territorial waters pending compensation of damage done by them to British ships or property elsewhere.[13]

As to practice, the business of the Court during the first years under the common lawyers remained at about the same level which it had reached just prior to Sir Robert Phillimore's retirement. For a random sample, there were 395 writs issued in 1887, 411 in 1891, and 404 in 1896, with the percentage of writs *in rem* remaining at about three-quarters of the total; there was a sharp rise in the number of writs *in rem* in 1903–4, but the total in the year of Jeune's retirement was again just under 400.[14]

Jeune retired as President in 1905, and died in the same year. The civilian influence, which had been maintained to some degree

---

[1] M.S.A., 1894, §745 and Schedule 22.   [2] §§31–46, esp. §33.
[3] §§155–63, esp. §§162, 156.   [4] §168.
[5] §472.   [6] §§356–8.
[7] §§464–8, 469–71, 475–9, esp. §§475(3), 478.
[8] See, *e.g.*, *The Seistan*, [1959] 2 Ll.Rep. 607.
[9] M.S.A., 1894, §494.   [10] §§502–9, 58.
[11] §504.   [12] §§510–71, esp. §§547, 556, 565.
[13] §§684–93, esp. §688.
[14] Figures supplied by Admiralty Registry, 1966.

by Sir Charles Butt, owing to his early practice in the Court under the civilians, dwindled and died during Sir Francis Jeune's tenure—not only in England, but also in Ireland, where, with the death of the last civilian Judge, Dr J. F. Townshend,[1] the High Court of Admiralty in Ireland was united and consolidated in 1893 with the Supreme Court of Judicature in Ireland.[2]

Coincidentally, a great era in United States Admiralty would soon end also. It was the intention of the framers of the Judiciary Acts of the late eighteenth century that the principal function of the District Courts should be the exercise of the Admiralty and maritime jurisdiction mandated by the Constitution; and so it was, until the early twentieth century.[3] The District Courts of the Atlantic coast were of course those which, in terms of business, flourished best; thus Maine, Massachusetts, and Southern New York were the early great Districts. But the Southern District of New York has always been the foremost Admiralty Court of the United States. This one Court—being the oldest Federal Court in the Nation—with a District comprising only Manhattan and a few surrounding counties of New York State, heard 245 Admiralty causes in 1860, 255 in 1870, 525 in 1880, 408 in 1890, 423 in 1900, 384 in 1910, and 1,904 in 1920.[4] Though essentially the Admiralty Court for the Port of New York, a host of proceedings involving foreign-flag vessels and causes arising outside territorial waters have been brought there; the names of a few—*Titanic*, *Andrea Doria/Stockholm, Torrey Canyon*—are fairly illustrative.

In the opinion of a leading American treatise upon the Rules of Nautical Road, 'Notwithstanding the fact that in this country we do not have special admiralty courts, but any federal judge may be required to hear a collision case, it will be found that the decisions have been, as a whole, sound in seamanship as well as in law.'[5] While that statement may be a generally accurate evaluation, it is undeniable that the lack of an Admiralty Judge or Judges in the English sense has historically been the greatest impediment to the development of Admiralty Law in the United States; whether or not a Judge comes to the bench of a great Admiralty District equipped to serve its maritime needs has always been largely a matter of fate, and fate has been kinder, by

[1] Yale, pp. 159–61.
[2] Williams and Bruce, 3rd ed., p. 325, n. (*u*).
[3] Hough, pp. 6–7.
[4] *Id.*, p. 34.
[5] Farwell and Prunski, pp. 220–1.

and large, than the system deserves.[1] That is why the eminent Admiralty Judges of American history (though little attention has ever been paid them) are so easily distinguishable—they are merely the ones whose decisions may be read and clearly understood. Of these there are perhaps ten who could be called great— Betts, Bee, Benedict, Hough, and H. B. Brown, in addition to those previously named.[2] Many, having Admiralty cases thrust upon them despite a total lack of qualification in the field, have been almost nightmarishly incompetent, with concomitant results for the Law. Indeed, only three can be said to have equalled the English civilians in stature; Story and Ware have already been spoken of, but the third, Addison Brown, was on the bench while the direct influence of the civilians in England waned and was extinguished.

Brown was born in West Newbury, Massachusetts, in 1830. He entered Amherst College in 1848, but transferred to Harvard in the following year, where he took his B.A. in 1852, LL.B. in 1854, and was awarded an LL.D. *honoris causa* in 1902. After law school he entered Admiralty practice in New York City, but he was better known as a gifted amateur botanist, on which subject he was the co-author of a noted three-volume treatise. He was appointed to the bench of the Southern District of New York in 1881, served as the last sole Judge of that Court (there are well over a score at present) retired in 1901, and died in 1913.[3] Upon his retirement he published a digest of his decisions, still a treasured possession for any American proctor, and which best shows the extent of his great capabilities in Admiralty.

But Addison Brown was unique in developing a special judicial expertise within Admiralty itself—he was probably the world's foremost judge of marine collision causes. His ability in this was fantastic, as only a reading of his decisions can serve to illustrate,[4] and the peculiar volume of collision cases in his Court gave him continual opportunity to perfect that area of the law, of which he is the modern father in America. In general, Brown took an expansive view of the Admiralty jurisdiction; its growth in the United States during his tenure owed chiefly to him,[5] and his retirement closed a chapter in its evolution.

[1] Wiswall, 'Procedural Unification,' pp. 44–5.   [2] *Supra*, p. 28.
[3] *D.A.B.*, *W.W.W.*
[4] See, *e.g.*, *The Aurania* and *The Republic*, 29 F. 98 (S.D. N.Y. 1886); also Brown, pp. 46–81.   [5] See Hough, p. 29.

In England, Jeune, P., was succeeded by Sir Gorell Barnes, first Judge of the 'new breed' of Admiralty specialists trained solely in the common law. Born in 1848, he took his degree at Peterhouse, Cambridge, was called to the bar by the Inner Temple in 1876, took silk in 1888, was appointed Admiralty Judge upon Butt's death in 1892, became President of the Division in 1905, was elevated to the peerage as Baron Gorell upon his retirement in 1909, and died in 1913.[1] Barnes was, as a former Admiralty barrister, a competent and dependable Admiralty Judge; and if not remembered today for any spectacular or very innovatory decisions, it is perhaps because he was better qualified to adjudicate Admiralty causes than was the President under whom he served.

Barnes' Presidency did see one notable procedural innovation, however, in the introduction of the Admiralty Short Cause Rules in 1908. These Rules represented the latest in the series of efforts begun in the early nineteenth century to streamline Admiralty procedure in hopes of achieving the truly summary proceeding which was the ideal of the civil law. The Short Cause Rules have never been a part of the Rules of the Supreme Court, but were instead established by order of the President of the Admiralty Division as directions to facilitate the dispatch of business.[2] As they enjoyed the technical status of directions rather than rules, the Short Cause Rules could not be imposed upon parties, but were applied in individual cases by request of the parties.[3] Except for claims and counterclaims, there were no pleadings in a short cause save by order of the Judge; after a mutual inspection of documents, the parties each made a simple statement of their case, including the values involved (which, in a normal proceeding, would be determined by reference), and the Judge might then call for and act upon any evidence desired. In all other respects, the Judge might apply at his discretion the normal rules of procedure, and his discretion was also complete as to the assignment of costs; the Judge could arbitrate any issues necessary, but there was no appeal from his determination of a short cause save by his leave, and then only upon questions of law.[4]

Sir Gorell Barnes' successor as President, appointed in 1910, was Sir Samuel Evans. Evans was born in 1859, and was admitted

---

[1] *D.N.B.*

[2] See Roscoe, *Practice*, p. 394.

[3] *S.C.R.*, 1908, r. 1.

[4] *S.C.R.*, 1908, rr. 2–10.

as a solicitor in 1883 before being called to the bar by the Middle Temple in 1891; he took silk in 1901, and became Solicitor-General in 1908.[1] By the greatest stroke of fortune, Evans had made the study of Prize Law something of a hobby, and with the outbreak of World War I, he was naturally called upon to handle a multitude of Prize causes. While he relied heavily upon the Prize precedents of Stowell, he yet established his individuality in that field, and is regarded second only to Lord Stowell as a Prize Judge.[2]

The Judge to whom fell the task of handling the Admiralty (instance) causes generated by the First World War was very fortunately a specialist and former member of the Admiralty bar, Sir Maurice Hill. Born in 1862, Hill was educated at Haileybury School and Balliol College, Oxford; he was called to the bar by the Inner Temple in 1888, made K.C. in 1910, and became Admiralty Judge in 1917; he retired from the bench in 1930, and died in 1934.[3] The volume of Admiralty business generated by World War I was considerable, reaching a peak of well over 900 writs issued in 1920, more than 800 being *in rem*; by comparison, the highest total of writs issued during the Second World War was just over 400, in 1940.[4]

Over a quarter-century after the removal of Admiralty jurisdiction to entertain suits *in rem* for wrongful death by the decision in *The Vera Cruz* (*No. 2*),[5] the United Kingdom became a party to certain international maritime conventions; these were given effect by a statute of 1911 which also confirmed and restored to the Admiralty Division jurisdiction in all causes of maritime personal injury or wrongful death.[6] The same Act introduced into Admiralty a two-year statute of limitations applicable to suits for salvage, personal injury or wrongful death, and a one-year statute of limitations applicable to actions for contribution of joint tortfeasors in such causes;[7] in addition, under the Brussels Collision Convention of 1910, the Act substituted the present rule of proportional fault damages in collision causes for the earlier practice

---

[1] *D.N.B.*
[2] See Roscoe, *Studies*, pp. 36, 40–3.
[3] *D.N.B.*
[4] Figures supplied by Admiralty Registry, 1966.
[5] (1884) 9 P.D. 96 [App.].
[6] Maritime Conventions Act, 1911, §5.
[7] Maritime Conventions Act, 1911, §8.

of awarding half-damages[1] under the both-to-blame rule[2] (which still—unfortunately—applies in American Admiralty[3]).

An Act earlier in 1911 designed to facilitate the compensation claims of stevedores and coal trimmers gave the Admiralty Court a concurrent jurisdiction over such claims, and created a right of recovery in the manner of claims for necessaries, with a statutory lien enforceable in Admiralty by suit *in rem*.[4] And nothing could have been more significant of the changes in environment since the time of the Court under the civilians than the grant to the Court in 1920 of a concurrent jurisdiction with the County Courts, by incorporation of the Merchant Shipping Acts, over salvage claims *by aircraft* in any case where a vessel rendering the service might have been able to claim salvage;[5] by the same Act all jurisdiction over air collisions might be delegated to Admiralty by an Order in Council,[6] but this was evidently a dead letter, for in the succeeding fifteen years no actions at all had been brought in Admiralty for air salvage or collision.[7] In another statute of the same year, however, jurisdiction over any claims involving charterparties, carriage of goods, or torts in respect of goods carried was given to Admiralty in suits *in rem* or *in personam* unless the ship- or share-owner defendants were English or Welsh domiciliaries at the institution of suit,[8] in which case the sole remedy lay at common law.

Acts of 1922[9] and 1925 gave Admiralty jurisdiction in cases arising under the conventions and treaties which they carried into effect, and the latter gave to seamen a specific right of wage recovery during the two months next after the termination of employment or shipwreck, provided that this period was within the time of his contract.[10]

[1] Roscoe, *Practice*, pp. 77–8.
[2] See, *e.g.*, *The Drumlanrig*, [1911] A.C. 16 [H.L.]; but *cf. The British Aviator*, [1965] 1 Ll. Rep. 271.
[3] See Gilmore and Black, §7–4, p. 402.
[4] Merchant Shipping (Stevedores & Trimmers) Act, 1911, §§1–3.
[5] Air Navigation Act, 1920, §11; of course seaplanes may be the *subjects* of salvage—see, *e.g.*, *Lambros Seaplane Base v. The Batory*, 215 F. 2d 228 (2 Cir. 1954).
[6] Air Navigation Act, 1920, §14 (2).
[7] See Merriman, P., *Address to the Canadian Bar Association*.
[8] Administration of Justice Act, 1920, §5(1), (2).
[9] Treaties of Washington Act, 1922, §2(3).
[10] Merchant Shipping (International Labour Conventions) Act, 1925, §1(1); see also §1(2).

This period just after the First World War saw also an emphasis upon the equitable nature of the Admiralty jurisdiction as strengthened by the acquisition of true equitable powers under the Judicature Acts. The doctrine of laches was applied by Sir Maurice Hill in connection with the two-year statute of limitations introduced in 1911 for salvage suits, where the salved vessel was immune from arrest as a Crown ship,[1] and injunctions were issued by the Court to prevent transactions affecting the ownership of a vessel[2] and to restrain interference with North Sea salvage operations.[3]

The procedure of the Court in instance causes continued to be governed by the 1883 Rules, but a series of Rules developed the procedure employed by the Court upon appeals from or rehearings of shipping casualties investigations. Rules were promulgated in 1894 which assigned to the Admiralty Division virtually all jurisdiction conferred upon the High Court by the 1894 M.S.A., and which detailed the procedure for making certain applications under the 1894 M.S.A. to the Admiralty Registrar.[4] An Act of 1906 made it possible to appeal to a Divisional Court of the Admiralty Division from decisions by Board of Trade rehearing tribunals, and from Naval Courts on questions of wages, fines or forfeitures;[5] and further Rules in 1908 permitted the consolidation of such causes on appeal to the Admiralty Division, and made it clear that the Divisional Court might enjoy the assistance of nautical assessors, receive new evidence, and make any necessary orders.[6] Such proceedings therefore came to be governed by a jumble of rules and statutes—a situation which prevailed until 1923, when a new set of Shipping Casualties and Appeals and Rehearings Rules consolidated and superseded the previous provisions. These 1923 Shipping Rules set down the procedure to be followed at original hearings as well as upon appeal. Appeal could be taken from any Board of Trade hearing to a Divisional Court of the Admiralty Division within twenty-eight days of the hearing decision,[7] and the use of nautical assessors upon appeal

---

[1] *H.M.S. Archer*, [1919] P. 1.
[2] *Beadell v. Manners* (*The Victoria*), Ll.L. 14 July 1919.
[3] *The Tubantia*, [1924] P. 78.
[4] R.S.C. (Merchant Shipping), 1894 (S.R.O. Rev. [1904], vol. 12, p. 680), rr. 1–3.   [5] Merchant Shipping Act, 1906, §§66, 68.
[6] M.S.R., 1908 (S.R.O., 1908, No. 446).
[7] S.C.R., 1923 (S.R.O., 1923, No. 752), rr. 19, 20(a), (b).

seems to be mandatory;[1] in all other pertinent respects, the procedure established by these Rules was either that previously obtaining under the older shipping casualties and merchant shipping rules, or that normally in use in the Admiralty Court.[2]

Sir Samuel Evans died in 1918, and his successor as President of the Admiralty Division was Sir Henry Duke, Lord Merrivale. Duke was born in 1855, was called to the bar by Gray's Inn in 1885, took silk in 1899, and may have had some Admiralty experience while at the bar. He served as Irish Secretary following the Easter Rebellion, from 1916 to 1918; he became a Lord Justice of Appeal in 1918, and in the year following his appointment in 1919 as President of the P.D.A. Division, the precedence of that Office was advanced by statute[3] to its present position next after that of the Master of the Rolls; he was elevated to the peerage as Baron Merrivale in 1925.[4]

The Admiralty Registrarship changed hands only twice in the fifty years following Sir Robert Phillimore's retirement as Judge; J. G. Smith succeeded H. A. Bathurst upon the latter's retirement in 1890, and Edward Stanley Roscoe, who had been appointed Assistant Registrar in 1890, succeeded Smith in 1904.[5] Roscoe was a prolific writer, leaving some thirty-eight published titles to his credit, and his works upon Admiralty Court jurisdiction, practice and history are valuable contributions to the body of knowledge in this field.

Early in the postwar period, it became obvious that the statutory structure of judicial administration, with a great host of enactments altering, modifying, and adding to the basic design of the Judicature Acts, had evolved into a grotesque and maze-like edifice. The entire structure was therefore razed and rebuilt in 1925 by a single consolidating enactment. Outwardly, the Consolidation Act changed very little of what had existed before; the High Court of Justice retained its three Divisions, though the President of the P.D.A. Division became an additional Judge of the Court of Appeal. To the Admiralty Division was assigned all of the Admiralty and Prize business, including all causes previously assigned and all which would have been within the exclusive jurisdiction of the High Court of Admiralty.[6]

---

[1] S.C.R., 1923, r. 20(e).   [2] S.C.R., 1923, r. 20(j).
[3] Administration of Justice Act, 1920, §7.
[4] *D.N.B.*   [5] Thompson, p. 22.
[6] Supreme Court of Judicature (Consolidation) Act, 1925, §§4, 6, 56(3)(a)–(c).

The greatest effect of the Judicature Consolidation Act upon the Admiralty Court was jurisdictional. The inclusive grant of Admiralty jurisdiction by the Judicature Acts remained the basis of jurisdiction,[1] but additions included claims for necessaries supplied to any foreign ship *anywhere* save in her home port and questions of title arising in necessaries suits,[2] claims for damage done *to* any ship,[3] and claims for salvage, life salvage, and services in the nature of towage and salvage regardless of where rendered.[4] The total Admiralty jurisdiction granted was therefore all that possessed formerly by the High Court of Admiralty, all that possessed by the High Court of Justice immediately prior to the Consolidation Act, and all that unrepealed and added by the Act itself.[5]

It is interesting to note, in addition, the definition by the Act of 'damage' as inclusive of personal injury and wrongful death,[6] and the definition of 'ship' as 'any description of vessel used in navigation, not propelled by oars.'[7] There were a few miscellaneous provisions governing the assignment of costs;[8] however, the discretion of the Judge still generally prevailed. Where a specific grant of pre-existing jurisdiction was made, portions of earlier statutes such as the Court Acts of 1840 and 1861 were correspondingly repealed;[9] but in no case does the Act appear to have affected the previous jurisdiction exerciseable *in rem*.[10]

One aspect of the Judicature Consolidation Act offers a point for speculation, because it differs in construction from the Judicature Acts. By the Judicature Acts of 1873 and 1875, the High Court of Admiralty was consolidated, together with other courts, into the Supreme Court of Judicature, and its jurisdiction transferred to the High Court of Justice,[11] though exercised primarily by the Admiralty Division.[12] But the Supreme Court of Judicature was reconstituted by the Judicature Consolidation Act, which vested in it the jurisdiction possessed before 1875 by a number of the old courts; the jurisdiction formerly possessed by the High Court of Admiralty was not specifically so vested, however,[13] and

---

[1] S.C.J. (Cons.) Act, 1925, §18.
[2] §22(1)(a)(vii), (i)
[3] §22(1)(a)(iii).
[4] §22(1)(a)(v), (vi).
[5] §22(1)(b), (c).
[6] §22(2).
[7] §22(3).
[8] §33(1)(a)–(c).
[9] See Schedule of Repeals.
[10] Price, *L.M.L.*, p. 95.
[11] Supreme Court of Judicature Act, 1873, §§3, 16.
[12] R.S.C., 1883, O. 5, r. 5; *cf.* S.C.J. Act, 1873, §34.
[13] S.C.J. (Cons.) Act, 1925, §18; *cf.* S.C.J. Act, 1873, §16.

the Admiralty jurisdiction of the High Court of Justice was separately provided for.[1] When the Acts of 1873 and 1925 are compared in this respect, the construction of the 1925 Act appears most peculiar; it may be that in specifying the Admiralty jurisdiction by particulars, it was hoped thereby to avoid confusion with the High Court's common law jurisdiction. Indeed, all of the High Court's civil law jurisdiction as exercised by the P.D.A. Division was set apart, and this may have prompted, in 1926, the decision (discussed p. 143) in the case of *The Sheaf Brook*.

The business of the Admiralty Court remained at a high (though declining) pitch in the years immediately after World War I, but after falling to roughly the prewar average of 400 writs issued in 1926–7, there began a decline which reached the low ebb of just over 200 writs issued in 1935.[2]

The nature of instance causes, in some respects, was reflective of scientific and technical progress; thus bottomry, after establishment of the rule that the master must make every reasonable effort to contact the shipowners and obtain money upon their personal credit before resorting to hypothecation,[3] was slowly made archaic by the establishment of world-wide telegraph links[4] in the same way that the great number of seventeenth and eighteenth century suits for holing by settling upon unbuoyed anchors had been eliminated in the nineteenth century by the advent of floating docks and non-grounding hulls.[5] Among the few twentieth-century bottomry cases, however, is one in which Lord Merrivale partially upheld bottomry bonds upon a yacht, finding necessity proven despite the vessel's non-commercial employment.[6] Other cases, such as one in which Hill, J., was required to rule whether the white ensign of a member vessel of the Royal Yacht Squadron gave her the status of a Crown ship, illustrate the somewhat trivial nature of many questions coming before the Court in that period.[7]

It is noteworthy that under the common lawyers, the Court has secured upon occasion a legislative enlargement of its jurisdiction

---

[1] S.C.J. (Cons.) Act, 1925, §22; see also §33(2).
[2] Figures supplied by Admiralty Registry, 1966.
[3] *The Oriental*, (1851) 7 Moo. P.C. 398, 411.
[4] Abbott, p. 207.
[5] See Marsden, 'Jurisdiction', 10 *L.Q.R.* 113 (1894).
[6] *The St. George*, [1926] P. 217.
[7] *H.M.S. Glatton*, [1923] P. 215.

following a restrictive decision; thus a twentieth-century decision by the Court of Appeal which held that the Admiralty Division could have no cognizance of claims *in personam* under the 1925 Consolidation Act by cargo owners against English shipowners, and that the President had no discretion to retain such a case but should transfer it to the King's Bench Division,[1] is said[2] to have resulted in the 1928 legislation which specifically declared the jurisdiction of the High Court of Justice to belong to all divisions alike,[3] thus enabling the Admiralty Division to entertain any claim *in personam* which could have been brought before any other Division. Similarly, the Court's own holding in 1886 that it had no jurisdiction to entertain an appeal from a refusal by the Board of Trade to order the rehearing of a shipping casualty investigation[4] resulted in legislation of 1894 giving a specific right of appeal to the Admiralty Division from such a refusal;[5] and the right of appeal from decisions of Board of Trade hearings was expanded by the Court in the post-World War I period to permit a censured but still licensed master to appeal as an 'interested party',[6] and the Court has power to revoke such censure when warranted.[7]

The twentieth century has also seen fundamental changes of theoretical Admiralty jurisprudence which evolved so gradually as to be almost unnoticeable. Thus the master of a vessel, once regarded as bailee for the owners, could therefore transfer possession—but the modern view sees the owner in possession of his ship at all times, and the master merely as a servant-custodian.[8] And the 'ship', a limited concept, has increasingly been replaced in the present century by the 'vessel',[9] a concept elastic enough to comprehend such undreamed-of innovations as the hovercraft. Concepts of the proper exercise of the Court's jurisdiction have also changed, so that Lord Stowell's restrictive view of the Admiralty jurisdiction over foreigners has been distinguished[10] until, at present, 'it is no longer necessary that the parties should consent, or that a foreign government should signify its assent.[11]

---

[1] *The Sheaf Brook*, [1926] P. 61 [App.]. [2] Roscoe, *Practice*, p. 123.
[3] Administration of Justice Act, 1928, §6. [4] *The Ida*, (1886) 11 P.D. 37.
[5] Merchant Shipping Act, 1894, §475(3).
[6] *The Royal Star*, [1928] P. 48.
See S.C.R., 1923, r. 19.
[7] *E.g.*, *The Seistan*, [1959] 2 Ll.Rep. 607.
[8] See Roscoe, *Practice*, p. 40. [9] *Id.*, p. 133.
[10] See, *e.g.*, *The Jupiter* (*No. 2*), [1925] P. 69, 74.
[11] Roscoe, *Practice*, p. 42.

Discretion is of course still exercised to refuse jurisdiction in the manner of *forum non conveniens* 'where foreigners have merely taken advantage of a vessel being temporarily in [England] . . . to obtain a decision on questions which depend upon the municipal law of a foreign state',[1] though where such questions arise in the normal course of a suit, the Judge may decide upon them.[2]

E. S. Roscoe, the last Admiralty Registrar to hold a life appointment to that post, died in 1932 at the age of 89; his Assistant Registrar, Henry Stokes, who similarly held his post under a life appointment, retired in 1939 at the age of 91. Subsequent appointees to these posts—the next being L. F. C. Darby as Registrar in 1933 and G. H. M. Thompson as Assistant Registrar in 1939— were required by statute to retire at age 75.[3] The 'dignified and urbane' Lord Merrivale retired as President in 1933 and died in 1939.[4] The new President, Sir Frank Boyd Merriman [Lord Merriman], sometime Solicitor-General,[5] was appointed in 1934 during another storm of controversy over the Admiralty Court.

The Second Interim Report of the Business of the Courts [Hanworth] Committee, published in December, 1933, contained a recommendation that the P.D.A. Division be abolished and its jurisdiction be assumed by the two other Divisions of the High Court; in particular, it proposed the transfer of Admiralty business to the King's Bench Division, with the appointment in that Division of a 'Judge in Admiralty' who alone should exercise the jurisdiction of the High Court in Admiralty, Prize, and 'Commercial Business'. The advantages of this scheme were supposedly the continued centralization of the specialty in London with the added assurance of a Judge skilled in Admiralty Law, though the 'Judge in Admiralty' would be assisted by other judges in the dispatch of 'commercial cases.'[6] In the ensuing furore, a counter-proposal was offered by 'a Member of the Admiralty Bar' for the establishment of a new Admiralty and Commercial Division of the High Court,[7] and this plan, which would have resulted in four Divisions rather than the two proposed by the Hanworth Committee, was endorsed by the London Chamber of Commerce in

[1] Roscoe, *Practice*, p. 42.
[2] S.C.J. (Consolidation) Act, 1925, §102.
[3] Thompson, pp. 22–3.
[4] *D.N.B.*   [5] See Heuston, p. 587.
[6] Parl. Paper, Cmd. No. 8809, ¶18, pp. 13–14; ¶11, p. 8 (1933).
[7] 177 *L.T.* 54 (1934).

a resolution sent to Lord Chancellor Sankey.[1] There was considerable—and justifiable—criticism of the Hanworth Committee, whose membership did not include any Admiralty lawyers or judges, for making such recommendations as the abolition of the Admiralty Court and Registry without having solicited sufficient testimony from the commercial and maritime interests and from the branch of the profession most concerned.[2] At length the furore died and the Hanworth Committee's proposals were shelved, but not forgotten.

It was observed in 1886 that the Rules of 1883 contained provisions not by their nature applicable to Admiralty practice and yet so worded as to appear to govern all practice in the High Court, the result being a confusion as to the extent to which the old Admiralty procedure remained in force.[3] The situation complained of three years after the promulgation of the 1883 Rules has not altered very materially in the succeeding eighty years, and the 1883 Rules are still the basis of Admiralty procedure,[4] though frequently amended during that period.[5] The undesirability of this situation has now been recognized for several years, and the first corrective steps began in 1962, pursuant to the recommendations of the [Evershed] Committee on Supreme Court Practice and Procedure in 1951.

It is most interesting that in some of the Evershed Committee's proposals, the pendulum has seemed to swing back past the 1859 Rules, pointing out as advantageous some of the procedures employed in the era of Lord Stowell. Thus the excess of reformative zeal which led to the printing rules of 1855 and 1859 is, after nearly a century, balanced by the Evershed Committee's observation that the printing of pleadings and apostles is a 'needless extravagance' which should be eliminated,[6] and the shift in emphasis from written to oral testimony which is particularly evident in the 1859 Rules contrasts with the 1951 recommendation encouraging the trial of salvage suits by documentary evidence alone[7]—much in the fashion, one would suppose, described by Dr Browne. Further parallels might be found in the recommendation that the Registrar be given jurisdiction to dispose of certain

---

[1] 77 *L.J.* 53 (1934). [2] See 177 *L.T.* 54 (1934).
[3] Williams and Bruce, 2nd ed., preface, p. vii.
[4] See *Annual Practice, 1966*, vol. 2, intro., p. v. [5] *Id.*, vol. 1, p. 1.
[6] Parl. Paper, Cmd. No. 8176, ¶¶30, 31, pp. 13–14 (1951).
[7] *Id.*, ¶23, p. 11.

cases in which there is no 'substantial' dispute[1] (a power resembling that of the Registrar as surrogate between 1861 and 1875), and that such proceedings be instituted upon *originating summons*[2] (a device similar to the old *monition* to appear and answer).

A few of the Evershed Committee's proposals have been adopted, most notably the use of the *originating motion* and *originating summons*[3] to institute certain proceedings. But the most significant development has surely been the consolidation of the Admiralty procedure begun in 1962 as part of a complete revision of the 1883 Rules; after patient 'weeding', the Admiralty rules have been separated from the body of Rules of the Supreme Court and consolidated in a single new Order 75, which took effect in 1964,[4] and subsequent steps have been taken to ensure that procedure in the Admiralty Court will follow that Order and not the procedure of the common law courts.[5] Ironically, an exactly opposite move was being made at the same time in the United States, where the old Supreme Court [General] Admiralty Rules have been abolished and, aside from special supplemental rules for actions *in rem* and a few other proceedings peculiar to Admiralty,[6] causes in Admiralty are now tried according to the rules and forms established for civil actions at common law and contained in the (1 July 1966) Federal Rules of Civil Procedure,[7] governing proceedings in all United States District Courts. In view of the previous experiences in both countries, it will be interesting to compare future procedural developments in England and America.[8]

It must be stressed that the consolidation of English Admiralty procedure has not been accompanied by a revision, and that the procedure currently in effect is still based upon the 1883 Rules. There have, however, been a few procedural developments which are deserving of comment with regard to the present Admiralty procedure. Thus the mechanism for pre-trial discovery has been improved by the application for orders for discovery of documents and the acceptance of written interrogatories as a method of discovery,[9] though the latter are not much used in practice.[10]

---

[1] Parl. Paper, Cmd. No. 8176, ¶36, p. 15 (1951).   [2] *Ibid.*
[3] See *id.*, ¶¶11, 12, p. 7; also McGuffie, *Practice*, §427, p. 190
[4] R.S.C. (Revision) 1962 [S.I. 1962, p. 2624].
[5] See *Annual Practice, 1966*, vol. 1, intro., p. xi.
[6] F.R.C.P. [1 July 1966], Adm. Rules A–F.
[7] F.R.C.P. [1 July 1966], Rule 1.
[8] See Wiswall, 'Procedural Unification,' pp. 46–8.
[9] Roscoe, *Practice*, pp. 316–20.   [10] McGuffie, *Practice*, §922, p. 402.

There is virtually complete discovery today, as 'the existence of all relevant documents must be disclosed even if it is intended to refuse production unless the court orders it to be given',[1] and the penalty for refusal to make discovery may be dismissal (plaintiff) or entry of judgment (defendant).[2] Several procedures, though still technically applicable, have fallen into practical disuse; it is doubted whether appearance under protest would be permitted now—though not abolished by the Judicature Acts—and a new 'conditional' form of appearance has been substituted, differing only in that it becomes unconditional within two weeks unless the Court's jurisdiction is successfully contested.[3] *Fieri facias* and other forms of execution are rarely employed, because even in the unusual instance of inadequate bail, the defendant normally makes voluntary satisfaction of the judgment.[4] And the Short Cause Rules of 1908, though amended in 1930–31, were observed by the Evershed Committee in 1951 to have been little used because of the difficulty of obtaining the consent by the parties to the implied waiver of the right of appeal;[5] this situation persisted until, in 1966, the President directed that the Short Cause Rules should cease to have effect, and they were at the same time replaced by a new Rule 31 in Order 75 of the Rules of the Supreme Court,[6] enabling the trial of any action in Admiralty as a Short Cause upon application.

While it appears that the majority of Admiralty actions *in personam* could be tried at common law in the Queen's Bench Division,[7] the procedural advantages of a suit in Admiralty— perhaps including the total absence of a civil jury—have evidently been sufficient to maintain a yearly average of about fifty *in personam* writs in Admiralty since 1935,[8] not counting over 200 writs *in personam* issued in the single cause of the disastrous wartime collision between the *Queen Mary* and the escort cruiser *H.M.S. Curacoa*.[9] There has been a recent increase in the issue of writs *in rem*, so that the total of writs issued has risen from a

[1] McGuffie, *Practice*, §841, p. 369.
[2] *Id.*, §901, p. 398.
[3] *Id.*, §300, p. 130; *The Vivar*, (1876) 2 P.D. 29 [App.].
[4] McGuffie, *Practice*, §§324, 325, p. 142.
[5] Parl. Paper, Cmd. No. 8176, ¶28, p. 13 (1951).
[6] R.S.C. (Amendment No. 2) 1966 [S.I. 1966, No. 1055].
[7] McGuffie, *Practice*, §42, p. 23, n. 47.
[8] Figures supplied by Admiralty Registry, 1966.
[9] *Ibid.*; *The Queen Mary*, (1947) 80 Ll.L.R. 178.

twentieth-century low of just over 100 in 1945–6 to over 350 in 1964–5.[1]

The evolution of case law in Admiralty has continued to have both procedural and substantive effect; thus the giving of bail, which was once held to be such 'a decisive step in the action' as to nullify the effect of an appearance 'under protest',[2] may now be tendered in certain cases under a special wording of the bond which will prevent conversion thereby of a conditional to an unconditional appearance.[3]

A much more extended and controversial case line deals with liability *in rem* in the absence of liability *in personam*. The line begins, characteristically enough, with a 'judicial pirouette' by Dr Lushington, who first held pursuant to a strained application of the law of agency that there could be no proceeding against the *res* where there could be no proceeding against the owners,[4] and who then held that there could be maintained an action *in rem* where there was no possibility of an action *in personam* upon the same cause if the owners had surrendered control to a sovereign charterer,[5] or if the owner was deceased.[6] Brett [Esher], L.J., reached the opposite conclusion in *The Parlement Belge*,[7] which like *The Ticonderoga*[8] involved a question of sovereign immunity, and held that there could be no action *in rem* without liability *in personam*. Sir Gorell Barnes made the next 180° turn in *The Ripon City*,[9] permitting the *res* to be sued in the absence of any personal liability by the owner. Sir Maurice Hill, however, in a case bearing a strong fact-situation resemblance to *The Ticonderoga*, disagreed with the position of Lushington and Barnes, and held that the vessel could not be sued *in rem* where the owner could not be sued *in personam*,[10] a view subsequently upheld by the Court of Appeal;[11] but a treatise on Admiralty practice published thereafter declared that suit *in rem* could in some instances be maintained without the availability of a remedy *in personam*.[12] Then, thirty-odd years later, in a case involving consideration of statutory rights *in rem*, Sir Bushby Hewson held against suit *in rem*

---

[1] Figures supplied by Admiralty Registry, 1966.
[2] *The Rosina*, (1921) 6 Ll.L.R. 346, 347.
[3] *The Bulgaria*, [1964] 2 Ll. Rep. 524.   [4] *The Druid*, (1842) 1 W. Rob. 391.
[5] *The Ticonderoga*, (1857) Swab. 215.   [6] *The Ruby Queen*, (1861) Lush. 266.
[7] (1880) 5 P.D. 197, 220 [App.].   [8] (1857) Swab. 215.
[9] [1897] P. 226, 242.   [10] *The Crimdon*, (1918) 35 T.L.R. 81
[11] *The Tervaete*, [1922] P. 259, 275 [App.]   [12] Roscoe, *Practice*, p. 104.

where a suit *in personam* was not possible.[1] Now, only a few years since, Sir Henry Brandon has made an exhaustive review of the authorities and perhaps settled the dispute, holding actions *in rem* maintainable without the possibility of suit *in personam*.[2]

Two pieces of legislation in the later 1940s affected Admiralty jurisdiction. In the first, a long concern over the application of the principle of limitation of liability to British vessels in foreign courts[3] was suddenly mirrored—in the wake of the *Queen Mary/ Curacoa* disaster—by concern over inapplicability of the same principle to claims involving Crown vessels in the Admiralty Courts of Britain, and limitation of liability together with immunity from suit *in rem* was made available to Crown vessels and aircraft.[4] The second statute reflected a weakness of the 1925 Judicature Consolidation Act, and enabled the Court to entertain claims by aircraft for salvage or life salvage of/from *other aircraft* as well as vessels.[5]

But in the entire panoply of legislation which has conferred jurisdiction upon the Admiralty Court, no other enactment has possessed the potential for judicial expansion of jurisdiction which is inherent in the most recent grant of jurisdiction to Admiralty, contained in Part I of the Administration of Justice Act, 1956. This Act confirms to the Court any jurisdiction possessed by the High Court of Admiralty prior to the Judicature Acts or subsequently vested in the High Court of Justice,[6] as well as a particular enumeration of questions or claims cognizable under the Act itself.[7] There are, however, a number of new or newly-phrased provisions enabling cognizance of claims: (1) for personal injury or wrongful death due to unseaworthiness or negligence of operations 'in or from the ship';[8] (2) by and against aircraft in the nature of salvage, towage and pilotage;[9] (3) for necessaries supplied for operation or maintenance;[10] (4) for construction, repair or equipment of a vessel, or for dock charges or [port] dues;[11] and (5) for general average.[12]

---

[1] *The St. Merriel*, [1963] 1 Ll. Rep. 63.
[2] *The Monica S.*, [1967] 2 Ll. Rep. 113, 132.
[3] See Parl. Paper [1874] (69) lx (H.C. 18 May).
[4] Crown Proceedings Act, 1947, §§5, 29.
[5] Civil Aviation Act, 1949, §51.
[6] Administration of Justice Act, 1956, §1(1)(*s*).
[7] §1(1)(*a*)–(*s*).   [8] §1(1)(*f*).
[9] §1(1)(*j*)–(*l*).   [10] §1(1)(*m*).
[11] §1(1)(*n*).   [12] §1(1)(*q*).

Even more important is the range of applicability of all cognizance, old and new, for it now extends to cover: (1) *all* vessels or aircraft, British or not, registered or not, whatever the domicile of their owners;[1] (2) all claims *wherever* arising (including cargo or wreck salved ashore);[2] (3) *all* mortgages or 'charges' (including maritime and statutory liens), registered or not, legal or equitable, foreign or domestic[3]—provided only that these provisions not be interpreted to extend recovery under the various Merchant Shipping Acts. Moreover, the jurisdiction of the Admiralty Court may now be invoked: (1) in *all* cases *in personam*,[4] save that in claims for damage (including that done to ship or cargo), personal injury, wrongful death or negligent operation (*arising out of or resulting in* **collision**) suit may be brought *in personam*— but only if: (A) the defendant resides or has a place of business 'in England and Wales' ('and' being employed to unify, and not to separate),[5] *or* (B) the cause arose within a port or territorial waters of England and Wales,[6] *or* (C) if the Court has ancillary jurisdiction over the person in a matter generated by the same cause;[7] (2) *in rem* in any suit for possession (including title, petition or restraint) of ship or share thereof, any suit upon a mortgage of ship or share thereof, any suit for condemnation, forfeiture or restoration of ship or goods, any suit for droits of Admiralty, or in any suit upon a maritime or statutory lien or other 'charge'.[8] And of the utmost significance is the introduction by the 1956 Act, in any case in which the owner is a resident of England and Wales and liable to suit *in personam*, of (1) the ability to invoke the Admiralty jurisdiction *in rem* against aircraft for claims in the nature of towage or pilotage,[9] and (2) (where the resident was, at the time the cause arose, owner, charterer, or otherwise 'in control'), the ability to invoke the Admiralty jurisdiction *in rem* against *sister ships* [any vessels also *wholly* owned by the possible defendant *in personam*] as well as against the offending vessel for any claims under the Act save those of possession, mortgage, forfeiture, condemnation, restoration, droits, or any other under §1(1)(*s*), or where the basis of the suit is a 'charge'

---

[1] Administration of Justice Act, 1956, §1(4)(*a*).
[2] §1(4)(*b*).   [3] §1(4)(*c*); *cf.* Dicey, comment p. 218.
[4] §3(1).   [5] §4(7), (1)(*a*).
[6] §4(7), (1)(*b*).   [7] §4(7), (1)(*c*).
[8] §3(2), (3); see comment in Dicey, at p. 218.
[9] §3(5).

incurred by a specific vessel and not within the scope of §1(1) (d)–(r).[1]

The 1956 Act also repealed the £50 minimum claim limit for jurisdiction over mariners' wage claims in the Admiralty Division, and gave the Court a specific authority to declare *forum non conveniens* in wages suits by personnel of foreign vessels,[2] though it seems clear that the question of *forum non conveniens* may be considered in a suit upon any claim involving foreign parties.[3] It should also be noted that the Act defines 'ship' as 'any description of vessel used in navigation',[4] dropping the 'not propelled by oars' qualification of the 1925 Consolidation Act[5] in deference to the gradual extinction of the oar as a propulsive mechanism.

Many provisions of many prior enactments were repealed by the 1956 Act, including the power given by §688 of the 1894 M.S.A. to detain in Britain foreign ships which had injured British-owned property anywhere in the world.[6]

For the total compass of current Admiralty jurisdiction, including that contained in the 1956 Act, reference should be made to *Halsbury's Laws of England*[7] and similar sources.

At the turn of the twentieth century, it was noted concerning the former jurisdiction of the Admiralty Court over suits by materialmen for necessaries—which was twice struck down by higher courts[8]—that: 'any jurisdiction the Admiralty possessed in respect of necessaries supplied on the high seas would be a portion of the jurisdiction, *ex contractu*, in matters on the high seas of which the Common Law Courts only obtained a share by the fiction of a false venue . . .'[9] Fifty-four years later, whether in recognition of the truth of that statement or not, the Admiralty jurisdiction over materialmen's suits was restored by the 1956 Act. But if the Act took pains to preserve such obsolete jurisdiction as that over suits for restraint,[10] and to re-enact the useful

---

[1] Administration of Justice Act, 1956, §3(4)(a), (b); see 1952 Brussels Convention on Arrest of Sea-Going Ships, Art. 3.

[2] §5(1), (2); see also Temperley, ¶306.   [3] See McGuffie, *Practice*, §493, p. 223.

[4] Administration of Justice Act, 1956, §8(1).

[5] S.C.J. (Consolidation) Act, 1925, §22(3).

[6] Administration of Justice Act, 1956, §7(1).

[7] Vol. 1, p. 50 *et seq.*; see also Dicey, pp. 213–20.

[8] *The Neptune*, (1834) 3 Kn. P.C. 94.

The Heinrich Björn, (1885) 10 P.D. 44 [App.].

[9] Williams and Bruce, 3rd ed., p. 197, n. (*l*).

[10] §1(1)(b); McGuffie, *Practice*, §642, p. 285.

jurisdiction over charter-party claims first given by the 1925 Act,[1] and to restore the lost jurisdiction over materialmen's claims and general average,[2] why did it not grant to the Court a jurisdiction equal to that of the common law over the remainder of mixed contracts, and specifically place within the cognizance of the Court such matters as questions of particular average and claims upon policies of marine insurance? Perhaps because the Act is elastic enough to permit such cognizance without great inter-pretive strain[3]—but it seems a missed opportunity that a flat jurisdiction over mixed contracts was not stated. At the heart of the matter lies the discretion, or lack of it, to transfer causes between Divisions of the High Court, and until cognizance of mixed contracts in general is statutorily placed within the Admir-alty jurisdiction there will continue to be grounds for demands for transfer of such causes out of the Admiralty Division and equal grounds for the refusal of transfer of such causes into the Admiralty Division.

The 1956 Act does, however, make such great restoration of jurisdiction to Admiralty that it may properly be termed 'a Coke's nightmare'. The territorial extension of jurisdiction alone is enough to cast doubt upon the definitive decisions in that area of the law,[4] and the new availability of proceedings *in rem* against aircraft has already involved the Court in an examination of the pertinent sections of the Act, and led to a suggestion that this jurisdiction ought to be extended to cover charges and mortgages upon air-craft as well.[5] In the case of the limitation of sister-ship arrest to claims upon which the owner may be liable on suit *in personam* as a domestic resident,[6] it is clear that the restriction was intended to answer the objections of a Parliamentary Committee on Arrestment which some years ago considered and rejected the device of sister-ship arrest in fear that it would create a new method of *obtaining* jurisdiction;[7] but it is not difficult to imagine that this provision, coupled with that which now enables suits upon claims for ship construction[8] (which American Admiralty has

---

[1] Administration of Justice Act, 1956, §1(1)(h).

[2] §1(1)(m), (q).   [3] *E.g.*, §1(1)(d), (g).

[4] *E.g.*, *The Fagernes*, [1927] P. 311 [App.]; *cf. Notarian v. Trans-World Airlines*, 244 F. Supp. 874 (W.D. Pa. 1965).

[5] *The Glider Standard Austria S.H. 1964*, [1965] P. 463.

[6] Administration of Justice Act, 1956, §3(4), (8); see *The St. Elefterio*, [1957] P. 179.   [7] Parl. Paper, Cmd. No. 3108, ¶7, pp. 4–5 (1928).

[8] Administration of Justice Act, 1956, §1(1)(n).

avoided since the earliest days of the Republic by holding such claims non-maritime[1]), may someday result in the arrest by the Marshal of a ship under construction—even if nothing of her yet exists save the architect's plans and models—in a suit upon a claim for construction of another ship of the same owner.

Since the early 1930s, the increase of divorce business in the P.D.A. Division has necessitated the appointment of several more judges under a timely provision of the 1925 Judicature Consolidation Act, which had already established the addition of one judge,[2] but there has been no increase in Admiralty business sufficient to warrant the appointment of an additional Admiralty Judge. One Admiralty Judge who served from 1945 until 1958, Sir Henry Gordon Willmer, thereafter had occasion to exercise his expertise in the subject as a Lord Justice of Appeal; his successor, Sir Joseph Bushby Hewson, was not only a member of the Admiralty bar but was educated and served as an Officer of the Royal Navy and in addition was the author of a valuable treatise upon navigation, and it is to be regretted that after only eight years of distinguished service as Admiralty Judge he was forced to retire owing to ill-health; the present Admiralty Judge, Sir Henry Brandon, is, in the tradition of his immediate predecessors, also an Admiralty specialist, and he brings to the bench a keen interest in that history.[3] Upon the death of Lord Merriman in 1962, Sir Jocelyn Simon, also sometime Solicitor-General, was appointed President of the Admiralty Division and continues in that Office at the present time, also hearing Admiralty matters upon occasion.[4] G. H. M. Thompson became Admiralty Registrar in 1948 upon the retirement of L. F. C. Darby, and the post of Assistant Registrar thereafter became obsolete; upon Thompson's retirement in 1957, the present incumbent, Kenneth C. McGuffie, assumed the Registrarship.[5] With the abolition of the Admiralty itself in 1964,[6] the Admiralty Registrar and Marshal now remain the only links with the High Court of Admiralty and its civilian history.

Though it was doubtful only ten years ago that the 1933 Report of the Hanworth Committee would ever be acted upon,[7]

[1] *Clinton v. The Brig Hannah*, 5 Fed. Cas. 1056 (No. 2898) (Adm. Ct. Pa., 1781).   [2] S.C.J. (Consolidation) Act, 1925, §§4, 5.
[3] See, *e.g.*, *The Monica S.*, [1968] P. 741.
[4] *W.W.*, 1966.   [5] Thompson, p. 24.
[6] Defence (Transfer of Functions) Act 1964.
[7] See Ivamy, 110 *L.J.* 330 (1960); see *supra*, pp. 144–5.

a proposal by the recent Government is strongly reminiscent. In its present form, this plan calls for the transfer of all Admiralty jurisdiction, the Admiralty Registry and staff (and the Silver Oar) to a new Admiralty Court within the Queen's Bench Division where the Admiralty Judge would hear maritime commercial cases in addition to the traditional Admiralty matters; probate would be transferred to the Chancery Division, which would in turn give up guardianship, wardship and adoption cases to a re-constituted Family Division—abolishing the Probate, Divorce and Admiralty Division altogether.[1] It is difficult to argue against the logic of any proposal which would give each of the respective divisions of the High Court complete cognizance of related matters; yet one must feel some twinge of apprehension at the dissemina-tion of the jurisdiction of the last united courts of civil law, and the thought of a final and complete acquisition of the Admiralty jurisdiction by Queen's Bench evokes ancient spectres as well. Much debate must follow, and if a new organization of the High Court does emerge it may differ from that just described. Time alone can tell whether chaos in the substance and pro-cedure of Admiralty will result, or whether the Court will again survive—as basically unaltered in its appearance and administra-tion of the maritime law as it has been for centuries—though perhaps in a new environment.[3]

There can be no doubt whatever that the future of the Admiralty Court will continue to be strongly influenced by social and techno-logical change; a hint of problems to come with the increase in pleasure-boating has already been seen in the present, in the Marshal's arrest—in the time-honoured manner—of a small sloop floating in an artificial indoor pool at a London boat show.[2] What the availability of such devices as hovercraft and helicopters to the general public will mean to the venerable Admiralty Court under its broad new jurisdiction is a subject for amusing speculation.[3]

In facing these and other new problems, the Court will apply a Law which, however ancient, has demonstrated its flexibility and adaptability to change; though, as will now be seen, changes in the Law of Admiralty itself may be as much the result of accident as of design.

[1] I am indebted to Lord Gardiner, L.C., for these details. And *cf*. Administra-tion of Justice Act 1969, §23.

[2] See *The Times*, 13 January 1966, p. 10, col. 5.

[3] See, *e.g.*, the jurisdiction conferred under the Hovercraft Act 1968, §2.

CHAPTER 6

THE EVOLUTION OF THE ACTION *in rem*

[An example of the effect of the historical development
of the Court upon the substantive Law of Admiralty]

> I will commence with the action *in rem*, being that which is most resorted
> to, and which constitutes the peculiarity of the Court of Admiralty,
> and gives to it an advantage over other Courts having concurrent juris-
> diction.[1]

FOR centuries, the ability to proceed in the Admiralty Court
directly against a ship has been the distinguishing feature of the
Admiralty jurisdiction. The action *in rem* seems to have been
employed in Admiralty before the Elizabethan era,[2] but only by
the nineteenth century had it become the dominant Admiralty
procedure;[3] and it was in the mid-nineteenth century—as a
result of the dominance of the action *in rem*—that the modern
theory of maritime liens [rights against the ship] began to evolve.
The beginning of consideration of the action *in rem* itself must lie
in the emergence of the theory of maritime liens, for the two have
since become inextricably intertwined.

It has been truly said that 'the beginning of wisdom in the law
of maritime liens is that maritime liens and land liens have little
in common';[4] for that reason, it is necessary to discard all pre-
conceptions and to consult one of the few works which deal with
the jurisprudence of maritime liens.[5] (The discussion of lien
jurisprudence in this work will be strictly limited to the nexus
between maritime liens and the action *in rem*.)

The principal English case in the area of maritime liens is still
The Bold Buccleugh, though the decision retains less force today
in England than in North America. The steamship *Bold Buccleugh*
ran down and sank the barque *William* in the Humber in 1848,
was seized under process in Leith in an action against her owners
upon that cause in the Court of Session in Scotland in January

---

[1] Coote, 1st ed., p. 10.
[2] See *The Black Book of the Admiralty*, vol. 3, p. 103.
[3] A. Browne, vol. 2, p. 396.
[4] Gilmore and Black, §9–2, p. 483.   [5] *E.g.* Hebert or Price.

1849, was bailed, released and sold to a *bona-fide* purchaser without notice of the cause or claim pending, was sent to Hull by her new owner in August, 1849, and was arrested by warrant of the High Court of Admiralty. The new owner appeared under protest, alleging a *lis pendens* [pending suit] in Scotland; the Scottish action was subsequently abandoned, and Dr Lushington overruled the protest and found for the owners of the *William*.[1] The cause was taken on appeal to the Privy Council,[2] which held that the Scottish action—being *in personam* with collateral seizure—could not bar a suit *in rem* in the Admiralty Court, and, in regard to a second defence asserted below but not considered by Dr Lushington, that the collision lien survived even a *bona-fide* sale without notice.

The opinion of the Judicial Committee in *The Bold Buccleugh* was delivered by Sir John Jervis, Chief Justice of the Common Pleas.[3] It may be, as has been authoritatively stated, that the lien for collision was established by *The Bold Buccleugh*;[4] the concept of the maritime lien, however, was well-established prior to Jervis' opinion,[5] and it may be doubted for once that the accusation of a judicial *volte-face* which has been levelled against Lushington in regard to collision liens[6] is justified, as there appears to be a serious discrepancy between Dr William Robinson's report of Dr Lushington's judgment in *The Volant* to the effect that collision does not give rise to a maritime lien[7]—upon which later criticism has been based—and the report of the same judgment given in another contemporaneous source,[8] which has been said by both Sir John Jervis[9] and Sir Robert Phillimore[10] to be more accurate, and which reports no such statement. At any rate, it is accepted that Lushington held for a collision lien upon the *Bold Buccleugh* at instance, before the case ever came before Jervis.[11]

In enunciating the characteristics of the maritime lien, Jervis was able to draw upon several accepted authorities, including

---

[1] *The Bold Buccleugh*, (1850) 3 W. Rob. 220.
[2] *The Bold Buccleugh*, (1850–1) 7 Moo. P.C. 267.
[3] (1850–1) 7 Moo. P.C. 267.   [4] Price, *L.M.L.*, p. 8.
[5] See, *e.g.*, A. Browne, vol. 2, p. 143.
[6] Price, *L.M.L.*, p. 36.
[7] *The Volant*, (1842) 1 W. Rob. 383, 387.
[8] *The Volant*, (1842) 1 Not. Cas. 503, 508.
[9] *The Bold Buccleugh*, (1850–1) 7 Moo. P.C. 267, 284.
[10] *The St. Olaf*, (1869) L.R. 2 A. & E. 360.
[11] Price, *L.M.L.*, p. 36.

Charles [Abbott], Lord Tenterden, and Mr Justice Story.[1] He
relied heavily upon Story's opinion in *The Nestor*,[2] which incor-
porates the famous judgment in *DeLovio v. Boit*,[3] and which laid
down the basic rule that the maritime lien gives rise to an action
in rem, and can be executed only by a Court of Admiralty; what
Jervis did, however, was to add his own observation that all
actions *in rem* had their genesis in maritime liens,[4] and though he
had shown earlier in the opinion that he was aware—as a common
lawyer—of the differences between liens in the common law and
liens in the civil law, this statement has been the cause of all of
the subsequent controversy over the authority of *The Bold
Buccleugh*.

What led Jervis to this observation was the assertion in argument
that the action *in rem* was a purely procedural device, intended to
secure the appearance of the owners and thus to gain personal
jurisdiction over them, similar to the manner of a foreign attachment, the object being to establish the defence of *lis alibi pendens*
with reference to the Scottish action by showing the English
action to be of the same character; and an earlier decision of Dr
Lushington's analogizing some aspects of the action *in rem* to
foreign attachment in the City of London Court[5] was cited in
support. Jervis took up this specific assertion at the outset of his
opinion, pointing out that with attachment, as in the Scottish
action, the process was directed initially at the person, and was
thus in the nature of an action *in personam*, whereas the Admiralty
action *in rem* was directed in the first instance at the ship—and he
then went on to make, in the course of his exposition of the nature
of maritime liens, the observation that every action *in rem* was
brought upon a maritime lien. But of the argument that the
action *in rem* was a procedural device, Jervis had this to say:

but it is said that the arrest of the vessel is only a means of compelling
the appearance of the owners ... and that the owners having appeared,
the question is to be determined according to the interests of the party
litigant, without reference to the original liability of the vessel causing
the wrong. For these propositions, dicta have been referred to, which

---

[1] *The Bold Buccleugh*, (1850–1) 7 Moo. P.C. 276, 284.
[2] 18 Fed. Cas. 9 (1 Sumn. 73, at 80–5) (No. 10126) (C. C. Me., 1831).
[3] 7 Fed. Cas. 418 (No. 3776) (C. C. Mass., 1815).
[4] *The Bold Buccleugh*, (1850–1) 7 Moo. P.C. 267, 284.
[5] *The Johann Friederich*, (1839) 1 W. Rob. 35, 37.

are entitled to great respect, but which, upon consideration, will be found not to support the propositions for which they were cited.[1]

If Jervis' observation that maritime liens were the foundation of actions *in rem* was itself a dictum, at least there was in *The Bold Buccleugh* a firm substantive decision that the action *in rem* was a proceeding directly against the ship, and not a procedural device to gain personal jurisdiction over the owners.

So matters stood for over forty years, until Sir Francis Jeune's fateful decision in *The Dictator*. The steamship *Dictator* had lost her propeller in East Dungeness Bay in November, 1891, and was saved from going ashore by three tugs of the Gamecock Steam Towing Company, who subsequently caused a writ of summons *in rem* to be issued upon a claim of salvage, the sum claimed in the indorsement of the writ being £5000. The action was tried before Sir Charles Butt, P., and two Elder Brethren of Trinity House, and a salvage award of £7500 was decreed, exceeding by £2500 the claim indorsed upon the writ and the sum in which the *Dictator*'s owners consequently undertook to give bail, but leave was granted to amend the indorsement, increasing the claim to £8500.[2]

The amount of the £7500 award was confirmed upon appeal, and the *Dictator*'s owners paid the costs but denied their liability to satisfy the award, in any proceedings upon the original writ, beyond the £5000 which they had undertaken to give as bail in substitution for the ship; the plaintiffs, however, moved in subsequent proceedings upon the original (amended) writ for leave to proceed to recover the full amount of the award as a personal judgment against the shipowners as defendants. Sir Francis Henry Jeune, in one of his very first sittings as new President of the Division, heard these subsequent proceedings.[3] It was the argument of Sir Walter (later Lord) Phillimore for the defending shipowners that, the action being *in rem*, the bail as substitute for the ship must stand as the limit of liability, and that it was not proper to decree a judgment *in personam* in an action *in rem*, but that separate proceedings in an action brought *in personam* were necessary to obtain satisfaction of the balance of the salvage award.[4] Gorell Barnes, Q.C. (later Lord Gorell, P.), for the plaintiffs,

[1] *The Bold Buccleugh*, (1850–1) 7 Moo. P.C. 267, 282.
[2] *The Dictator*, [1892] P. 64.   [3] *The Dictator*, [1892] P. 304.
[4] [1892] P. 304, 307–8.

argued that the cost of new proceedings *in personam* ought
to be avoided by granting complete relief in the present action,
that (citing *The Bold Buccleugh*) a maritime lien arose for the
full amount of the claim—as amended—indorsed upon the writ,
and that the judgment for the balance of the award might, under
the 1861 Admiralty Court Act (§15), be enforced as at common
law; Barnes, it seems, treated the matter *in toto* solely as a question of procedure.[1]

The President's judgment also dealt with the matter solely as a
question of procedure, though in two segments: (1) the Court's
personal jurisdiction over the defending shipowners in an action
in rem, and (2) the measure of liability in the action at bar; these
segments will now be examined separately.

The Privy Council had firmly established in *The Bold Buccleugh*
that the action *in rem* was not a procedural device for obtaining
personal jurisdiction over shipowners, but a unique proceeding
directly against the ship.[2] What has come to be known as the 'procedural theory' holds that the precise reverse is true, and 'this
proposition was first advanced by Sir Francis Jeune, in *The
Dictator*'.[3] Bearing in mind that *The Bold Buccleugh*, as a decision
of the Privy Council when the highest court of appeal in Admiralty,
should have had in Admiralty matters following the Judicature
Acts the same status as a decision of the House of Lords,[4] it is well
to examine Jeune's arguments for the procedural theory.

In evolving the procedural theory, Jeune based his reasoning
upon 'the early practice of the Admiralty Court',[5] and commenced his investigation of the Court's procedural history with
Clerke's *Praxis*, compiled by an Elizabethan Proctor-in-Admiralty,
which describes a proceeding to seize the *res*, usable only when the
defendant in a proceeding *in personam* was unavailable for personal
arrest; failing to appear in response to a citation, the defendant
was held in contempt and his *res* defaulted.[6] Jeune evidently felt
that Clerke's reputation was in need of some support, for he
cited an opinion of Lord Hardwicke referring to Clerke as 'an
author of undoubted credit'.[7] How undoubted Clerke's credit

---

[1] *The Dictator*, [1892] P. 304, 308–9.
[2] *The Bold Buccleugh*, (1850–1) 7 Moo. P.C. 267, 282.
[3] Hebert, pp. 390–1; see also Price, *L.M.L.*, p. 13.
[4] *English & Empire Digest*, vol. 1, p. 117; *cf. The Cayo Bonito*, [1903] P. 203,
215, 220 [App.].   [5] *The Dictator*, [1892] P. 304, 310.
[6] *Praxis*, pp. 61, 63, 65, 67, 69, 73.   [7] [1892] P. 304, 311.

really was to Admiralty practitioners of the last days of Doctors' Commons may perhaps be judged from the following:

The miserable compilation which passes by the name of Clerke's Praxis . . . is inconsistent with the fact that the Civil Law was the fountain of the Admiralty jurisprudence, and also, that from the time of the Commonwealth, the hypothecal principle had been employed by the court, without doubt on its part or a question on the part of others.[1]

To support Clerke, Jeune then cited a passage from Ridley's *View of the Civile and Ecclesiasticall Law* (1639) which neither mentioned Admiralty proceedings specifically nor had any reference to the action *in rem*,[2] and followed with citations to Godolphin (1685) and Spelman (1641), whose remarks Jeune interpreted to mean that arrest of the ship was only a means to compel the owner's personal appearance.[3] Such was the entire body of evidence relied upon by Sir Francis Jeune to substantiate his assertion that the action *in rem* was a device to obtain personal jurisdiction.

What the President utterly failed to mention were the sources of equal antiquity which militate against his conclusion; indeed, no less an authority than *The Black Book of the Admiralty*—a work of considerably greater antiquity than Clerke's *Praxis*, says quite clearly that 'the ship has to pay' when arrested, not the shipowner.[4] Again, in an action of Clerke's day in the King's Bench to obtain a prohibition against suit in the High Court of Admiralty, Serjeant Nichols described the action *in rem*: 'the ship only is arrested, and the libel ought to be only against the ship and goods, and not against the party.'[5] Moreover, in citing no authorities for the proposition less than two hundred years of age, Jeune implied that the question had not arisen since, much less in modern times; in fact, the nature of the action *in rem* was considered in the nineteenth century, and the opinion of all who considered it save Sir Francis Jeune was, to the best of my ability to determine it, unanimous in its support for the holding of the Privy Council in *The Bold Buccleugh*. Maxwell, in giving the advantages of an Admiralty action *in rem* in his treatise of 1800, says 'the ship itself is responsible in the admiralty, and not the

---

[1] 17 *L. Rev.* 421, 423 (1855).
[2] *The Dictator*, [1892] P. 304, 312.   [3] *Ibid.*
[4] Twiss, vol. 3, p. 103; also pp. 245, 345.
[5] *Greenway & Barker's Case*, (1613) Godb. 260.

owners';[1] Browne, in 1802, says that 'no person can be subject to that [Admiralty] jurisdiction [*in rem*] but by his consent';[2] Sir John Nicholl, in a judgment of 1834, said 'the ship is liable for wages and costs';[3] and Coote, in 1860, recites that 'a maritime lien, as being the tacit hypothec of the civil law, is a secret interest in a *res* which may be enforced against it *corporaliter*, the *res obligata* being the defendant and not its owners.'[4]

Nor did Jeune make any attempt to reconcile his theory with the ancient and (now obsolete, but) still extant proceeding *in rem* upon bottomry; the point did not escape Sir John Jervis, who recognized that suits upon bottomry bonds had to be brought *in rem*, for 'the advance is made upon the credit of the ship, not upon the credit of the owner; and the owner is never personally responsible.'[5] Perhaps the most remarkable omission in Jeune's argument, however, is any reference to the Privy Council's clear holding in *The Bold Buccleugh* directly against the proposition which he was advocating, and such an omission is all the more remarkable because Jeune considered the bearing of the *Bold Buccleugh* upon the second segment of his decision— that involving the amount of liability—and concluded, incredibly, 'that the Privy Council [had not] . . . intended to lay down that an action in rem could affect only the res.'[6]

It is of interest to look briefly into some of the history of Jeune's procedural theory subsequent to the decision in *The Dictator*. The most notable historian of the Admiralty Court to date, R. G. Marsden, reached the conclusion that the very early Admiralty action *in rem* was a procedural device because:

Arrest of goods was quite as frequent as arrest of the ship . . . , [and] the fact that goods and ships that had no connection with the cause of action, except as belonging to the defendant, were subject to arrest, points to the conclusion that arrest was mere procedure, and that its only object was to obtain security that judgment should be satisfied.[7]

Marsden also seems to have based his argument largely upon Clerke's *Praxis*,[8] and the heart of his point seems to be that the

---

[1] p. 8. [2] Vol. 2, p. 100.
[3] *The Margaret*, (1834) 3 Hag. Adm. 238, 240.
[4] 1st ed., p. 3.
[5] *Stainbank v. Fenning*, (1851) 11 C.B. 51, 89.
[6] *The Dictator*, [1892] P. 304, 320.
[7] Marsden, *Select Pleas*, vol. 1, intro., p. lxxi.
[8] See Price, *L.M.L.*, pp. 8–9.

proceeding *in rem* against the vessel had no unique qualities, because proceedings were as often *in rem* in Admiralty against other goods of the defendant owner. But again, it may be questioned whether the description of the action *in rem* given by Clerke fits the original practice, because *The Black Book of the Admiralty* indicates that property of the defendant owner other than his ship was originally exempt from arrest,[1] and even the applicability of Clerke's statement in his own day must be judged against the argument of Serjeant Nichols that 'execution [of a judgment at law] ought to be only of the goods, for the ship only is arrested . . .'[2] But in no case does Marsden attempt to show or to intimate that the early jurisprudence of Admiralty endured without change until the 1890s, and his remarks are entirely concerned with the Court's very early practice, though they were subsequently cited in support of the historical accuracy of Jeune's opinion.[3]

The historical accuracy of Jeune's procedural theory is certainly open to question, especially as regards the authority and practice of the nineteenth century, but even if this doubt is overlooked, the question of the jurisprudential validity of the procedural theory itself has been the subject of some scrutiny, *e.g.*:

The procedural theory, **assuming its historical accuracy,** requires a statement that a ship is liable in an action *in rem*, and subject to a maritime lien, only if the owner is personally liable at the time when the action is brought. *The Bold Buccleugh*, however, shows that this formula must be modified to read that a ship is liable *in rem* and subject to a maritime lien only if the person who was the owner at the time when the facts giving rise to the cause of action occurred could have been held answerable at common law. It will thus be apparent that the procedural theory which has been adopted in England involves considerable difficulties.[4] (emphasis supplied)

It is interesting to compare, without going into very great detail, the English and American theories of actions *in rem*. The American theory, known as the 'personification theory'[5] began to develop in the eighteenth century following the Revolution. The origins of the personification theory may be seen in the early

---

[1] Twiss, vol. 3, pp. 103, 245, 345.
[2] *Greenway & Barker's Case,* (1613) Godb. 260.
[3] *The Dupleix,* [1912] P. 8, 13–14.
[4] Price, *L.M.L.*, p. 16; *cf. The Monica S.*, [1967] 2 Ll. Rep. 113, 130.
[5] See *The Ville de St. Nazaire,* 124 F. 1008 (D. Ore. 1903).

decisions that contracts for ship construction were not maritime and hence not enforceable in Admiralty,[1] though it was not until the beginning of the present century that the last Admiralty specialist to sit upon the bench of the United States Supreme Court—Mr Justice Henry Billings Brown—gave the definitive opinion which declares the ship 'born' when she is first launched, and that thereafter 'she acquires a personality of her own . . . and is individually liable for her obligations.'[2] Correlatively, a 'dead' ship [permanently withdrawn from navigation] is now considered non-maritime property, and hence not individually liable in tort or upon warranty of seaworthiness.[3]

The idea of the ship as debtor became well developed in American Admiralty during the early nineteenth century, though the idea was almost certainly derived from the nature of the English proceedings of the period, which have been described, *e.g.* in Prize [the basic nature being similar to instance as to the *res*], as '*in rem*; in other words, the ship was considered to be a veritable defendant'.[4] Even before Mr Justice Story's opinion in *The Nestor* established the formal requisites for and character of the maritime lien,[5] the concept of the ship as an individual—the owner coming in to defend his *res* as a guardian would to defend his ward—had given rise to virtually as many varieties of maritime lien which could be executed only *in rem*[6] as there were causes upon which the owner himself could be sued *in personam*. It is thus that maritime liens in America became more numerous and diverse than in England, and not, as one scholar has suggested,[7] because there was no history of restraint of the Admiralty jurisdiction in America by common law prohibition; prohibition, though relatively rare, was employed by the common law courts to restrain the Admiralty jurisdiction in both colonial[8] and republican[9] times. With *The Nestor*, the maritime lien became the recognized foundation of the action *in rem*, and an American Admiralty court has ever since been the sole forum in the United States

[1] See, *e.g.*, *Clinton v. The Brig Hannah*, 5 Fed. Cas. 1056 (No. 2898) (Adm. Ct. of Pa., 1781).
[2] *Tucker v. Alexandroff*, 183 U.S. 424, 438 (1901).
[3] See, *e.g.*, *Noel v. Isbrandtsen Company*, 287 F. 2d 783 (4 Cir. 1961).
[4] Nys, p. 113, ¶3.
[5] 18 Fed. Cas. 9 (No. 10126) (C. C. Me., 1831).
[6] See Gilmore and Black, §9–2, pp. 482–3.
[7] Price, *L.M.L.*, p. 116.   [8] See Ubbelohde, p. 19.
[9] *E.g.*, *U.S. v. Peters*, 3 Dall. (3 U.S.) 121 (1795).

possessing cognizance of claims upon maritime liens arising under state, federal or international law.

Ironically, while the action *in rem* can give no jurisdiction *in personam*[1] in American Admiralty, the reverse has always been true. Admiralty attachment *in personam*, which fell into disuse in English Admiralty practice prior to the nineteenth century,[2] survived the practice of the Colonial Vice-Admiralty Courts to become a feature of post-Revolutionary practice. The really fascinating thing about this procedure, which is well described by Dr Browne,[3] is that it is certainly the same procedure described by Clerke and erroneously identified by Sir Francis Jeune as a proceeding *in rem*, upon which he based the procedural theory. 'Maritime attachment' was and is a remedy unique to Admiralty, without an exact counterpart in the civil law as a whole,[4] and is clearly designated by both Browne and Clerke (from whose *Praxis*, the standard reference work for Colonial Proctors and Advocates,[5] it was doubtless introduced into American Vice-Admiralty) as an adjunct to the proceeding *in personam*.

Throughout its continued use in American Admiralty, attachment has been carefully and consistently preserved in its original capacity as an adjunct to the action *in personam*. Oddly, the definitive decision as to the use of Admiralty attachment in the United States was contained in an opinion of Mr Justice Johnson, a foe of the Admiralty jurisdiction who led the opposition—eventually unsuccessful—to Mr Justice Story and those who advocated an unrestricted jurisdiction for Admiralty. Mr Justice Johnson was perhaps the least qualified member of the Supreme Court to discourse upon Admiralty procedure and the civil law, of whose history he was ignorant, and it was he who has caused such subsequent confusion about the nature of Admiralty attachment by referring to it as 'foreign attachment'—which it is not and has never been, though the two have often been analogized[6]—a term which has fortunately been supplanted in the present century by 'maritime attachment'.[7] But the main point did not escape even Johnson, 'The process of foreign [maritime] attachment in admiralty is governed by its own rules and principles, and does

---

[1] Price, *L.M.L.*, p. 117.
[2] See A. Browne, vol. 2, p. 435.
[3] *Id.*, pp. 434–5.
[4] *Ibid.*
[5] See Setaro pp. 28–9.
[6] See, *e.g.*, A. Browne, vol. 2, p. 434.
[7] See F.R.C.P. [1 July 1966] Adm. Rule A. (1).

not depend on, and is not derived from, the custom of London, or the local laws of the different [American] States.'[1] The procedure itself (which has earlier been described[2]) has been the same, evidently, since Clerke's day: the goods and chattels—including ships, if any—of a defendant who is absent from the jurisdiction of the Admiralty court may be attached to compel his appearance, and if the defendant does not respond to the citation to appear personally, the articles so attached are sold by order of the court to satisfy the claimants *in personam*, following the entry of a default judgment.[3] Sir Francis Jeune's error (and presumably that of R. G. Marsden as well) lay in the assumption that the seizure of a ship and goods under process of maritime attachment constituted an arrest *in rem*; this procedure has never been termed an action *in rem* by any authority which has come to my attention until so termed by Jeune in *The Dictator*, but it seems from subsequent authorities that this particular assertion by Jeune has never been questioned—doubtless because the only persons who might reasonably have raised the question were the already-extinct Fellows of Doctors' Commons.

The procedure of maritime attachment is similar in outline to that of the action *in rem*; indeed, because it involves seizure of a vessel, it is often referred to as a proceeding *quasi in rem*,[4] but the '*quasi*' is a vital distinction, for the *res* is attached and seized by special process of the court rather than arrested by warrant,[5] and sale under a default judgment is not a sale of the vessel in an action *in rem*, and so does not execute any maritime liens which may remain unsatisfied. Maritime attachment, like foreign attachment, is a device designed to compel the appearance of a defendant in an action *in personam*, and is by no means a proceeding *in rem*; it is this crucial distinction which was so deftly grasped by Sir John Jervis, and so unfortunately ignored by Sir Francis Jeune.

One mystery remains: it is clear that by the beginning of the nineteenth century the action *in rem* as known today had become the dominant feature of Admiralty practice, and yet Clerke makes no mention in the *Praxis* of the proceeding *in rem* nor does he describe such a proceeding therein. As to the origin of the action

[1] *Manro v. Almeida*, 10 Wheat. (23 U.S.) 473, 490 (1825).
[2] See *supra*, pp. 16–17.
[3] F.R.C.P. [1 July 1966] Adm. Rule B. (1), (2).
[4] See, *e.g.*, F.R.C.P. [1 July 1966] Adm. Rule E.
[5] See Rules B. (1), E. (4) (a), also A. Browne, vol. 2, pp. 344–5.

in rem, therefore, only two alternatives appear: (1) that it came into being during the late seventeenth or early eighteenth century, or (2) that it did in fact exist concurrently with maritime attachment in Clerke's day—and possibly before—but was for some reason omitted from mention in the *Praxis*. Considering the statements in *The Black Book of the Admiralty* and in *Greenway & Barker's Case* (and the opinion of Clerke held in 1855)—previously quoted—the evidence would seem to point to the second alternative given above. But I should acknowledge my general incapacity to declare beyond the scope of this work, and the mystery, if such it is, will have to be solved by scholars more competent to deal with the very early history of English Admiralty.

It was of course necessary to Sir Francis Jeune's theory that he offer some explanation of the 'shift' from seizure of a *res* primarily to compel the appearance of the owner, to arrest of a *res* primarily to satisfy a debt which had arisen in the course of its operation. The reason given by Jeune for this development was that the obsolescence of the proceeding *in personam* by personal arrest[1] gave rise to the modern action *in rem* commencing with arrest of the ship and proceeding directly against the ship rather than the owner, and that the emergence of the action *in rem* gave rise in turn to the doctrine of maritime liens[2]—in short, that the Court turned to the action *in rem* because it could no longer proceed directly against the person. There is a twofold difficulty in this explanation: (1) it does not, if Jeune's earlier theory about the origin of the action *in rem* was accurate, explain why the action *in rem* as a procedural device to gain personal jurisdiction had become obsolete, and (2) it ignores the development of the personal action by way of monition. In fact, as Dr Browne says,[3] it was Admiralty **attachment** *in personam* which had fallen into disuse, perhaps because it was found generally more expeditious to proceed directly *in rem*, and it seems reasonable that, the only means of acquiring jurisdiction *in personam* then being by personal arrest, the action *in personam* was simply abandoned (until its re-incarnation in the 1859 Rules[4]) and the vacuum filled by the development of the personal action by way of monition—which, as it did not commence with personal custody, could not terminate

---

[1] See *The Clara*, (1855) Swab. 1, 3.
[2] *The Dictator*, [1892] P. 304, 313; also Price, *L.M.L.*, p. 9.
[3] A. Browne, vol. 2, p. 435.   [4] See *supra*, p. 64.

in a default judgment, and was usable only as an alternative to a warrant of arrest *in rem*, was in fact an adjunct to the action *in rem*, in which form it always appeared.[1] Indeed, just as maritime attachment was the procedural device to secure a kind of 'jurisdiction *in personam*' in the absence of the defendant, so the proceeding by monition was the procedural device to secure a kind of 'jurisdiction *in rem*' in the absence of the vessel.

Because it is fundamental to Admiralty jurisprudence that a maritime lien can be executed only by valid proceedings *in rem*,[2] any searching discussion of one must inevitably involve the other. The relevant characteristics of the maritime lien, then, are these: (1) it is an inchoate right which adheres to the ship *eo instanti* of the incident giving rise to it, and at execution relates back to the instant of adherence for determination of its priority[3] (on priorities in satisfaction of maritime liens, see Price generally), (2) it may be extinguished prior to execution by payment in full satisfaction,[4] (3) it is not extinguished by fruitless actions *in personam*,[5] (4) laches may prevent the execution of a maritime lien,[6] (5) it may be extinguished by giving bail for the ship's release following arrest upon a warrant *in rem*,[7] and (6) it is completely executed by sale of the ship by order of the Court pursuant to an action *in rem*,[8] which sale vests a perfect and indefeasible title in the purchaser of the ship, free from all maritime liens, 'suits and claims of every kind'; and upon sale the liens released from the ship attach to and may be enforced against the proceeds of the sale while in the hands of the Court.[9] In England the Admiralty Court will look to the *lex fori* to determine whether a maritime lien exists in any particular case,[10] but the American rule is that the *lex loci* will determine the existence of a lien, and the *lex fori* its priority.[11] (On maritime liens generally, see Robinson, Price, and Gilmore and Black.)

---

[1] See, *e.g.*, *The Trelawney*, (1801) 3 C. Rob. 216n.; *The Meg Merrilies*, (1837) 3 Hag. Adm. 346; also *supra*, pp. 63–5.

[2] Robinson, §48, p. 363.

[3] See *The Bold Buccleugh*, (1850–1) 7 Moo. P.C. 267, 284–5.

[4] See, *e.g.*, *William [Moakes's] Money*, (1827) 2 Hag. Adm. 136.

[5] Price, *L.M.L.*, p. 88.

[6] See, *e.g.*, *The Two Ellens*, (1872) L.R. 4 P.C. 161, 169.

[7] See, *e.g.*, *The Point Breeze*, [1928] P. 135.

[8] See, *e.g.*, *The Saracen*, (1847) 2 W. Rob. 451.

[9] Williams and Bruce, 3rd ed., p. 319.

[10] *The Acrux*, [1965] P. 391.   [11] Robinson, §62, p. 434.

One other feature of maritime liens, especially of importance since the 1861 Admiralty Court Act, is that they may be extended in application by statutes extending Admiralty jurisdiction.[1] New jurisdiction granted by statute, however, such as that over aircraft or over ship mortgages, does not confer a maritime lien but instead a 'statutory right *in rem*', which differs from a maritime lien in that it adheres upon and only relates back to arrest of the *res*,[2] may be defeated by a *bona-fide* sale of the *res* for value,[3] and does not attach to the proceeds of sale of the *res* by the Court[4] (for other aspects, see Price, 'Statutory Rights'). The leading work states that statutory rights *in rem* are peculiar to English Admiralty and have no counterpart in American Admiralty,[5] but it is doubtful whether this observation is still accurate.[6] There is yet another type of right *in rem*, very scarce in England but fairly common in America, which is conferred by statute but specified therein to apply and have effect as if a maritime lien;[7] this right, to avoid confusion, may be called a 'semi-maritime lien'.

It was of course the grant of statutory rights *in rem* by the 1861 Court Act and subsequent enactments which invalidated Sir John Jervis' statement that the basis of every action *in rem* was a maritime lien[8]—rather a semantic quibble, but one which has been useful to detractors of *The Bold Buccleugh*. And even Sir Gorell Barnes, who declared in 1901 that both a maritime lien and an independent right *in rem* arose upon collision,[9] recognized that the statements made by Sir John Jervis as to the nature of maritime liens, which had been unconditionally re-affirmed by the House of Lords,[10] were still good law. E. S. Roscoe, however, in the introduction to the fifth edition of his *Practice*, attempted to demonstrate that some of the accepted characteristics of maritime liens were inaccurate—notably the feature of non-transferability.[11] In one case so cited to support transferability the lien was not in fact transferred,[12] and in another the right involved

---

[1] See, *e.g.*, *The Tolten*, [1946] P. 135.   [2] Price, 'Statutory Rights', p. 25.
[3] Price, *L.M.L.*, p. 90.   [4] *Id.*, pp. 92–3.
[5] Price, 'Statutory Rights', p. 21.
[6] See F.R.C.P. [1 July 1966] Adm. Rule C. (1)(b).
[7] Price, *L.M.L.*, p. 90.
[8] See *The Scotia*, 35 F. 907 (S.D.N.Y. 1888).
[9] *The Veritas*, [1901] P. 304, 310.
[10] *Currie v. M'Knight*, (1896) 24 Rett. 1; [1897] A.C. 97.
[11] Roscoe, *Practice*, pp. 28–9.
[12] *The Cornelia Henrietta*, (1866) L.R. 1 A. & E. 51, 52.

was actually a statutory right *in rem* under the 1861 Court Act and not a maritime lien at all;[1] moreover, the principle of non-transferability of maritime liens had been upheld by Sir Maurice Hill only a short time previously.[2]

Most other developments in the law of maritime liens have been paralleled in both England and America; it had long been established in the United States, for example, that maritime liens did adhere to sovereign vessels, but could not be sued upon unless and until such vessels were sold to private owners,[3] and the same view came to be held in England.[4] But the obvious inequities of that position led to a decision by the U.S. Supreme Court in 1921 that maritime liens did not adhere to sovereign vessels at all;[5] this is surely the more logical position under American theory, for a sovereign vessel could only be personified as a government officer, enjoying the protection of immunity unless deliberately waived as in the institution of suit by the sovereign upon the same cause of action, thus opening the sovereign vessel to counterclaims.[6] A similar position was taken in England very shortly thereafter, in a notable opinion by Atkin, L.J.,[7] which recognized that the procedural theory (in normal cases) is inconsistent with the enforceability of maritime liens following a transfer in ownership of the *res.*[8]

In extending the procedural theory in 1901 to hold charterers of a vessel personally liable to pay a salvage award in an action *in rem* against the vessel,[9] it was necessary for Sir Francis Jeune to retreat from an earlier holding[10] in agreement with Dr Lushington that the action *in rem* was 'the ancient foundation of a salvage suit';[11] but on the whole the procedural theory continued to fare quite well until the first test of the practicality of one of its essential corollaries, *i.e.*, that in the original action *in rem* it was possible to arrest property of the defendant other than his ship. It had been stated in 1885 as a gratuitous and unsupported dictum in an

---

[1] *The Wasp*, (1867) L.R. 1 A. & E. 367.   [2] *The Petone*, [1917] P. 198.
[3] *The Siren*, 7 Wall. (74 U.S.) 152 (1868).
[4] *The Crimdon*, (1918) 35 T.L.R. 81.
[5] *The Western Maid*, 257 U.S. 419 (1921).
[6] *E.g.*, *The Thekla*, 266 U.S. 328 (1924).
[7] *The Tervaete*, [1922] P. 259, 275; also Price, *L.M.L.*, p. 16.
[8] And see *The Monica S.*, [1967] 2 Ll. Rep. 113, 132.
[9] *The Cargo ex Port Victor*, (1901) 84 L.T.R. 363, 365.
[10] *The Elton*, [1891] P. 265, 269.
[11] *The Fusilier*, (1865) Br. & Lush. 341 [P.C.].

opinion of Fry, L.J., that 'any property of the defendant within the realm' might be arrested to enforce a statutory right *in rem*;[1] whether (as seems likely) Fry had also confused the very early action *in rem* with maritime attachment *in personam*, this aspect of the procedural theory, strengthened by the statements of R. G. Marsden,[2] eventually prompted the arrest in an action *in rem* of collateral property of a shipowner, in the particular case a sister-ship.[3] The Court of Appeal, in order to avoid sanctioning collateral arrest, found it necessary to modify the procedural theory—which it had previously accepted without question.[4] Abandoning the assertion of Marsden (and Jeune) that arrest in early actions *in rem* was purely a procedure to obtain security for any judgment which might be given, the Court of Appeal adopted instead[5] a suggestion made by E. S. Roscoe in the introduction to the third edition of his *Practice*,[6] that arrest of the *res* was a procedural device to obtain personal jurisdiction, but was not developed until such time as 'any attempt to assume jurisdiction *in personam* was prohibited by the common law courts'. Indeed, if the indications of *The Black Book of the Admiralty* and *Greenway & Barker's Case* are wholly incorrect, then Roscoe's version of the procedural theory would give an acceptable basis for the origin of the action *in rem*, though if accurate, it does not explain the necessity for resurrecting the procedural device long after the Admiralty Court had regained complete jurisdiction directly *in personam*; what seems more likely is a confusion by Roscoe of the action *in rem* itself with the personal action by way of monition, which probably developed as an adjunct to the action *in rem* when actions *in personam* by arrest became obsolete. This confusion was passed along to Merriman, P., who delivered the judgment in *The Beldis*, and who mentioned the personal action by way of monition[7] without recognizing it as the forerunner of the modern action *in personam*. *The Beldis*, in accepting Roscoe's version of the procedural theory, was able to disapprove Fry's dictum in *The Heinrich Björn* (which had been cited in support by Jeune in *The Dictator*[8]), permitting the theory itself to survive without

---

[1] *The Heinrich Björn*, (1885) 10 P.D. 44, 54 [App.].
    See, directly *contra*, *The Victor*, (1860) Lush. 72, 76.
[2] *Viz.*, *Select Pleas*, vol. 1, intro., p. lxxi.
[3] *The Beldis*, [1936] P. 51.   [4] *The Gemma*, [1899] P. 285.
[5] [1936] P. 51, 73–4.   [6] At p. 44.
[7] [1936] P. 51, 75.   [8] [1892] P. 304, 313.

sanctioning collateral arrest, and it is the procedural theory as expressed in *The Beldis* which has found general acceptance,[1] though the entire portion of Lord Merriman's judgment dealing with the theory is itself dictum.[2]

The entire subject of maritime liens seems to be a source of great confusion in English Admiralty at the present time—so much so, in fact, that one of Her Majesty's Judges is reported to have remarked at a recent meeting of the *Comité Maritime International*: 'You Americans are crazy on the question of maritime liens. You shouldn't have any. You should follow the British rule; wipe them all out.'[3] It is very difficult to reconcile these words with the language of the 1956 Administration of Justice Act, which makes specific reference to the jurisdiction of the Admiralty Court to entertain proceedings *in rem* for enforcement of maritime liens.[4] Greater confusion may arise, however, in attempting to reconcile the very basis of maritime liens—that they are an inchoate right adhering to the wrongdoing ship and not transferable from her—with the action *in rem* against sister-ships permitted by the 1956 Act;[5] it would appear that actions against sisterships could not execute any maritime liens adhering to the offending vessel, and that maritime lienholders whose claims are unsatisfied may thereafter proceed against a succession of sisterships until the debt is paid—a paradox which strains the fabric of the Admiralty jurisprudence.[6]

The second segment of Sir Francis Jeune's decision in *The Dictator* is also of importance to the jurisprudence of Admiralty, for it was the first clear and supported holding that liability in an action *in rem* might exceed the value of the vessel against which the action was brought. Again, before examining this phase of Jeune's decision, it is useful to establish what the previous position was. The body of authority on the question is relatively small, and the first nineteenth-century case in which the issue was directly considered seems to have been *The Triune*,[7] a cause of collision in which Sir John Nicholl awarded damages in excess of the value of the ship and decreed a monition to the owner commanding

---

[1] Price, *L.M.L.*, p. 10. [2] Price, 'Statutory Rights', p. 23.

[3] M.L.A.U.S. Doc. No. 496, p. 5290 (March, 1966). [4] §3(3).

[5] See *Practice Direction (Arresting 'Sister' Ship: Pleadings) (No. 2)*, [1969] 1 W. L.R. 613.

[6] And see *The Putbus*, [1969] P. 136 [Inst.], *rev'd.* [1969] P. 144 [App.].

[7] (1834) 3 Hag. Adm. 114.

him to pay the balance of the judgment upon pain of contempt. That case has a number of peculiarities: the shipowner was also the master whose negligence caused the collision; no bail was given for the ship and yet the owner entered an appearance to an action in which the claim exceeded the value of his ship; and no reasoning and no citation of authority was given by Sir John Nicholl in support of his judgment. Moreover, in the same year, Nicholl made the statement that 'the ship is liable for wages and costs',[1] which, if *expressio unius est exclusio alterius*, would indicate that the owner had no personal liability in a wages suit *in rem*.

The question next arose six years later before Dr Lushington in *The Hope*,[2] but Sir John Nicholl's decision in *The Triune* was neither cited in argument nor referred to by Dr Lushington in the judgment. *The Hope* was also a collision cause, but bail had been given for the ship following arrest in an amount which was nearly double her value; recognizing no precedent for enforcement of a judgment *in rem* beyond the value of the *res*, Lushington refused to do so because, in his view, this would be 'engrafting' an action *in personam* on to one *in rem*.

Ironically, the first judicial comment upon Sir John Nicholl's decision in *The Triune* seems to have come from America rather than England, and the comment came from no less than Mr Justice Story, who made specific reference in one opinion to *The Triune*—which had been cited in argument—saying, 'I confess that I do not well see how a proceeding, originally *in rem*, could be prosecuted *in personam* against a party, who in such proceeding intervened only for and to the extent of his interest. . . . At all events, I am not prepared to accede to the authority of this case . . . , [as] I do not understand how the proceedings can be blended in the libel.'[3] The question soon came before Dr Lushington again, and the conflict between *The Triune* and Lushington's earlier decision in *The Hope* did not escape him; noting the conflict, he said, 'It is, I think, my duty to consider the question an open question, and to pronounce that decision which in my judgment is most conformable to law . . .'[4] In addition to his misgiving expressed in *The Hope* that to hold for personal liability

---

[1] *The Margaret*, (1834) 3 Hag. Adm. 238, 240.

[2] (1840) 1 W. Rob. 154.

[3] *Citizen's Bank v. Nantucket Steamboat Company*, 5 Fed. Cas. 719, 733 (No. 2730) (C. C. Mass. 1841).

[4] *The Volant*, (1842) 1 W. Rob. 383, 386–7.

in such a case would be engrafting an action *in personam* on to an action *in rem*, Dr Lushington adverted in *The Volant* to the significance of bail posted to secure the release of a vessel from arrest; for bail may never be demanded in an amount greater than the value of the ship, and 'If bail could not be demanded beyond the value of the ship, I do not see how the owners, in that proceeding, can be made further responsible. It appears to me, therefore, that there is no personal liability beyond the value of the ship . . .'[1] With the decisions in *The Hope* and *The Volant*, the position had become well established, in the words of Baron Parke, that 'the Court of Admiralty proceeds in rem, and can only obtain jurisdiction by seizure and the value, when seized, is the measure of liability.'[2]

It would have been quite in character for Dr Lushington to have subsequently altered or reversed the position taken by him in *The Hope* and *The Volant*, but his consistency upon this question was absolute throughout his tenure as Admiralty Judge. When it next arose, in *The Kalamazoo*, he refused to give judgment beyond the amount of the bail—let alone beyond the value of the ship— and expanded upon his earlier reasoning:

The bail represents the ship, and when a ship is once released [from arrest] upon bail she is altogether released from that action. [¶] But it is said that the party ought to receive the whole amount of the damage done, to the full extent of the value of the ship in fault. To this there are two answers. First, it was their [plaintiffs'] own fault if they did not arrest her to the full value of the ship; and, secondly, there is no authority to shew, that, having obtained bail for the ship, you can afterwards proceed against the owner [in the same action] to make up the amount of the loss. I cannot think that I can engraft a personal action upon an action *in rem*.[3]

And in a later case Lushington squarely laid down the collateral rule that the liability of the bail was limited to the value of the ship even where bail had been given in excess of the ship's value.[4] Clearly, the decisions in *The Hope*, *The Volant*, and *The Kalamazoo* constitute a firmly established case-line for the doctrine that liability in an action *in rem* cannot exceed the value of the *res*.

[1] (1842) 1 W. Rob. 383, 388–9.
[2] *Brown v. Wilkinson*, (1846) 15 M. & W. 391, 398.
[3] *The Kalamazoo*, (1851) 15 *Jur*. 885, 886.
[4] *The Duchess De Brabant*, (1857) Swab. 264, 266.

The sole exception to this doctrine appeared to lie in recovery of costs of an action *in rem*; it will be recalled that Sir John Nicholl, in *The Margaret*, said that 'the ship is liable for wages and costs'.[1] But this rule was not established as clearly as the *Hope–Volant–Kalamazoo* doctrine, for in an action *in rem* wherein Dr Lushington awarded costs which—added to the judgment—exceeded the value of the ship, Denman, L.C.J., upon a rule *nisi*, directed the issue of a prohibition out of the Queen's Bench to prevent execution.[2] And it is significant that Lushington's reasoning in awarding costs beyond the value of the ship was that also relied upon by Sir Francis Jeune in asserting that a *judgment* might exceed the value of the ship, *i.e.*, that the appearance of the owners to defend their ship in an action *in rem* introduces an element of 'personal responsibility'—but the extent of that responsibility was at least strictly limited by Lushington to the *costs* of an action, which liability is, jurisprudentially, entirely distinct from that upon the merits of the cause. It is perhaps fortunate for Jeune's decision in *The Dictator* that writs of prohibition against the Admiralty Court were effectively abolished by the Judicature Acts.

In a subsequent case, Dr Lushington refused to award costs beyond the amount of the bail,[3] but characteristically, fifteen years after his first attempt, he again awarded costs in excess of bail where the defending owner had deliberately chosen to indulge in a lengthy and expensive proceeding by plea and proof[4] and said that he was only applying 'the principle enforced in many cases—that the owners are liable for the full amount of the value of the ship and freight, and also for costs.'[5] It seems eminently fair that a party obstructing the progress of a suit in such a manner should pay the cost of harassment, and this reasoning of Dr Lushington's was given the force of statute a few years later.[6]

Prior to *The Dictator*, then, even the textwriters were in perfect accord that: (1) bail in an action *in rem* could not be required in an amount exceeding the value of the *res*,[7] (2) liability did not extend beyond the amount of the bail unless to pay costs incurred

---

[1] *The Margaret*, (1834) 3 Hag. Adm. 238, 240.
[2] *The John Dunn*, (1840) 1 W. Rob. 159 [Inst. & Prohib.].
[3] *The Mellona*, (1846) 10 *Jur.* 992.   [4] See *supra*, pp. 14–16, 56.
[5] *The Temiscouata*, (1855) 2 Sp. 208, 210.
[6] Admiralty Court Act, 1861, §19.
[7] Williams and Bruce, 2nd ed., p. 283.

by the conduct of the defence,[1] and (3), on the point vital to Jeune's holding in *The Dictator*, the position was such 'Hornbook Law' that it was thus clearly presented in *The Student's Guide to Admiralty* in 1880:

Q: Can an action **in rem** be changed into an action **in personam,** or vice versa?

A: *It cannot; but must be continued in the form in which it was begun.*[2]

In this light, the second segment of Sir Francis Jeune's holding in *The Dictator* must be examined. That the case of *The Dictator* established the modern view of personal liability in actions *in rem* is acknowledged,[3] and it is clear from Jeune's own words that this holding is in turn based upon his procedural theory:

I cannot help thinking that the fallacy lies in considering that to enforce a judgment beyond the value of the res, against owners who have appeared and against whom a personal liability, enforceable by Admiralty process, exists, is the grafting of one form of action on to another. The change, if it be a change, in the action, is effected at an earlier stage, namely, when the defendant, by appearing personally, introduces his personal liability.[4]

Oddly enough, Judge Addison Brown had considered this very question in New York just a decade previously; he rejected Nicholl's holding in *The Triune*, but accepted Lushington's position and quoted extensively from the *Hope* and *Volant* judgments, finding it 'the established practice in the English admiralty' that liability in an action *in rem* was limited to the value of the *res*, and citing *The Wild Ranger*[5] in support. Then Brown explained his rationale, citing various English and American decisions:

In actions at common law, and in actions in admiralty *in personam* a general appearance, though it cannot cure any essential defect of jurisdiction of the subject-matter, [*cit.*] cures any irregularities in the service of process, or even the want of any service. [*cit.*]

In these cases, the action being general against the person, a general appearance is co-extensive with the nature of the action. But even in such actions, where the defendant's person or property has been arrested [*capias*] or attached irregularly, the defendant may appear specially to

---

[1] Coote, 1st ed., pp. 89–90.   [2] Haynes, ¶149, p. 44.
[3] Hebert, pp. 390–1; Price, *L.M.L.*, p. 13.
[4] *The Dictator*, [1892] P. 304, 319.   [5] (1863) Br. & Lush. 84.

vacate the proceedings, and the court will not acquire thereby any jurisdiction to proceed to a personal judgment. [*cit.*] But an action purely
in rem is itself limited to a proceeding against the *res*, and a *general*
appearance in such an action should, it seems to me, be deemed no more
general than the limited nature and scope of the action itself, and of no
greater effect than a *special* appearance to vacate an unauthorized arrest
or attachment upon a general suit *in personam.*[1]

It is this simple question implicit in Judge Brown's holding—
viz., why should the shipowner's appearance in an action *in rem*
be deemed 'more general than the limited nature and scope of
the action itself'?—which is unanswered by Jeune, P., and is so
difficult to reconcile with his judgment. And if the action *in rem*
is purely a procedural device, then once its function of coercing
the owner to appear and defend is fulfilled, the action, according
to Jeune's reasoning, changes into and proceeds as an action *in
personam*; yet the form and procedure of an action *in rem* is
retained throughout the remainder of the proceedings, and so, in
fact, an action *in personam* has been superadded to one *in rem*.
The conflict between the views of Dr Lushington and Sir Francis
Jeune could not, therefore, be more direct.

   At the heart of Jeune's view of the action *in rem*, it seems, lay
his training in the common law and his deficiency of knowledge
of the civil law in general and the Law of Admiralty in particular.
The idea of a procedural theory of actions *in rem* would occur
most easily to a common lawyer, for 'at common law, proceedings
are against persons; and if any property is taken, it is only as a
method of coercing the debtor.'[2] Jeune himself makes affirmation
of his aim to give in a single action in Admiralty as complete
relief as could be given in the common law courts by quoting
portions of Dr Lushington's decision in *The Aline*[3] contrasting
the complete relief *in personam* afforded by the common law with
relief in an Admiralty action *in rem* limited to the value of the
ship and freight.[4] Moreover, the confusion of Admiralty and common law terminology which had been generated by the Judicature
Acts and the 1883 Rules[5] was particularly severe with regard to
the nature of the action *in rem*, for a certain type of **judgment**
at common law was also known—and still is—by the same name.

---

[1] *The Monte A.*, 12 F. 332, 335 (S.D.N.Y. 1882).
[2] 5 *Am. L. Rev.* 581, 584 (1871).   [3] (1839) 1 W. Rob. 111, 117–18.
[4] *The Dictator*, [1892] P. 304, 316.   [5] See *supra*, pp. 121–2.

Both the distinction and the confusion between the common law judgment and Admiralty action *in rem* are very well illustrated in the comments of the editors of the fourteenth edition of *Abbott* (themselves common lawyers), which first show that their concept of 'an action *in rem*' is that it is simply an action *in personam* which, as in suits for divorce, may terminate in a judgment which is binding upon third parties (whereas the Admiralty action *in rem* in truth commences with the arrest of and continues to proceed against a definite *res*); failing to show that the two concepts are not identical, the note then uses the common law concept of a **judgment** *in rem* in explanation of the rule of international maritime law which holds an Admiralty decree *in rem* 'binding against all the world.'[1] Others have also confused the two *in rem* concepts in discussing the history of Admiralty and its doctrines; the language used by Sir William Holdsworth in discussing the Admiralty decree *in rem* makes it plain that he applied to it the common law concept.[2] The appearance to Sir Francis Jeune of the action *in rem* as one which was basically *in personam* is therefore not remarkable; but what must be borne in mind from this point forward is that, just as the maritime lien has little in common with the common law lien, so the Admiralty concept of the **action** *in rem* bears very little relation to the common law **judgment** concept.[3]

Faced with such clear words as those of Baron Parke in *Brown v. Wilkinson*,[4] previously quoted, to the effect that the limit of liability *in rem* was the value of the *res*, Jeune could only attempt to show that view as historically unfounded. This he did by making reference primarily to two decisions of the first half of the nineteenth century, and of these the first was that of Lord Stowell in *The Dundee*.[5] Lord Stowell's statement as quoted by Jeune certainly appears to declare that in an action under the general maritime law of Europe a full personal recovery could be had; what Jeune nowhere indicates, and what becomes clear when Lord Stowell's words are read in context, is that his consideration was devoted solely to an interpretation of the specific language of §§7 & 8 of the limitation of liability statute of 1813,[6]

[1] *Abbott*, p. 28, n. (*l*).   [2] *H.E.L.*, vol. 11, p. 271.
[3] See *The Belfast*, 7 Wall. (74 U.S.) 624, 644 (1868).
[4] (1846) 15 M. & W. 391, 398.
[5] (1823) 1 Hag. Adm. 109, 124–8.
[6] Responsibility of Shipowners Act, ×1813, §§7, 8.

in an effort to find jurisdiction over some barrels of fishing gear not specifically named in the warrant of arrest. Read in context, Lord Stowell's statement in *The Dundee* does not support Jeune's contention that in nineteenth-century England the measure of liability *in rem* was not limited by the value of the *res*; indeed, in subsequent proceedings in the case of *The Dundee*,[1] not cited by Sir Francis Jeune in his references to the instance proceedings,[2] Lord Stowell explicitly stated—in his last decision as Admiralty Judge—that the shipowners could not be made liable beyond the value of the *res*.

Citation of *The Dundee*, a proceeding for limitation of liability, does prompt, however, consideration of the reasons for the pre-*Dictator* rule that there was no liability in an action *in rem* beyond the value of the ship and freight. One reason is terminological-procedural, and apparent in the designation of the action, namely, that the action *is* in fact '*in rem*'—'against the thing[/ship]'—and to proceed beyond the worth of the *res* is obviously to proceed against something else—the owner—which is clearly not the *res*; the elementary reason for the pre-*Dictator* view is therefore that the position taken by Sir Francis Jeune would have been a contradiction in terms. Another reason, not so obvious, is bound up with consideration of the enactment of statutes granting limitation of liability to shipowners. In a nutshell, the pre-*Dictator* view was an outgrowth of the public policy which developed during the eighteenth century and had as its aim the encouragement of Britain's maritime commerce. Of course the principle of limitation *in rem* to the value of the *res* is itself of much greater antiquity, antedating statutory law; Judge Ware saw its origin in the Roman Law regarding obligations *ex delicto*,[3] and Mr Justice Holmes analogized it to the surrender of a sheep-killing dog to offset liability at common law in the reign of Edward III.[4] And a sort of limitation, evidently under Article 32 of the Laws of Oleron, was applied in early times to free the ship and certain tackle from contribution in general average.[5]

But it is perhaps easier to envisage development of the principle

---

[1] *The Dundee*, (1827) 2 Hag. Adm. 137 [subs. proc.].

[2] *I.e., The Dictator*, [1892] P. 304, 313–15.

[3] *The Rebecca*, 20 Fed. Cas. 373, 376 (No. 11619) (D. Me. 1831).

[4] *Liverpool &c. Navigation Co. v. Brooklyn Terminal*, 251 U.S. 48, 53 (1919).

[5] See, *e.g., Barons of the Cinque Ports v. Rokesle, et al.*, Coram Rege Roll, no. 93 (Trinity 1285), m. 1 [K.B.].

across the long years of sea-trading in the inability to proceed *in personam* against foreign shipowners over whom the maritime courts could gain no jurisdiction whatever; the *res* being all of the owner which could be had, his liability became personified therein and the actual value became also the constructive limit. The extension of that benefit to domestic ship-owners decrying the unfair advantage of foreigners would then have been only a matter of time—this, however, is merely my own speculation, prodded by such echoes as: 'What more natural and just, when the ship has been the cause or occasion of the loss or damage, than to look to the ship for reparation?'[1]

The common law of England, having no cognizance of such actions *in rem*, naturally could not comprehend the principle of limitation of liability to the value of a *res*; and Admiralty, prohibited during the seventeenth century from exercising its jurisdiction *in personam*,[2] came during the eighteenth to act almost exclusively *in rem*.[3] The upshot was that the shipowner, as defendant in an action at common law, was without the protection which he came to enjoy in Admiralty. The obvious remedy would have been a statutory extension of the principle applicable in actions *in rem* to those *in personam*,—under the circumstances then prevailing, to create a new type of proceeding at law, with the jurisdiction originally assigned to Chancery for reasons earlier discussed.[4]

Dr Lushington described the origin of the limitation of liability statutes as 'political',[5] *i.e.*, commercial, and one method of stimulating expansion of the merchant navy was to offer to shipowners a statutory protection of their personal assets by limiting their liability upon suit to the amount of their interest and investment in the ship, her tackle, and the particular voyage in which she was engaged at the time the cause of action arose (as represented by the freight)—a public policy perfectly analogous to that which led to the protection of business investors by the formation of limited liability corporations. The specific language of the limitation of liability statutes, most notably that of 1813, allowed shipowners against whom actions had been brought upon causes arising out of the operation of their vessels to claim the protection of the

---

[1] *The Rebecca*, 20 Fed. Cas. 373, 376 (No. 11619) (D. Me. 1831).
[2] See *supra*, pp. 5–7.
[3] See *supra*, p. 62.
[4] See *supra*, p. 22.
[5] *The Amalia*, (1863) 1 Moo. P.C. (n.s.) 471, 473.

statute unless it could be proved that they were privy to the actual negligence out of which the cause arose;[1] privity to the act of negligence could of course be shown in virtually every case in which the shipowner was also her master, and he then could not claim limitation of his liability under the statute, which seems the likely explanation for Sir John Nicholl's decision in *The Triune*.[2] But the policy remained a general one, and in the Admiralty Court the principle of limitation was broadly applied *in rem* also; that this was so prior to the enactment of the limitation statutes is indicated by Dr Lushington in *The Volant*,[3] and if Lushington was correct in that case in finding that the form of the warrant, commanding the Marshal to cite for appearance 'all persons in general who have any right, title or interest' in the arrested ship, implied a limitation of their liability to the extent of that 'right, title or interest',[4] then it is not without significance that this form is set out by Marriott in his *Formulare* of 1802,[5] and it may be presumed to antedate limitation statutes even prior to that of 1813.

Had the *res* not been considered the sole object of actions *in rem* before the decision in *The Dictator*, and had its value not likewise been considered the limit of liability, there would have been no obstacle to a succession of arrests of the same ship upon the same cause of action. But in fact the rule, recognized by Dr Lushington in the case of *The Kalamazoo*,[6] was that there could be no re-arrest following bail for release in any action *in rem*; though in two later cases he made heavily qualified exceptions to this rule,[7] and though Sir Robert Phillimore maintained that it was always possible to re-arrest for costs of the suit,[8] the view taken in the present century repudiates these later decisions and reverts to the rule of *The Kalamazoo* that re-arrest after bail for release is not permissible.[9]

At the end of his judgment in *The Dictator*,[10] Sir Francis Jeune attempted to show that in the last case in which Dr Lushington

---

[1] Responsibility of Shipowners Act, ×1813, §1.
[2] (1834) 3 Hag. Adm. 114; *cf. The Annie Hay*, [1968] P. 341.
[3] (1842) 1 W. Rob. 383, 389.
[4] *Ibid.; The Dictator*, [1892] P. 304, 317–18.
[5] Pp. 326–7.   [6] (1851) 15 *Jur.* 885.
[7] *The Hero*, (1865) Br. & Lush. 447, 448.
   The Flora, (1866) L.R. 1 A. & E. 45, 46.
[8] *The Freedom*, (1871) L.R. 3 A. & E. 495, 499.
[9] *The Point Breeze* [1928] P. 135.   [10] [1892] P. 304, 318–19.

considered the question of the limit of liability in actions *in rem* he had retreated from his earlier holdings in *The Hope, The Volant,* and *The Kalamazoo.* But in the case cited, *The Zephyr,* Lushington refused an application to amend the praecipe to institute so as to insert the names of the owners and thereby render them personally liable, on the grounds—wholly consistent with his earlier decisions—that to amend the praecipe and issue a *citation in personam* would be to engraft an action *in personam* onto one *in rem,* only one anomalous instance of which, *The Triune,* was known to him—and of which he disapproved.[1] What Lushington did do in *The Zephyr*—quite inexplicably (as Jeune acknowledges[2]) —was to declare that the 1861 Court Act, §15, gave him power to issue a monition to the owners (which he does not, in fact, appear to have done), obliging them to pay the balance of the judgment upon pain of contempt, though the judgment exceeded the value of the ship. That statement of Lushington's was unsupported dictum, but in refusing the motion to amend he upheld the substance of the *Hope-Volant-Kalamazoo* doctrine—and even in cases not calling for direct consideration of the question, such as *The Clara,* Lushington took the opportunity to express his view that the limit of liability in an action *in rem* was 'the extent of the value of the ship.'[3]

The final authority relied upon by Sir Francis Jeune was the second of the two decisions of Lord Stowell which were cited, and this one, *The Jonge Bastiaan,* was said by Jeune to be 'on all fours' with the case at bar because it was a cause of salvage in which Lord Stowell made an award in excess of the claim and bail;[4] what Jeune did not point out was that the circumstances of the decision in *The Jonge Bastiaan* were most peculiar—the action was brought and a claim entered by the first salvors alone, but Lord Stowell later permitted the second salvors to join, thus necessitating an award beyond the amount of the original claim and consequent bail.[5] Clearly there were no similar circumstances to justify Jeune's holding in *The Dictator,* and of his assertion that *The Jonge Bastiaan* is 'clear authority' for the proposition that 'the claim in the praecipe could be exceeded with or without formal amendment',[6] it need only be pointed out that the praecipe was

---

[1] (1864) 11 L.T.R. 351.
[3] (1855) Swab. 1, 3.
[5] (1804) 5 C. Rob. 322, 323–4.

[2] [1892] P. 304, 319.
[4] *The Dictator,* [1892] P. 304, 322.
[6] [1892] P. 304, 323.

not introduced into Admiralty procedure until well after Lord Stowell's day.

Finally, there are three notable features of Sir Francis Jeune's decision: (1) *The Hope, The Volant*, and *The Kalamazoo*[1] were a clear line of precedent establishing that an action *in rem* could not be converted into one *in personam*, and *The Dictator* violates the principle that 'the Admiralty Court is bound to adhere without deviation to a course of precedents adopted by its predecessors, though not to a single decision';[2] (2) it was unnecessary to make the owners liable *in personam* in *The Dictator*, for it was clear at that time that an action *in personam* could have been brought against the owners for the balance of the judgment over the amount of the bail;[3] and (3) because *The Dictator* was a salvage cause, and—in Jeune's own words in the very case—'the salvage award never goes beyond the value of the property salved',[4] no award in that case could possibly have been made in excess of the value of the *res* (as distinct from the lesser amount of the bail), and the entire portion of the decision purporting to state that recovery in an action *in rem* could exceed the value of the *res* is therefore dictum, and not binding.

Jeune's procedural theory was quickly accepted by Smith, L.J., in *The Gemma*:

The President, in a judgment full of learning and research, in which he dealt with all the cases from the earliest time, whether in conflict or not with each other, has held in the case of *The Dictator* [*cit.*] that a person appearing in an action in rem becomes personally liable. I do not doubt that the President came to the correct conclusion, and I adopt it.[5]

Jeune himself viewed this uncritical acceptance as complete substantiation of the procedural theory,[6] and thereafter it remained only for some cause other than salvage to arise in which the claim was greater than the value of the ship. This occurred in *The Dupleix*, in which Sir Samuel Evans, P., declared that *The Dictator* 'stated that the law was that in a **collision** action *in rem*, where the

---

[1] *The Dictator*, [1892] p. 304, 321.
[2] *English & Empire Digest*, vol. 1, p. 118; *cf. The Leucade*, (1855) 2 Sp. 228, 229 [Prize].
[3] Williams and Bruce, 2nd ed., p. 81; see *supra*, pp. 158–9.
[4] [1892] P. 304, 310.   [5] [1899] P. 285, 292 [App.].
[6] *The Cargo ex Port Victor*, (1901) 84 L.T.R. 363, 365.

defendant appeared', liability could exceed the value of the ship, and he proceeded to put Jeune's theory into execution for the first time.[1] Lord Merrivale found the *Dictator–Gemma–Dupleix* line of 'precedent' as binding authority, and rebuffed the argument of Sir Gainsford Bruce in the introduction to the third edition of his *Practice* that *The Dictator* was both legally and historically inaccurate,[2] with the statement that 'the trend of modern cases is entirely contrary'.[3]

The current view of the action *in rem* has adopted the procedural theory, and is based upon the *Dictator–Gemma–Dupleix* case line.[4] It is interesting to note that a modern American Admiralty decision permitted a recovery in excess of bail in an action *in rem*, citing the *Dictator–Gemma–Dupleix* case line[5] and the only prior American case to so hold,[6] which had in turn cited *The Jonge Bastiaan*. The decision was approved upon appeal in its own Circuit[7] and cited with approval by another Circuit Court,[8] but the most recent appellate decision comes from a most authoritative Circuit in Admiralty, the Second (which includes New York), and it overrules the earliest decision and repudiates the more recent ones.[9]

'Arrest', Sir Francis Jeune declared in *The Dictator*, 'became the distinctive feature of the action *in rem*'—and yet the steamship *Dictator*, though her owners appeared in the action, was never in fact arrested.[10] This fact has a significance which requires examination of the procedure by which the Admiralty Court assumes jurisdiction *in rem*. Some attempts have been made to trace certain fundamentals of the Admiralty action *in rem* out of the Roman Law,[11] but no definite source has appeared for the most characteristic feature—arrest of the ship—which is said by Lord Stowell to be the 'ancient' method of acquiring jurisdiction *in rem*.[12] That arrest was a step of greatest importance is reflected in

---

[1] [1912] P. 8, 12. [2] Williams and Bruce, 3rd ed., pp. 18–26.
[3] *The Joannis Vatis (No. 2)*, [1922] P. 213, 214.
[4] See McGuffie, *Practice*, §325, p. 142 & n. 14.
[5] *The Fairisle (Dean v. Waterman SS Co.)*, 76 F. Supp. 27 (D.Md. 1947).
[6] *The Minnetonka*, 146 F. 509 (2 Cir. 1906).
[7] *The Fairisle*, 171 F.2d 408 (4 Cir. 1948).
[8] *Mosher v. Tate*, 182 F.2d 475 (9 Cir. 1950).
[9] *Logue Stevedoring Corp. v. The Dalzellance*, 198 F.2d 369 (2 Cir. 1952); and see 'Personification of Vessels', 77 *H.L.R.* 1122 (1964).
[10] [1892] P. 304, 313, 305. [11] *E.g.*, see Conkling, pp. 427–32.
[12] *The Dundee*, (1823) 1 Hag. Adm. 109, 124.

Stowell's first standing order as Admiralty Judge, by which he appears to have introduced the affidavit to lead warrant into Admiralty practice.[1] Dr Browne makes it clear that 'when the proceeding is against the ship, ... process commences by a warrant directed to the marshal of the court, commissioning him to arrest the ship ...'[2]

Arrest of the ship is a unique process, not—as has previously been stressed—to be confused with seizure in maritime attachment, or with the power of detention which all Courts of Record once possessed by statute,[3] or with the power which still exists to detain foreign ships 'in respect of salvage.'[4] Arrest of a ship under Admiralty warrant is not merely a restraint analogous to injunction, but vests an actual custody of the ship in the Admiralty Marshal,[5] including custody of any tackle and rigging which may have been removed from the ship prior to arrest,[6] and the Marshal is absolutely responsible for ships and property while in *custodia legis*.[7] Warning is given to all persons that the arrested vessel is not to be moved or interfered with while under arrest,[8] and moving the vessel without the permission of the Marshal, whether to remove her from possible danger[9] or under the mistaken impression that she has been bailed,[10] constitutes a contempt of the Court, even if the warrant has not been formally served but notice of its imminent arrival has been given.[11] An official such as a sheriff or Harbour-Master commits contempt by attempting a seizure of the arrested ship or her tackle,[12] and the mere incitement of arrest-breaking is likewise contumacious.[13] And because arrest is such a restrictive condition, damages for wrongful arrest of a ship may be recovered in an action *in personam*.[14]

But as in the case of *The Dictator*, it is also possible for the Admiralty Court to assume 'jurisdiction *in rem*' without arresting the *res*; the method evolved to permit this was the substitution for

---

[1] See Marriott, p. 31.   [2] Vol. 2, p. 397.
[3] Shipowners' Negligence (Remedies) Act, 1905, §1.
[4] McGuffie, *Practice*, §259, p. 196.
[5] *The Arantzazu Mendi*, [1939] A.C. 256, 266 [H.L.].
[6] *The Alexander*, (1811) 1 Dod. 278.
[7] *The Hoop*, (1801) 4 C. Rob. 145.   [8] R. G. M. Browne, p. 104.
[9] *The Selina Stanford*, (1908) *The Times*, 17 November.
[10] *The Jarlinn*, [1965] 1 W.L.R. 1098.   [11] *The Seraglio*, (1885) 10 P.D. 120.
[12] *The Harmonie*, (1841) 1 W. Rob. 179.
[13] *The Bure*, (1850) 14 Jur. 1123, 1124.
[14] *The Walter D. Wallet*, [1893] P. 202.

the *res* of a promise to appear personally and defend the action, and upon the strength of this promise, or undertaking, a *caveat*, or warning against arrest, would be entered in a ledger under the ship's name. This caveat procedure makes its first formal appearance in the 1855 Rules, [Fees] r. 4, which declares that the *caveat warrant book* shall be kept in the Admiralty Registry, that proctors may secure the entry therein of an undertaking to appear and answer and give bail to any claim which may be entered against a particular ship, and that, without 'good and sufficient cause' the extraction of a warrant and arrest of a ship on whose behalf a caveat has been entered renders the plaintiff liable to condemnation in costs. Caveats might also be entered in a *caveat release book* to ensure that a named ship would not be released from arrest without notification to second claimants,[1] and in a *caveat payment book* to prevent payment of proceeds or other monies out of the fund of the Court.[2] The principle is in each case the same, as the entry of a caveat is procured on behalf of a party or interested person; but in the context of the action *in rem*, consideration will be limited to caveats against the arrest of a *res*.

Of the antiquity of the caveat procedure, all that can presently be stated with any certainty is that it must have arisen subsequent to the practice of arresting the ship by warrant; the appearance of the procedure in the 1855 Rules is completely 'out of the blue', for neither the Admiralty Registry nor the Public Record Office have any record of *caveat warrant books* prior to 1855, and no mention of the practice is made by Dr Browne or other text-writers previous to the same year. Nor does there appear to be any mention of the caveat against arrest in the reports prior to 1855, even in cases where one might expect to see the practice utilized, such as those in which there was no arrest of the ship, and the proceeding was a personal action by way of monition;[3] yet in one case Lord Stowell speaks of a caveat against payment,[4] which indicates that the basic idea was not an 1855 innovation. Mr Lionel Bell of the Public Record Office, a scholar of the Court's early history and records to whom this writer turned for information quite beyond the reach of his own expertise, has produced

---

[1] See, *e.g.*, Williams and Bruce, 1st ed., p. 197.
[2] See, *e.g.*, R.S.C., 1883, O. 22, r. 21.
[3] *E.g.*, *The Trelawney*, (1801) 3 C. Rob. 216n.
[4] *The Hercules*, (1819) 2 Dod. 353, 368.

evidence of the caveat warrant procedure from two seventeenth-century warrant books of the Admiralty Court. The procedure then seems to have been entirely informal, and the caveat itself took the form of an entry in the warrant book of the notation: *cave ne aliquod warrantum extranatur ad arrestandum navem the Tiger*...[1] or similar wording, with the name of the proctor to be notified. One of these entries is accompanied by a note in the margin to the effect that the caveat is by order of the Admiralty Judge,[2] though it is suggested by Mr Bell that in some of the cases entry might be explained by a mild corruption of Registry clerks by some proctors, and it is plausible that the procedure may have originated in this way. The caveat against arrest, says Mr Bell, was not frequently entered, and the more ordinary procedure seems to have been that of the caveat against release on bail.[3] It is interesting to note that in one instance the notation in the warrant book was accompanied by the entry of the single word '*caveat*' in the margin,[4] which would seem to remove any doubt that this is the origin of the modern practice.

That the caveat was a creature of the civil law in general is doubtful; certainly the procedure never developed in the Colonial Vice-Admiralty Courts, nor in the High Court of Admiralty of Ireland, which, like that of England, was entirely in the hands of the civilians.[5] The caveat did enter Canadian Admiralty practice, however, via adoption of most of the English 1883 Rules.[6]

The origin of the execution of a formal undertaking to appear, make answer and give bail to the claim—a procedure necessary under the 1855 Rules to procure entry of a caveat[7]—is even more obscure, though Dr Browne makes reference to a 'stipulation' to submit to the Court's jurisdiction.[8] After the introduction of praecipes into Admiralty practice, the undertaking took the form of a praecipe for entry of a caveat against arrest, by which the defendants promised to appear and give bail to the claim within three days of the institution of any action; the caveat thus pro-

---

[1] *The Tiger*, (1622) W.B. 14, p. 51; [P.R.O.] H.C.A. 38/14/51.
[2] *Ex parte Trinity House*, (1624) W.B. 15, p. 22; H.C.A. 38/15/22.
[3] Letter to me of 21 June 1966.
[4] *The John and Humphrey*, (1624) W.B. 15, p. 43; H.C.A. 38/15/43.
[5] Parl. Paper [1864] (219) xxix (R.C.), p. 20.
[6] See Howell (1893) for Canadian Rules.
[7] See 1855 Rules, [Fees] r. 4.
[8] Vol. 2, p. 100.

cured was valid for six months and could be renewed thereafter,[1] and the current procedure is virtually identical, even to the preservation of the praecipe.[2]

The caveat procedure became very popular, and it is noteworthy that a 1920 text on commercial maritime law takes it for granted that the procurement of a caveat following a claim upon a cause of collision was standard.[3] But at some time in the late nineteenth century, the entry of caveats began to be bypassed with the giving of undertakings in private form by the defendant's to the plaintiff's solicitors directly upon notification that a claim would be brought, and in return for such an undertaking to appear and give a bail for the claim, the plaintiff would agree not to take out a warrant for the arrest of the ship in that particular cause; it appears that this is what took place in the case of *The Dictator*, and by 1931 undertakings were said to be 'the usual practice'.[4]

Though the procedure is still available, caveats are becoming increasingly rare in the present day,[5] as the allied practice, whereby cash may be deposited in the fund of the Court by a defendant in lieu of the execution of a bail bond, has always been.[6] It must be stressed that the bail given in pursuance of an undertaking is no guarantee that the ship will not be arrested, even if the entry of a caveat has been procured, and the defendant's only recourse if his ship should be arrested over an undertaking or caveat lies in an application for release of the ship and consequential damages.[7] The breach of an undertaking, on the other hand, renders the undertaking solicitor liable to immediate personal attachment committal,[8] and the undertaking continues in binding force despite sale of the ship by order of the Court in an unrelated action.[9] Undertakings in individual suits brought upon causes of action *in rem* are now the usual practice,[10] and this is reflected in the issue of warrants for arrest, which number less than 20% of the quantity of writs *in rem* issued since 1960,[11] and in the figures for 1964, when in the 310 actions listed as *in rem* there were but 47 arrests

---

[1] See Williams and Bruce, 1st ed., pp. 197–8.
[2] See R.S.C. 1965, O. 75, r. 6 and Ap. B, form 5.
[3] Saunders, pp. 45, 49.   [4] Roscoe, *Practice*, p. 271.
[5] McGuffie, *Practice*, §239, p. 102.   [6] *Id.*, §291, p. 125; §344, p. 153.
[7] *Id.*, §322, p. 139.   [8] R.S.C., 1883, O. 12, r. 18.
[9] *The Ring*, [1931] P. 58.   [10] McGuffie, *Practice*, §243, p. 104.
[11] Figures supplied by Admiralty Registry, 1966.

(and there were releases from arrest in 34 of those cases).[1] It is certainly true that arrest once was the 'distinctive feature of the action in rem', as stated by Sir Francis Jeune;[2] it certainly is no longer the distinctive feature, and its absence in *The Dictator* proves one of the most distinctive aspects of that case.

Though the caveat procedure as such never developed in American Admiralty, a partial counterpart had evolved by the late eighteenth century. The American version has two procedures, a 'special bond' and a 'general bond'. The special bond was originally known as a 'stipulation', which strongly indicates that it may have been a descendant of the 'stipulation' described by Dr Browne;[3] it was formally introduced in Rule 12 of the old General Admiralty Rules in 1845, but this was probably codification of a pre-existing procedure.[4] The procedure was and is in essence an undertaking, which can be given pending the issuance of a process for maritime attachment or a warrant for arrest of the ship, and which will stay the execution of process in the hands of the Marshal or effect the release of the vessel if the process has been served. The amount of the special bond under Rule 12 was stipulated by the parties, but a statute of 1847 also permitted a bond to the same effect without agreement by the parties if posted in double the amount of the claim[5]—a procedure which was obviously not very popular with Rule 12 as an alternative;[6] the two procedures are now consolidated in the new unified Rules of Civil Procedure, which permit the parties to stipulate the amount of the bond or the Court to fix it in any amount not exceeding twice the sum of the claim—and in no case exceeding the value of the *res*.[7] An 1899 amendment to the 1847 statute first permitted a general bond to be posted,[8] and its substance is the same under the new rules; in form it is an undertaking, to appear and answer generally any action which may be entered against a named vessel, upon security approved by the Court.[9]

The general bond is not equivalent to a caveat, because (1) the

---

[1] C.J.S., 1964 [Cmd. No. 2666], pp. 42–5.

[2] *The Dictator*, [1892] P. 304, 313.

[3] Vol. 2, p. 100; and see *Lane v. Townsend*, 14 Fed. Cas. 1087 (No. 8054) (D. Me. 1835).   [4] See Benedict, vol. 1, §373, p. 445.

[5] Act of March 3, 1847, c. 55.

[6] See Gilmore and Black, §9–89, p. 650.

[7] F.R.C.P. [1 July 1966], Adm. Rule E.(5)(a); see also 28 U.S.C., §2464.

[8] Act of March 3, 1899, c. 441.

[9] F.R.C.P. [1 July 1966], Adm. Rule E.(5)(b).

effect of a caveat is usually the prevention of issuance of the warrant of arrest, whereas the process for Admiralty attachment or warrant of arrest is never prevented by a general bond, which only stays execution in the hands of the Marshal; (2) the caveat may not prevent arrest, whereas the general bond absolutely prevents arrest or maritime attachment; and (3), the caveat is entered upon payment of a set fee and is valid for six months, whereas the general bond remains valid for so long as the security posted under it equals at least twice the sum of all claims pending against the named vessel (a feature which eliminates the usefulness of the general bond when the aggregate of claims becomes equivalent to the value of the vessel); despite these differences, the general bond and caveat are designed to serve the same basic purpose. And the special bond, commonly known as an 'undertaking', is roughly equivalent to the procedure of the same name in England, being the usual practice in American actions *in rem* also;[1] but there is a fundamental distinction—liability on the special bond cannot exceed the value of the *res* it protects.[2]

The special bond may also serve as bail for release of an arrested *res*; in both England and America, however, bail is more commonly in the form of a 'consent' of the parties to release (pursuant to privately-agreed security), with payment of the costs of detention —and this has long been, according to Mr Justice Story, the 'known course of the Admiralty.'[3] But it is unfortunate that a long-standing confusion in America is perpetuated by the newly-unified Federal Rules of Civil Procedure, which use the terms 'consent' and 'stipulation' interchangeably with reference to the release of a *res* from arrest[4] (except in possessory, petitory or partition suits, where release is only upon Court order[5]); the result is that the vital distinction between a stipulation to *prevent* arrest (*i.e.*, a general or special bond) and a stipulation to *release from* arrest (*i.e.*, a consent; or, rarely, a special bond) is very generally ignored. Without having the distinction in mind at the outset, it is often difficult to ascertain the meaning and significance of nineteenth-century decisions; in the present century, where a

---

[1] See *The Agwisun* [*In re. Atlantic Gulf & West Indies SS. Lines*], 20 F.2d 975 (S.D.N.Y. 1927).

[2] F.R.C.P. [1 July 1966], Adm. Rule E.(5)(a).

[3] *The Palmyra*, 12 Wheat. (25 U.S.) 1, 10 (1827).

[4] F.R.C.P. [1 July 1966], Adm. Rule E.(5)(c).

[5] *Id.*, Rule E.(5)(d).

Court of Admiralty may speak of a 'special bond', 'undertaking', or 'stipulation' all with reference to the same procedure, the difficulties are even greater; clearly, an overhaul of nomenclature is indicated.

In England, it was declared by the 1883 Rules that service of process in actions *in rem* should not be required where the defendant has executed an undertaking;[1] but that is far from saying that arrest is in general unnecessary in actions *in rem*, a proposition which has since been advanced largely on the strength of a single decision by Sir Gainsford Bruce, sitting as relief Judge in Admiralty.[2] The proposition so advanced by Bruce in the case of *The Nautik*[3] has serious jurisprudential implications and must therefore be examined. In that case an undertaking had been given by the owners of the *Nautik*, and a writ *in rem* was issued and served upon them, whereupon they withdrew their undertaking; a warrant of arrest was then extracted, but before it could be served the vessel had left the jurisdiction of the Court. Upon these facts Sir Gainsford proceeded to try the action as if the warrant had been served, on the basis that service of the writ was notice of the claim and that it was not necessary that the vessel should be 'actually in the possession of the Court or under the arrest of the Court'. Taking the last point first, Bruce based the conclusion quoted above upon the statements of two eminent judges, whom he quoted in turn—and which shall be examined in turn.

'It is enough that it [the ship] should, according to the words of Lord Chelmsford, in the case of *Castrique v. Imrie*, "be within the lawful control of the State under the authority of which the Court sits." '[4] In *Castrique v. Imrie*, the question was one of a conflict of laws arising out of the sale of a vessel in a French action *in rem*, and the decision of the House of Lords affirmed the principle of comity in international maritime law that the sale of a vessel by a Court vested with authority to act *in rem* will—provided that jurisdiction *in rem* was validly acquired—universally be held valid and binding. It is clear from the context of Lord Chelmsford's statement[5] that the portion quoted by Sir Gainsford Bruce in *The Nautik* was made in reference to the general principle of comity

---

[1] R.S.C., 1883, O. 9, r. 10.
[2] See McGuffie, *Practice*, §50, p. 26; §378, p. 165.
[3] [1895] P. 121.   [4] *Ibid.*
[5] *Castrique v. Imrie*, (1870) L.R. 4 H.L. 414, 448.

and not to the Admiralty Law of England; to attempt to negate the procedural requirements of English Law because the requirements of international maritime law are less specific is clearly preposterous.

But Bruce placed even greater reliance upon another authority: 'The same view is expressed by Jessel, M.R. in *The City of Mecca*. That learned Judge says: "An action for enforcing a maritime lien may, no doubt, be commenced without an actual arrest of the ship." '[1] The question in *The City of Mecca*, like that in *Castrique v. Imrie*, was one of comity, and required an examination of the character of the foreign action. A proceeding had been entertained in Portugal, and the Portuguese judgment was sought to be enforced in England under the principle of comity by an action *in rem* against the *City of Mecca* in the Admiralty Division. A considerable portion of the opinion of Jessel, M. R., was given over to consideration of the Admiralty Law of Portugal, and Bruce's quotation was lifted directly from that portion;[2] it must be made clear that when Jessel, M.R., said that 'an action for enforcing a maritime lien may, no doubt, be commenced without an actual arrest of the ship', he was referring specifically to **Portuguese Law,** and not to the Admiralty Law of England. What makes this misleading excontextual quotation even more incredible is that Bruce himself actually argued as counsel in *The City of Mecca*, both at instance[3] and on appeal,[4] and lost—appropriately enough—to the team of Judah P. Benjamin, Q.C. (onetime Attorney-General, Secretary of War, and Secretary of State of the Confederate States of America during the American Civil War) and Edward S. Roscoe (later Admiralty Registrar and Bruce's thumbnail biographer in *Studies*).

Clearly, Sir Gainsford Bruce's decision in the case of *The Nautik*, attempting to subordinate the procedural requirements of English Admiralty Law to those of the international maritime law and the Law of Portugal, cannot continue to be sustained as support for the proposition that arrest is wholly unnecessary in actions *in rem*.[5]

The argument that a writ of summons *in rem* is by itself as effective as a warrant of arrest is tantamount to an assertion that

---

[1] *The Nautik*, [1895] P. 121.   [2] (1881) 6 P.D. 106, 112 [App.].
[3] (1879) 5 P.D. 28.   [4] (1881) 6 P.D. 106 [App.].
[5] But see *The Monica S.*, [1967] 2 Ll. Rep. 113, 127.

the warrant is nothing more than a redundant notice. It is impossible to reconcile such an argument with the fact of the warrant's alteration in the status of the arrested vessel and of the powers which arrest confers upon the Marshal in respect of the vessel in *custodia legis* as previously discussed,[1] or with the specific rules for the service of such process—unchanged for centuries[2]—violation of which has consistently been held to nullify the efficacy of the process even in the present day.[3]

Under the civilians, the English position was quite clear: 'But as no prudent person will hesitate to proceed *in rem if the res be within the jurisdiction of the Court,* so a personal proceeding is never adopted *unless the res be inaccessible to arrest.*'[4] The vessel had to be physically present within the Court's jurisdiction to enable a proceeding *in rem*; if it was not, the alternative was a personal action against the owner. Such was the established rule observed by the civilians. But since the case of *The Nautik,* the attitude toward the institution of proceedings against the vessel has changed; Hill, J., perhaps relying upon *The Nautik,* declared (reasonably, but without citation of authority in support) that he could 'see no reason why the writ cannot be issued [in the absence of the vessel] and then served when the *res* comes within the jurisdiction.'[5] But in cases where an undertaking is executed, the present position is far more extreme:

In fact, it is common practice for an owner of a res threatened with arrest to give an undertaking either direct or through his solicitors to accept service of any writ issued, to enter appearance and to provide bail, even *before the writ has been issued.* Such an undertaking sometimes includes an agreement to accept English jurisdiction as, for example, *where the defendant is here but his res is threatened with arrest in some foreign court.*[6]

The significance of this statement is that it now appears possible to conduct an entire proceeding upon a cause of action *in rem*—from start to finish—during the whole of which the vessel proceeded against has been absent from the jurisdiction of the Court.

---

[1] See *supra,* p. 184.   [2] See A. Browne, vol. 2, p. 398.
[3] See, *e.g., The Prins Bernhard,* [1963] 2 Ll. Rep. 236.
[4] Coote, 1st ed., pp. 131–2 (emphasis supplied).
[5] *The Espanoleto,* [1920] P. 223, 225.
[6] McGuffie, *Practice,* §232, p. 98 (emphasis supplied).

The American rule has always been that no proceeding *in rem* may be maintained unless the *res* be physically present within the Court's jurisdiction. Compliance with this requirement was assured under the old General Admiralty Rules by the demand of Rule 22 for inclusion in every instance libel [writ] a statement upon oath by the plaintiff's proctor that the *res* was present within the jurisdiction of the Court, and a similar requirement has been prescribed for complaints in Admiralty actions *in rem* under the unified rules.[1] This was clearly the practice in the Colonial Vice-Admiralty Courts of North America,[2] and has passed not only into American practice but into that of Canada as well, where the presence of the *res* within the jurisdiction of the Court is absolutely required by statute before a writ of summons *in rem* may be issued.[3]

The firm American view is that: 'an Admiralty court in order to have jurisdiction in rem must be in a position to secure the res'[4]; and the corollary is that: 'the foundation of jurisdiction *in rem* is the taking of the vessel into the custody of the court'.[5] The advantage of this custody, perfected by arrest, has long been the distinctive feature of the action *in rem* in the United States,[6] and even an action in which the owner has posted a general or special bond cannot be instituted by a plaintiff unless the vessel is or will be present in the Court's jurisdiction. This position is even clearer under the unified rules,[7] eliminating the misinterpretation which led to one anomalous decision.[8] Moreover, the position is clear that the posting of a general or special bond does not constitute a personal submission to the jurisdiction of the Court save to enforce the security specified in the bond,[9] and in case of an award in an action in which there has been a special bond (which cannot exceed the value of the *res*[10]), the surety is liable only to the extent of the stipulated sum even if the award exceeds that sum.[11] Arrest

---

[1] F.R.C.P. [1 July 1966], Adm. Rule C.(2).   [2] See Dunlap, p. 91.

[3] The Admiralty Act, *R.S.C.* 1952, c. 1, §20(1)(a).   [4] Robinson, §59, p. 415.

[5] Benedict, vol. 1, p. 16; and see *The Resolute*, 168 U.S. 437, 439 (1897).

[6] *Jennings v. Carson*, 4 Cranch (8 U.S.) 2 (1807); *The General Pershing [Criscuolo v. Atlas Imperial Diesel Engine Co.]*, 84 F.2d 273, 275 (9 Cir. 1936).

[7] F.R.C.P. [1 July 1966], Adm. Rule C.(2).

[8] *The Providence*, 293 F. 595, 596 (D. R.I. 1923); erroneously followed in *The New England*, 47 F.2d 332, 335 (S.D.N.Y. 1931).

[9] Conkling, p. 448.

[10] F.R.C.P. [1 July 1966], Adm. Rule E.(5)(a).

[11] *Brown v. Burrows*, 4 Fed. Cas. 360 (No. 1996) (C. C. S.D. N.Y. 1851).

of the ship is not a procedural device,[1] and any appearance of an owner to defend an Admiralty or maritime claim upon which his ship has been arrested or seized may be entered as a 'restricted' appearance which will not submit him to the jurisdiction of the Court for any other purpose,[2] so that a defending owner in an American action *in rem* cannot be held personally liable beyond the value of his ship against his will.

At this point it is necessary to digress momentarily, and to examine the nature and function of bail before discussing the modern English proceeding upon causes of action *in rem*. The standard axiom in both American and English Admiralty Law is that bail is a substitute for the *res* and that, when posted in an action *in rem*, it becomes the subject of the proceeding and the *res* itself is thereupon discharged from the action,[3] which is why, in both America[4] and England,[5] re-arrest of a ship released upon bail is not permissible upon the same cause of action. What is significant about the cases establishing this axiom of bail as a substitution for the *res* is that in each instance, whether declared by Lord Stowell,[6] Dr Lushington,[7] or common lawyers upon appeal[8] or at instance,[9] the ship proceeded against had been duly arrested by warrant *in rem*. Bail, of course, can only be given upon entry of an appearance in any action,[10] and the question which quite naturally arises must be whether bail given in a proceeding upon a cause of action *in rem* in which the *res* has not been arrested differs from bail given after arrest by warrant *in rem*.

In *The John Dunn*,[11] the case in which Dr Lushington attempted to award costs which, when added to the judgment, would have exceeded the value of the *res*, but against the enforcement of which award a prohibition was issued, the rationale of Lushington's decision was that the defending shipowner's appearance rendered him personally responsible, and he referred to bail given in another case to secure the release of an arrested ship as a substitution of

---

[1] *Reed v. The Yaka*, 307 F.2d 203 (3 Cir. 1962); *rev'd. on other grounds*, 373 U.S. 410 (1963).
[2] F.R.C.P. [1 July 1966], Adm. Rule E.(8).
[3] See, *e.g., The Christiansborg*, (1884) 10 P.D. 141, 155 [App.].
[4] *The Thales*, 23 Fed. Cas. 884 (No. 13856) (C.C.S.D.N.Y. 1872).
[5] *The Point Breeze*, [1928] P. 135.   [6] *The Peggy*, (1802) 4 C. Rob. 304.
[7] *The Wild Ranger*, (1863) Br. & Lush. 84, 87.
[8] *The Christiansborg*, (1884) 10 P.D. 141, 155.
[9] *The Point Breeze*, [1928] P. 135.   [10] McGuffie, *Practice*, §232, p. 97.
[11] (1840) 1 W. Rob. 159 [Inst. & Prohib.].

'personal responsibility'. And in the present century, when undertaking rather than arrest has become the dominant feature of practice, the same notion is put forward by a leading textwriter, who states flatly that 'bail is the substitution of personal security for that of the *res*'.[1] This view, of course, dovetails very neatly with the procedural theory—bail as the substitution of personal security is logical if the appearance upon which bail is posted has itself the effect of converting the action into one *in personam*.[2] But the same neatness is not present with regard to the proceeding upon a cause of action *in rem* in which there has been no actual arrest of the *res*. This is so because the Admiralty Court 'perfects' its jurisdiction over the *res* by taking it into custody, and the instrument by which that custody is obtained is arrest upon Admiralty warrant;[3] only such arrest can give the Court custody, for only in cases in which the Court has perfected its jurisdiction by arrest of the *res* can the *res* be defaulted and sold by order of the Court.[4] The question therefore arises as to the plausibility of bail as a 'substitution' in cases in which the Court has no custody of the *res* for which to substitute custody of the bail—it is difficult to 'substitute' X for Y, if Y does not exist. But if bail in actions without arrest of the vessel is not a substitute, then it must have some independent nature—a nature which is present today in most of the actions described as *in rem*, for in most of these there is no arrest of the ship.[5]

A hint of the answer is given in one of the first works on Admiralty practice to be published after the Judicature Acts and 1883 Rules: 'The Writ of Summons is addressed "to the owners and parties interested in" the property against which the Action is in effect brought. In terms, therefore, even an Action *in rem* is commenced as though it were a personal Action.'[6] Each action in the Admiralty Court since the Judicature Acts has begun with a writ of summons addressed to the defending party, and thereafter the actions have fallen into one of four categories: (1) the action in which the Court acquires jurisdiction of the cause *in personam* —there is no arrest, the only process served is the writ of summons, and whether by default or adverse judgment the defendant is

---

[1] Roscoe, *Practice*, p. 272. [2] See *The Dictator*, [1892] P. 304, 319.
[3] See Marsden, *Collision*, ¶274, p. 205.
[4] *Annual Practice 1966*, vol. 1, pp. 1863–4.
[5] McGuffie, *Practice*, §232, p. 97.
[6] R. G. M. Browne, p. 19.

personally liable to the extent of the award; (2) the action in which the Court acquires jurisdiction of the cause *in rem*—there is arrest, and both a writ and warrant are served, but the action is undefended and the vessel sold by order of the Court pursuant to a default judgment, and the limit of liability is thus the value of the *res*;[1] (3) the action which is commenced by writ of summons and a warrant *in rem* arresting the vessel—the action is defended and there is personal liability under the procedural theory to pay the amount of the judgment whether or not exceeding the value of the *res*; and (4) the action in which an undertaking has been given—there is no arrest, the only process served is the writ of summons, and if (a) the action is defended there is personal liability to the extent of the award. Now if category (4)(a) is compared to the others, it will be seen to be substantially identical to (1)—the action *in personam*; but the action in category (4) is commenced by a writ of summons *in rem* and the name of the defendant's vessel appears in the title of the cause and in practice the action is designated as an action *in rem*; therefore, if (b) such an action is undefended it would seem to follow that upon a default judgment the Court may without further ado order the sale of the vessel as in category (2). In fact, this cannot be done—for the Court in category (4) has never had jurisdiction over the *res* at all. Authority is unanimous to the effect that in such case:

The judgment is only in the nature of a judgment *against the defendant* on whose behalf the [undertaking or] *caveat* has been entered, [and] it seems that the property cannot be sold, nor can any final judgment be pronounced absolutely affecting the rights of other persons interested in the property until ... similar steps [have been] taken to those required in other actions *in rem* where the property has been arrested.[2]

This statement, in virtually identical wording, is repeated in the latest treatise upon Admiralty practice,[3] and it is clear that both past[4] and present[5] rules of procedure support the statement, as does the general practice manual.[6] Moreover, the point is illustrated in at least one decision,[7] referring to another case[8] in which

---

[1] See Price, *L.M.L.*, p. 118.

[2] Williams and Bruce, 2nd ed., p. 281 (emphasis supplied); see also *The Reina Victoria*, 299 F. 323, 324 (S.D.N.Y. 1924), *per* Learned Hand, D.J.

[3] McGuffie, *Practice*, §645, p. 288.   [4] R.S.C., 1883, O. 29, r. 17.

[5] R.S.C. (Revision) 1962, O. 75, r. 20.

[6] *Annual Practice 1966*, vol. 1, pp. 1863–4.

[7] *The City of Mecca*, (1879) 5 P.D. 28.   [8] *The Troubador*, (1878) [unrep.].

'the Court directed the issue of a warrant after judgment, for the purpose of enforcing payment of an award of salvage.'

In practice, the difficulties of enforcing a default judgment in an action in category (4) are great if attempted against the *res*, for what is required appears to be a complete new action in category (2), and, as the vessel may not be within reach of the Court's process, and cannot be compelled to present herself for service,[1] a considerable delay may ensue. Since the judgment is 'in the nature of a judgment against the defendant',[2] it has, both in the past[3] and in the present,[4] been found more expedient to enforce the judgment in the manner of a default judgment in an action *in personam*. As a result, default judgments *in personam* may not in substance be as rare in modern practice as hitherto thought.[5]

What the nature of the proceeding upon a cause of action *in rem* in which there has been no arrest of the *res* actually is, may be deduced from its characteristics; there is personal service of a copy (and in some cases, the original) of a writ of summons directed to the person, a personal undertaking is given, and there is either a personal appearance or a default judgment against the person, with a personal liability enforceable against the person— all the attributes of an action '*in personam*'. Yet the action—said to be *in rem*—does not proceed against the *res*, does not take the *res* into custody nor give the Court any jurisdiction over it, and cannot result in a default and sale of the *res* unless and until the Court's jurisdiction over it is perfected by arrest—none of the attributes of an action '*in rem*'. Manifestly, an action which proceeds against the person rather than the thing ought not to be called an action *in rem*; this category of action deserves some distinctive term of reference—*quasi-in-rem* would be ideal if not already in use in America to describe maritime attachment[6] and also foreign attachment at common law[7]—and therefore, in deference to its present classification in English Admiralty practice, I suggest the term '*para-in-rem*', by which name this category of action will be hereafter identified in this work; the intended

---

[1] See *Thyssen Steel Corp. v. Federal Commerce & Nav. Co., Ltd.*, 274 F. Supp. 18 (S.D.N.Y. 1967).   [2] Williams and Bruce, 2nd ed., p. 281.
[3] See Williams and Bruce, 1st ed., p. 229.
[4] See McGuffie, *Practice*, §645, p. 289.
[5] See *id.*, p. 247, n. 27a.
[6] See *supra*, p. 165.
[7] See *Hanson v. Denckla*, 357 U.S. 235, 246, n. 12 (1958).

literal significance of this term is that the shipowner, in executing an undertaking (whether or not to procure a caveat), volunteers to submit himself as the subject of an action rather than his ship—and thereby offers his personal liability—in return for which the plaintiff agrees to forego a proceeding against the ship.

Indeed, the action *para-in-rem* is closer in substance to an action *in personam* than was the old 'personal action by way of monition' which was utilized in causes of action *in rem* where the ship was unavailable for arrest. This is so because the action *para-in-rem*, like that *in personam*, may if undefended result in a default judgment against the person, whereas the monition—being only an order to appear and not a process against the person—could if disobeyed result only in a personal attachment for contempt. The most important distinction, however, is that the action *para-in-rem* proceeds directly against the person, whereas the 'traditional' action *in rem* proceeds directly against the *res*—a substantive distinction, which has been hinted at (but not clearly drawn) by such notable English lawyers as Patrick (now Lord) Devlin, K.C.,[1] and Dr Griffith Price.[2]

The greatest irony, therefore, of Sir Francis Jeune's labour to evolve the procedural theory in order to find personal liability in *The Dictator* is that the action in that case, being *para-in-rem*, was at its institution a direct proceeding against the person of the shipowner, who had already undertaken to submit his personal liability. But the procedural theory has ultimately prevailed, and there have been no judicial decisions inconsistent with Jeune's decision in *The Dictator*, according to all of the treatises which have subsequently examined or stated the procedural theory. In fact, that is *not* the case, for two decisions having a considerable bearing upon both the authority of *The Dictator* and the procedural theory exist in the reports—and have elsewhere been virtually ignored.

The first of these decisions was *The Longford*, in which a vessel belonging to the City of Dublin Steam Packet Company was arrested upon an Admiralty warrant *in rem*; the defence of the owners in the Admiralty Court was based upon a portion of a local and personal Act of Parliament dealing with 'any action against the Company'. In giving judgment for the plaintiff, Sir

---

[1] See *The Tolten*, [1946] P. 135, 136.
[2] See Price, *L.M.L.*, p. 42.

Charles Butt held, very simply, that an action *in rem* is a proceeding solely against a *res*, and hence could not in any way be construed as an action against the Company. This view was unanimously affirmed upon appeal, and the appeal dismissed, Lord Esher, M.R., saying: 'That action [*in rem*] is now what it always was, except that the Judicature Act has slightly altered the procedure in regard to it.'[1] Remarkably, though *The Longford* was decided only three years before *The Dictator*, it was neither cited as authority in the argument nor considered by Sir Francis Jeune in the course of his decision; but even more surprisingly, with *The Longford* and *The Dictator* obviously in conflict, *The Longford* was not cited in argument before or cited or considered by the Court of Appeal in *The Gemma*,[2] which wholeheartedly adopted the procedural theory and approved *The Dictator*.

Thus matters stood until 1907, and the second and more direct decision upon the procedural theory in *The Burns*, in which a vessel owned by the London County Council was arrested in an action *in rem*; the Council's defence was based upon a statute of limitations barring actions against 'any person' where the cause arose out of the performance of a public duty. The cause was tried at instance in the Admiralty Division by Sir Bargrave Deane, who held that an action *in rem* could not be an action against a person, and with specific reference to the procedural theory he said:

I see the difficulties and quite appreciate the force of the arguments which have been addressed to me by counsel for the defendants, and on looking at *The Dictator* [*cit.*], which was approved by the Court of Appeal in *The Gemma* [*cit.*], it is clear that in the opinion of the learned judge in that case if the owners appear in an action *in rem* to contest the suit, by their appearance they become responsible not only for the amount of the *res*, but beyond that for extra damage which the *res* might not cover.[3]

Despite the approval of the procedural theory in *The Gemma*, this decision of Deane, J., was clearly in conflict with the notion of personal liability in actions *in rem*; as would be expected, therefore, the cause was taken up on appeal. Again as might be expected, the argument of Scrutton, K.C., before the Court of

---

[1] *The Longford*, (1889) 14 P.D. 34, 37 [App.].
[2] [1899] P. 285 [App.].
[3] *The Burns*, [1907] P. 137, 139.
    cf. The Monte A., 12 F. 332 (S.D.N.Y. 1882); p. 175, *supra*.

Appeal on behalf of the County Council premised that *The Gemma*'s approval of Jeune P's. rationale in *The Dictator* was binding as to Jeune's statement that arrest of the *res* was solely a device to compel the personal appearance of the owner, and that the action *in rem* was, in the end, merely a different way of proceeding against the person.[1] The Court of Appeal, however, affirmed the decision of Deane, J., below—and the crucial point was dealt with by Lord Justice Fletcher Moulton, who said of Scrutton's argument:

> I am of opinion that this view cannot be supported. The two cases upon which counsel have chiefly relied—*The Dictator* [*cit.*] and *The Gemma* [*cit.*]—appear to me to negative and not to support that proposition. They both of them treat the appearance as introducing the characteristics of an action in personam. In other words, it is not the institution of the suit that makes it a proceeding in personam, but the appearance of the defendant. And further, I think that *the contrary is conclusively established by the case of The Bold Buccleugh* [*cit.*], supported and approved as it was by the House of Lords in the case of *Currie v. M'Knight* [*cit.*].[2]

Thus Moulton, L.J., repudiated the essential of the procedural theory—that the action *in rem* is a procedural device—and in effect overruled Jeune's holding in that regard.

As to the matter of personal liability, it was the view of Dr Lushington, expressed in *The Volant*,[3] that the process in an action *in rem* only called upon the owners to appear to defend their interest, and that, the extent of their interest being the value of the ship, their liability ought not to be greater than the interest possessed by them in the ship which they appeared to defend. But the Judicature Acts and 1883 Rules changed the form of the process (though the 'persons interested' are still cited[4]), so that it might be thought the introduction of a personally-served writ had altered the situation, connoting thereafter a proceeding directed against the persons of the owners. This point was also taken up by Moulton, L.J., as follows:

> I am ... of opinion that the action in rem is an action against the ship itself ... it is evident from the language of that [pre-Judicature Acts] warrant that the process was regarded then as being directed against the

---

[1] *The Burns*, [1907] P. 137, 141 [App.].
[2] *Id.*, at 148 (emphasis supplied).   [3] (1842) 1 W. Rob. 383, 388.
[4] R.S.C. 1966, form of Admiralty writ *in rem*.

ship itself. That old form was abandoned, and a new form of writ was employed, by . . . the Judicature Act . . . in 1883 . . . the rule was passed which directed the present form of writ to be issued in Admiralty actions in rem. The direction itself shews that . . . the writ was intended to apply to the old-established Admiralty action in rem, and was not intended to have the effect of creating a new type of action or altering the nature of the action . . .[1]

Though the cases of *The Longford* and *The Burns* arose upon points of statutory interpretation, they nevertheless stand as authority contrary to the procedural theory of actions *in rem*, and have never been judicially considered in any attempt to resolve the conflicting views. *The Longford* was cited in argument in the case of *The Dupleix*,[2] which first gave recovery beyond the value of the ship under the procedural theory, but Sir Samuel Evans, P., neither cited nor considered *The Longford* in the course of his decision; and neither *The Longford* nor *The Burns* was cited in argument or decision in *The Joannis Vatis* (*No.* 2),[3] which approved, per Lord Merrivale, P., the *Dictator–Gemma–Dupleix* case line and the procedural theory.

What is more surprising is that textwriters of the present century have likewise made no attempt to resolve the conflict of authority; but there is perhaps an explanation for this. The leading text upon Admiralty Practice for many years was that of E. S. Roscoe, who, having been appointed Admiralty Registrar by Sir Francis Jeune, P., in 1904, could scarcely have been unaware of the decision in *The Burns* in 1907; but either through oversight or in deference to the procedural theory, which he heartily endorsed, Roscoe omitted in his subsequent editions any mention of either *The Longford* or *The Burns* in his consideration of the nature of the proceeding *in rem*, and instead, citing the *Dictator–Gemma–Dupleix* case line as authority, he asserted that 'an action *in rem* is not a limited process against a particular thing, but a process auxiliary to the ordinary process against individuals'[4]—a view diametrically opposed to the decisions of the Court of Appeal in *The Burns* and *The Longford*. The influence of Roscoe's text, particularly as the author was Admiralty Registrar, has naturally been very great, and it may be that this influence was felt by the author of a later and most competent study of the

---

[1] *The Burns*, [1907] P. 137, 149.   [2] [1912] P. 8.
[3] [1922] P. 213.   [4] Roscoe, *Practice*, p. 272.

law of maritime liens, Dr Griffith Price, who likewise did not consider either *The Longford* or *The Burns* in the course of his lengthy discussion of the procedural theory. Certainly the effect of Roscoe's text upon judicial decision was considerable, for in the case of *The Majfrid*, Bucknill, J., granting recovery in excess of bail in an action *in rem*, cited the statement in Roscoe's text quoted above, saying: 'I have taken my statement of the law very largely from Mr. Roscoe's book.'[1]

Textwriters of the present day have cited *The Longford* and *The Burns* for the proposition that 'an action *in rem* is an action against a *res*',[2] and that changes in form by the Judicature Acts and 1883 Rules did not alter the previous character of actions *in rem*,[3] but as yet no attempt has been made to reconcile the major incongruities.

Unless and until the incongruities affecting the modern English Admiralty action *in rem* [and *para-in-rem*] are resolved, some difficulty with regard to the effectiveness of English Admiralty judgments may arise abroad, and by way of illustration I will point to difficulties which might arise in North American courts. Primarily, these may occur because of the fact that Admiralty Courts in the United States and Canada 'have universally followed the doctrine of *The Bold Buccleugh*',[4] regarding the execution of maritime liens in actions *in rem*, and the collateral rule that liens are not executed by 'fruitless actions *in personam*'.[5] Arguments to the effect that bail 'is equivalent to the arrest of the res'[6] to the contrary notwithstanding, this writer has yet to see a decision or hear a cogent argument holding that bail in an action *in personam* (or *para-in-rem*) works execution of a maritime lien upon a vessel over which the Court has not perfected jurisdiction. The point has been made by English authority, such as Lush, J., 'I do not see how it was possible for them to carry and execute a maritime lien when they [Portuguese Courts] had not possession of the thing'.[7] And by American authority such as Judge Ware, who said—relying upon Lord Stowell—that the ship must be within

---

[1] *The Majfrid*, (1943) 77 Ll. L.R. 127, 129.

[2] *Annual Practice 1966*, vol. 1, p. 1863, n.

[3] McGuffie, *Practice*, §9 , p. 10.

[4] *Partenreederei Wallschiff v. The Pioneer*, 120 F. Supp. 525, 527 (E.D. Mich., S. Div. 1954).   [5] Price, *L.M.L.*, p. 88.

[6] *The Christiansborg*, (1884) 10 P.D. 141, 155 [per Fry, L.J.].

[7] *The City of Mecca*, (1881) 6 P.D. 106, 118 [App.].

the jurisdiction of the Court in order to operate directly upon it; indeed, Judge Ware's statement has direct applicability to the action *para-in-rem* in which the ship is proceeded against while absent from the Court's jurisdiction: 'In proceedings in rem, the forum rei sitae is the natural and proper forum, for it is the only one which can make its jurisdiction effectual by operating directly on the thing [*cit.*]. A court sitting in another jurisdiction can only reach the thing through the person of the owner.'[1] The same is agreed by Dr Price, who said that to him it 'seems logical, that to proceed *in rem* a plaintiff must be in a position to arrest a wrong-doing *res*'.[2]

Essentially, it is the current popularly-accepted English view that the action *in rem* commences with the issuance of the writ of summons—that this alone is sufficient to 'seize' the jurisdiction of the Admiralty Court, and that actual arrest (or the lack thereof) cannot therefore make the action any more or less *in rem* than at its institution. Moreover, the view has been expressed to this writer that the 1956 Act, in setting forth the conditions whereby an action is brought *in rem*,[3] has eliminated any controversy which might have existed under the prior law—and the same view has recently received judicial expression.[4] But I must say, that view appears to disregard the significance of the warrant as the instrument by which the Court has since the earliest times perfected its jurisdiction over the *res*; it is the indifferent—or, if one prefers, disagreeable—existence of the *fact* that the Court cannot act directly upon the *res* (*i.e.*, *in rem*) without perfecting jurisdiction by arrest under warrant,[5] which transcends semantic dispute over the form in which the plaintiff institutes his action and thereby indicates the direction in which he **wishes** it to proceed. It seems to follow that what is embodied in the writ is the **potential** of the action, and that the **actual** proceeding against the *res* does not commence until process enables the Court to exercise directly upon the vessel the jurisdiction *in rem* conferred by the 1956 Act.

The situation which actually prevails in the United States is more difficult to evaluate, principally because the *res* must be in a

---

[1] *The Bee*, 3 Fed. Cas. 41, 43 (No. 1219) (D. Me. 1836).
[2] Price, *L.M.L.*, p. 42.   [3] Administration of Justice Act, 1956, §§3(2), (3), (4).
[4] *The Monica S.*, [1967] 2 Ll. Rep. 113, 131–2.
[5] *Supra*, p. 196.

position to be arrested before an action *in rem* can be maintained.[1] But it is still necessary for arrest under warrant to have been effected in order for the Court to be able to decree a sale of the *res*,[2] and one must therefore conclude that any action in which the defendant has given a general or special bond to prevent arrest is merely *para-in-rem*, with personal liability the absolute and fundamental consequence.[3]

It is even more remarkable that the basic question has thus far escaped the focus of attention in America, because a flurry of excitement has been aroused by the innovation at common law of personal liability in excess of *res* value in actions *quasi-in-rem* [foreign attachment] upon **default** judgments taken after notice to the defendant; the theory has a familiar ring—notice converts an action *quasi-in-rem* into one *in personam*.[4] Moreover, there have been holdings in American Admiralty that personal liability may exceed *res* value in actions *in rem*,[5] that actual arrest is not necessary in actions *in rem*,[6] and even that the action *in rem* employs the fiction of personification to satisfy a claim whose true nature is *in personam*.[7] The overwhelming weight of authority, however, establishes in the Admiralty Law of the United States that the value of the *res* is the limit of liability in actions *in rem*,[8] that personification, while patently a fiction, nonetheless gives rise to an action which is truly against the ship rather than the owner,[9] and that arrest is the foundation of jurisdiction *in rem*.[10] The roots of this modern doctrine tap the jurisprudential wisdom of Mr Justice Story,[11] Judge Ware,[12] and others.[13] It reflects poorly indeed upon the Admiralty Bar as well as upon the Bench, that in general the names—much less the decisions—of the most eminent Admiralty jurists of the nation have been almost completely forgotten in present-day American practice. There are certain types of cases which call for close examination of the fundamentals

---

[1] F.R.C.P. [1 July 1966], Adm. Rule C. (2).   [2] *Id.*, Rules C.(5), E.(9).
[3] *The Ulrik Holm*, 298 F. 849, 851, 853 (1 Cir. 1924), and cases cited therein.
[4] See *Fishman v. Sanders*, 15 N.Y. 2d 298; 258 N.Y.S. 2d 380; 206 N.E. 2d 326 (Ct. App. N.Y. 1965). But *cf.* N.Y. Civil Practice Law and Rules, R. 320 (c) (1) [1969].   [5] See *supra*, p. 183, nn. 5–8.   [6] See *supra*, p. 193, n. 8.
[7] See *The Caribe* (*Pichirilo v. Guzman*), 290 F.2d 812 (1 Cir. 1961).
[8] See *supra*, p. 183, n. 9.
[9] See *supra*, p. 194, n. 1.   [10] See *supra*, p. 193, n. 6; *infra*, p. 206, n. 2.
[11] *The Palmyra*, 12 Wheat. (25 U.S.) 1 (1827).
[12] *The Orpheus*, 15 Fed. Cas. 492 (No. 8330) (D. Mass. 1858).
[13] *The Berkeley*, 58 Fed. 920 (D. So. Car. 1893).

of jurisdiction *in rem*, the most common perhaps being those involving transfer of actions *in rem* between Districts; this is a problem over which American Courts of Admiralty have long agonized, and yet the distinction between those cases in which the *res* has actually come within the jurisdiction of the Court by arrest under warrant, and those in which the owner has substituted personal liability to prevent arrest, has not been clearly drawn as a step toward solution.[1]

Aside from the probability that an American Court considering the effect of an action *para-in-rem* upon a maritime lien would not hold the lien executed by such an action and would permit arrest of the ship in an action *in rem* upon the same cause earlier tried in the English action—to the obvious detriment of shipowners who had given undertakings in England—it is likely that an American Court would refuse to permit enforcement *in rem* of a judgment given in an English action *para-in-rem*. The enforcement of foreign Admiralty judgments by American Courts is a policy of long standing,[2] and in keeping with the principle of comity in international maritime law, but even English precedent acknowledges that a foreign judgment given in an action against the person will not be enforced by a domestic action *in rem*,[3] and the same rule is established in the United States by a case with both *para-in-rem* and English involvements, *The Harrogate*.[4] In that case, the owners of the *Hazelmere*, with which the *Harrogate* had been in collision, caused a writ of summons *in rem* to issue from the Admiralty Division; however, as a later American decision noted, 'there was no arrest of the ship, but, as in the United States practice, the owners gave bail as substitution for the seizure and appeared'.[5] The judgment in the Admiralty Division held the *Harrogate* solely at fault, and subsequently the owners of a damaged cargo of oats aboard the *Hazelmere* caused the *Harrogate* to be libelled *in rem* and arrested in the Eastern District of New York. Upon the hearing, only the English decree was submitted to the District Court as evidence of fault, and enforcement of that judgment was prayed; the District Court held the English decree not *res judicata* and dismissed the libel. The U.S. Court

[1] But *cf. Internatio-Rotterdam v. Thomsen*, 218 F. 2d 514 (4 Cir. 1955).
[2] See *Penhallow v. Doane's Administrators*, 3 Dall. (3 U.S.) 54 (1795).
[3] *The City of Mecca*, (1881) 6 P.D. 106 [App.].   [4] 112 F. 1019 (2 Cir. 1901).
[5] *The General Pershing (Criscuolo v. Atlas Imperial Diesel Engine Co.)*, 84 F.2d 273, 276 (9 Cir. 1936).

of Appeals, Second Circuit, affirmed the dismissal on grounds that there had been no arrest or publication of arrest, etc., in the English action; the Supreme Court of the United States denied a petition for review by *certiorari*,[1] and *The Harrogate* therefore enunciates a binding principle which has been recognized in a number of subsequent decisions that affirm arrest of the *res* as a necessary prerequisite to jurisdiction *in rem*.[2]

For the same reasons which indicate that an English *para-in-rem* proceeding might not bar a subsequent action *in rem* elsewhere, the reverse proposition seems to have been recognized in the recent case of *The Mansoor*.[3] There an undertaking was given in Antwerp to prevent arrest of the *Mansoor* in Belgium upon a cause of collision; subsequently, plaintiffs who had accepted the undertaking in Belgium obtained a writ *in rem* against the *Mansoor* in the Admiralty Division. Mr Justice Cairns, on a motion to set aside the writ and stay proceedings, first observed that the defendants ought to have been aware of the possibility of a subsequent action, and then said:

I am satisfied that the plaintiffs were entitled to bring an action in respect of their damage in the Courts of another country notwithstanding their acceptance of the defendants' undertaking . . . But did the fact that the present action is an action *in rem* make it a breach of faith? In my opinion it did not.[4]

In dismissing the motion, Cairns, J., then put a finger upon the vital distinction in the case at bar, *viz.*:

It is not as if the only way of proceeding in an action *in rem* were arrest of the ship or the obtaining of further bail. The *plaintiffs deliberately refrained from arresting* the *Mansoor* when they could have done [in England] . . . If I dismiss this application the action will become one *in personam* as well as *in rem*.[5]

Thus in *The Mansoor*, a foreign action *para-in-rem* was no bar to the subsequent English action [*para-*] *in rem*, actual arrest never having been effected in either.

The basic philosophy of the American position has been well put by the late Chief Justice Charles Evans Hughes:

The proceeding *in rem* which is within the exclusive jurisdiction of

---

[1] *Cert. den.* 184 U.S. 698.
[2] *E.g., The Transfer No. 7*, 176 F. 2d 950 (2 Cir. 1949), and cases cited therein.
[3] [1968] 2 Ll. Rep. 218.   [4] *Id.*, at p. 227.   [5] *Ibid.* (emphasis supplied).

Admiralty is one essentially against the vessel itself ... By virtue of dominion over the thing all persons interested in it are deemed to be parties to the suit; the decree binds all the world, and under it the property itself passes, and not merely the title or interest of a personal defendant ... [Even] actions in personam with a concurrent attachment to afford security for the payment of a personal judgment are in a different category.[1]

Under a strict reading of the American position, then, the action *para-in-rem* would be viewed as an action *in personam*, and even the typical English action with arrest of the ship but terminating in a personal judgment might be viewed as a form of Admiralty attachment in a proceeding essentially against the person, and therefore not enforceable by action *in rem* elsewhere—a very real possibility in view of the procedural theory's declaration that a personal appearance in an action *in rem* changes its character to that of an action *in personam*.

The delightful irony of the American position is, of course, that its jurisprudence is as easily applicable to the proceeding *para-in-rem* in the United States as to that in England; but ironies aside, the potential for serious problems remains—albeit in the background—for so long as the two modern views stay unreconciled with each other as well as with their internal contradictions. One approach to resolution lies via the judiciary, but there may be considerable resistance to overcome, *viz.*:

Where general principles of law have been laid down by learned judges in considered judgments, it does not appear to me to be right, or in the public interest, to look minutely at the facts of the particular case and to say that the case might have been decided on narrower grounds, and that the general principles need not have been enunciated, and that, therefore, they are to have no judicial authority.[2]

This position, the writer submits, though put forth by a worthy Admiralty Judge—Sir Samuel Evans, P.—is itself unworthy of the jurisprudence of the common law; one cannot, however, ignore the difficulties which beset judges in ruling upon such matters, and the restrictions pointed out by Brandon, J., are valid, *viz.*:

It is no doubt helpful to see what views have been expressed in textbooks

---

[1] *Rounds v. Cloverport Foundry & Machine Co.*, 237 U.S. 303, 304 (1915).
[2] *The Dupleix*, [1912] P. 8, 13.

over the years. But in the end I have to determine this question not on the views of textbook writers and editors, however eminent, but by construing the relevant statutes with the guidance of the cases decided on them.[1]

Ultimately, though, with the realization that even the finest scholars of English Admiralty have based the whole of their considerations in the area of the action *in rem* upon the premise that the procedural theory as propounded in *The Dictator* was both historically accurate and judicially unchallenged,[2] the necessity must also be realized for some judicial review of the present position which will either successfully reconcile its incongruities, or will put into practice the principles recently enunciated by the House of Lords regarding the status of judicial precedent.[3] The alternative would seem to be a diplomatic approach, seeking to embody the solution in an international convention; this, however, would be much more difficult of accomplishment—the writer well knows that Americans, for example, are notoriously talkative but inactive in this regard.

But whatever the future holds for English Admiralty, the historical point must be made that the substantive Law of Admiralty has undergone considerable change in the period since the scholarly training of the civilians was replaced by the interpretive faculties of the common lawyers. The action *para-in-rem* is a civilian legacy, but the procedural theory (and its ramifications) was and is essentially a creature of the common law.

It is that amalgamation of civilian legacy and common law creativity which has profoundly affected the Admiralty Law of England during the period spanned by this work.

---

[1] *The Monica S.*, [1968] P. 741, 768.
[2] *E.g.*, Price, *L.M.L.*, p. 117.
[3] *Practice Statement (Judicial Precedent)*, [1966] 1 W.L.R. 1234 [H.L.].

CONCLUSION

THE theme of this study becomes apparent only at the last: the development of Admiralty jurisdiction and practice since 1800 has not been confined to the dry stuff of enactments and repeals, or even to the more interesting matter of establishment, following of or departure from judicial precedents. Men, as types and individuals, have been responsible for the Law during every second of every day; it is the change in the philosophy of men—sometimes slow and sometimes abrupt—which gives substance to raw and otherwise uninspiring data.

Some have viewed one important change as a great conquest of the civilians by the common lawyers, and lamented the change in the status and structure of the Admiralty Court. But while the facts of history may legitimately give rise to lament for the passing of a noble body of scholars and the venerable status of the Court as a direct instrument of the Royal Prerogative, it must be observed that this development has had no great effect upon either the function or operation of the Court. It was noted after Sir Robert Phillimore's retirement that the intimate atmosphere of the Court under the civilians had not wholly changed with the move to the Strand and a common lawyer upon the bench,[1] and the picture today is still one of a calm and unhurried administration of maritime justice, free from the drama and sensation of juries and crowds of spectators, and with a small and select professional attendance. And yet it cannot be denied that there have been developments apart from changes in simple philosophy—the transition in doctrine from: 'the ship itself is responsible in the admiralty, and not the owners',[2] to: 'an action *in rem* is not a limited process against a particular thing, but a process auxiliary to the ordinary process against individuals',[3] is one of the more dramatic illustrations.

The observation of R. G. Marsden that 'the chequered career of the court accounts for much of this uncertainty in its law',[4] is both shrewd and accurate. But the degree of change in the Admiralty Law as a whole would certainly have been much greater had not

---

[1] Roscoe, *H.C.A.*, p. 14.　　　　[2] Maxwell, p. 8.
[3] Roscoe, *Practice*, p. 272.　　　[4] 'Six Centuries', p. 176.

the common lawyers, once the Court of Admiralty had passed into their hands, shown an unexpected concern for the preservation and extension of the legal system bequeathed by the civilians. Only in relatively few respects has the procedure and substance of the common law intruded into Admiralty. And even where change has taken place as a result of misapprehension of Admiralty jurisprudence, such as in the classification by the 1883 Rules of a proceeding for apportionment and distribution of salvage as an action *in rem*,[1] there has been a good deal of rectification; the action just described, for example, has now been properly reclassified as one *in personam*.[2] Adaptation and extention of the principles of the Law of Admiralty are also evident in the statutory provisions which have given the Court jurisdiction over claims involving aircraft,[3] and the liberal scope of recent enactments such as the 1956 Administration of Justice Act evokes visions of a comprehensive Admiralty jurisdiction which might at some time in the future see the Court again trying causes such as slander at sea (a maritime tort), even as they came before Dr Lewes four centuries ago,[4] and come before American judges today.[5]

F. W. Maitland called Lord Stowell's service as Admiralty Judge the civilians' 'chief contribution to the jurisprudence of the world'.[6] Yet in the present that great heritage, together with the entire jurisprudence of the civil law in general and of the Law of Admiralty in particular, strives for recognition against the most formidable barrier which can be imagined—an almost total lack of interest. In great measure, this is due to the shortsightedness and perhaps even the selfishness of the last of the civilians themselves, for had they not voted to dissolve the College of Advocates, Doctors' Commons might have fulfilled the great role envisioned for it by Dr Lee, who pleaded in 1858 that 'The wants of the age point to the necessity of a collegiate institution for furnishing the means of education in those branches of jurisprudence, which are the sources and contain the principles of maritime and international law.'[7]

The wants of the present in this regard are no less severe than

[1] R.S.C., 1883, O. 5, r. 16(38)(d). [2] McGuffie, *Practice*, §425, p.189.
[3] *E.g.*, Administration of Justice Act, 1956, §§1(1)(*j–l*), (3) (5).
[4] *E.g.*, *Raynes c. Osborne*, (1579) 2 *Sel. Pl. Adm.* 156.
[5] *E.g.*, *Foster v. United States*, 156 F. Supp. 421 (S.D.N.Y. 1957).
[6] See Senior, p. 109.
[7] Parl. Paper [1859] (19) xxii (H.C. 20 January), p. 14.

were those of Dr Lee's day, but they have not been supplied. Where the great scholars of the maritime law who were both Fellows of Doctors' Commons and teachers of the law once answered the need for instruction, not one of the Universities of England is today prepared to give instruction in the Law of Admiralty. The bald statement that the Admiralty Court of the present is a court of civil law evidently has the power to elicit surprise and even shock, but it is nonetheless a true statement, and will continue to be for so long as the law applied by that Court is that portion of the civil law which is the Admiralty Law; unless some entirely novel code is invented to supplant the Law of Admiralty which has descended from the prerogative power of the Lord High Admiral, and which will not take as its basis the mercantile and maritime law, the law of the Admiralty Court will remain a part of the civil law. With this must come the realization that the extinction of the English civilians did not ordain the extinction of the English civil law, and with that realization must come in turn an understanding that a living branch of the English legal system is deserving of more formal study than it has enjoyed in the present century.

Illustrations of the necessity for this abound even in the honest efforts of the common lawyers of the present day to preserve the essentials of the Law of Admiralty while extending its operation, such as the construction of the Administration of Justice Act, 1956, which purports to allow an action *in personam* upon causes of bottomry.[1] It was elementary knowledge even to the common lawyers of the last century that the shipowner could never be held personally liable upon a bottomry bond, because the essence of bottomry is the pledge of the keel of the ship rather than the credit of the owner;[2] thus one result of indifference to Admiralty jurisprudence in the twentieth century—encouraged in this instance by the virtual disappearance of bottomry suits—has been the enactment of a monstrous paradox.

Perhaps the final irony of reconstruction of the courts of civil law and their consolidation with the common law courts in a single structure has been the 'discovery' of an unreconstructed court of civil law in which—long after the extinction of the civilians —common lawyers technically do not possess the right of audience.

---

[1] Administration of Justice Act, 1956 §§3(1), 1(1)(r).
[2] See, *e.g.*, *Stainbank v. Fenning*, (1851) 11 C.B. 51, 89.

This is, of course, the High Court of Chivalry [Constable and Marshal], which was not dealt with at all by the Judicature or Consolidation Acts because it had fallen into dormancy in the eighteenth century and was not awakened until a cause within its exclusive jurisdiction came to hearing in 1954. The story of its revival has been well and interestingly told in a work which also reveals how similar was the constitution and procedure of the Court of Chivalry to the old Court of Admiralty.[1] A familiarity with the procedures and principles of the civil law might have been somewhat useful to many of those concerned with the handling of the Court of Chivalry's most recent case (but the fitting and proper course was at any rate taken of reporting the decision together with those of the P.D.A. Division[2]).

The greatest goal ahead lies not in further extensions of Admiralty jurisdiction, nor in refinements of procedure or practice, but in the fostering of knowledge and appreciation of Admiralty jurisprudence. If the old hostility between Admiralty and the common law has 'even in our own days ... shown a spark or two of life',[3] then it is because even such a great scholar of the common law as Mr Justice Oliver Wendell Holmes, in saying of the Law of Admiralty that: 'There is no mystic overlaw to which the United States must bow',[4] had thereby to indicate that the Law of Admiralty was to him a mysterious thing. Removal of the mystery will only be accomplished through the achievement of an understanding of the jurisprudence of Admiralty; perhaps this examination of the development of the Court of Admiralty, with some light upon its jurisprudence, will prove useful in that direction.

It is with that wish—and in quest of that goal—that this work has been undertaken.

[1] Squibb, pp. 12–13, 17.
[2] *Manchester Corporation v. Manchester Palace of Varieties, Ltd.*, [1955] P. 133 [High Court of Chivalry].
[3] Marsden, 'Six Centuries', p. 169.
[4] *The Western Maid*, 257 U.S. 419, 432 (1921).

BIBLIOGRAPHY

Abbott, Charles [Lord Tenterden]: *Abbott's Law of Merchant Ships and Seamen*, 14th (Aspinall and Moore) edition, London, 1901.

Ackermann, Rudolph: *Microcosm of London*, vol. 1 of 3, London, 1808.

'Admiralty Court and its Reform', 5 *L. Mag. & Rev.* 34 (1858).

'Admiralty Court', 77 *L.J.* 53 (1934).

Benedict, Erastus C.: *The American Admiralty: its Jurisdiction and Practice with Practical Forms and Directions*, 5th (McCloskey) edition, vol. 1 of 3, Albany, New York, 1925.

Betts, S. R.: *U.S. Admiralty Practice in the Southern District of New York*, New York, 1838.

Black, H. C.: *Black's Law Dictionary*, 4th edition, St Paul, 1957.

Boyd, A. C.: *The Merchant Shipping Laws*, London, 1876.

Brown, [Judge] Addison, *Index-Digest of Decisions*, Lancaster, Pennsylvania, 1902.

Browne, Arthur, LL.D.: *Compendious View of the Civil Law and the Law of the Admiralty*, 2nd edition, vol. 2 of 2, London, 1802.

Browne, R. G. M.: *Admiralty Procedure against Merchant Ships and Cargoes*, London, 1887.

Campbell, Lord John: *Lives of Lord Lyndhurst and Lord Brougham*, London, 1869.

Chronological Table of the Statutes, 1235–1965, London, 1966.

Civil Judicial Statistics, London [annual].

Clerke, Francis: *Practice of the High Court of Admiralty [Praxis Supremae Curiae Admiralitatis]*. Oughton, ed., London, 1829.

Coke, Sir Edward: *The Fourth Part of the Institutes of the Laws of England, Concerning the Jurisdiction of Courts*, London, 1797.

Conkling, Alfred: *Admiralty Jurisdiction, Law and Practice* [U.S.], 1st edition, Albany, New York, 1848.

Coote, H. C.: *Practice of the High Court of Admiralty*, 1st & 2nd editions, London, 1860, 1869.

Dicey: *Conflict of Laws*, 7th edition, London, 1958.

Dictionary of American Biography, New York, 1958 *et seq.*

Dictionary of National Biography, [Sir L. Stephen & Sir S. Lee, eds.], London, 1882 *et seq.*

Dunlap, Andrew: *Admiralty Practice in the United States*, 2nd (S. F. Dunlap) edition, New York, 1850.

Dunne, G. T.: 'Joseph Story', 77 *Harvard Law Review* 240 (1964).

Edwards, Edwin, LL.D.: *Jurisdiction of the High Court of Admiralty of England*, London, 1847.

English and Empire Digest, vol. 1 [*Admiralty*], London, 1961.

'Evidence Receivable in Admiralty', 50 *L. Mag.* 57 (1853).

Farwell, CAPT. R. F. and Prunski, LCDR. A.: *Rules of the Nautical Road*, 4th edition, Annapolis, Md., 1968.

Fifoot, C. H. S., ed.: *Letters of Frederic William Maitland*, London, 1965.

Gilmore, Grant, and Black, C. L.: *The Law of Admiralty* [U.S.], Brooklyn, New York, 1957.

Gloag, W. M., and Henderson, R. C.: *Introduction to the Law of Scotland*, 6th (Gibb & Walker) edition, Edinburgh, 1956.

Hall, J. E.: *Practice and Jurisdiction of the Court of Admiralty* [U.S.], Baltimore, 1809.

Halsbury's Laws of England, 3rd (Simonds) edition, London, 1952 & cumulative supplements.

Halsbury's Statutes of England, 2nd (Burrows) edition, London, 1948 & cumulative supplements.

Haynes, J. F.: *Student's Guide to Admiralty*, London, 1880.

Hebert, Paul M.: 'The Origin and Nature of Maritime Liens', 4 *Tulane Law Rev.* 381 (1930).

Heuston, R. F. V.: *Lives of the Lord Chancellors 1885–1940*, Oxford, 1964.

'High Court of Admiralty', 76 *L.T.* 286 (1884).

'History of Admiralty Jurisdiction in the Supreme Court of the United States', 5 *Am. L. Rev.* 581 (1871).

Holdsworth, Sir W. S.: *Charles Dickens as a Legal Historian*, New Haven, 1929.

Holdsworth, Sir W. S.: *A History of English Law*, 7th (Goodhart & Hanbury) edition, 16 volumes, London, 1956–66.

Holt, F. L.: *System of the Shipping and Navigation Laws of Great Britain*, 2nd edition, London, 1824.

Hough, C. M.: *The United States District Court for the Southern District of New York, 1789–1919*, New York, 1934.

Howell, Alfred: *Admiralty Law* [Canada], Toronto, 1893.

Ivamy, E. R. H.: 'Admiralty Court: Sixth Centenary', 110 *L.J.* 330 (1960).

Kent, [Chancellor] James: *Commentaries on American Law*, 8th (W. Kent) edition, New York, 1854.

McGuffie, K. C.: *Notes on Four Admiralty Registry Letter Books*, London, 1964.

McGuffie, K. C., Fugeman and Gray: *Admiralty Practice*, London, 1964 and supplement 1965.

McGuffie, K. C. *et al.*: *The Annual Practice, 1966*, London, 1965, 1966.

MacLachlan, D.: *A Treatise on the Law of Merchant Shipping*, 7th (Pilcher & Bateson) edition, London, 1932.

McMillan, A. R. G.: *Scottish Maritime Practice*, Edinburgh and Glasgow, 1926.

Marriott, Sir James: *Formulary of Instruments* [*Formulare Instrumentorum*], London, 1802.

Marsden, R. G.: *Select Pleas in the Court of Admiralty (1390–1602)*, 2 volumes, London, 1894 and 1897.

Marsden, R. G.: 'Jurisdiction of Admiralty; The Zeta', 10 *L.Q.R.* 113 (1894).

Marsden, R. G.: 'Six Centuries of the Admiralty Court', *Nautical Magazine*, February 1898 *et seq.*

Marsden, R. G.: *Digest of Cases relating to Shipping and Marine Insurance from Elizabeth I to end of 1897*, 1st edition, London, 1899.

Marsden, R. G.: *The Law of Collisions at Sea*, 11th (McGuffie) edition, London, 1961 and supplement 1965.

Maxwell, J. I.: *The Spirit of Marine Law*, 1st edition, London, 1800.

Merriman, Sir F. B. [Lord Merriman]: *Address to the Canadian Bar Association, 28 August 1935.*

Moore, E. G.: *An Introduction to English Canon Law*, Oxford, 1967.

Nys, Ernest: *Le Droit Romain, le Droit des Gens, et le Collège des Docteurs en Droit Civil*, Brussels, 1910.

Papers Relating to the Proposed 1855 H.C.A. Rules, London, 1855.

Parry, Clive, ed.: *British Digest of International Law*, volumes 7 & 8, London, 1965.

Parsons, Theophilus: *A Treatise on the Law and Practice of Admiralty* [U.S.], vol. 2 of 2, Boston, 1869.

'Personification of Vessels', 77 *H.L.R.* 1122 (1964).

Price, Griffith: *The Law of Maritime Liens*, London, 1940.

Price, Griffith: 'Statutory Rights *in rem* in English Admiralty Law', 27 *J.C.L. & I.L.* (3rd ser.) 21 (1945).

Pritchard, W. T., and Hannen, J. C.: *Digest of Law and Practice of the Court of Admiralty*, 3rd edition, 2 volumes, London, 1887.

'Prospects of the Admiralty Court', *10 L. Mag. & Rev.* 262 (1861).

Public Record Office: *Guide to Contents*, 2 volumes, London, 1963.

Reddie, James: *Researches in Maritime International Law*, vol. 1 of 2, Edinburgh, 1844–1845.

Reeve, F. A.: *Cambridge*, London, 1964.

Roberts, David: *A Treatise on Admiralty and Prize* [U.S.], New York, 1869.

Robinson, Gustavus Hill: *Handbook of Admiralty Law in the United States*, St Paul, 1939.

Roscoe, E. S.: *The High Court of Admiralty—The Last Phase*, London, 1927.

Roscoe, E. S.: *Admiralty Jurisdiction and Practice*, 5th (Hutchinson) edition, London, 1931.

Roscoe, E. S.: *Studies in the History of the Admiralty and Prize Courts*, 2nd edition, London, 1932.

Roscoe, E. S.: *Lord Stowell, His Life and the Development of English Prize Law*, London, 1916.

Rothery, H. C.: *Suggestions for an Improved Mode of Pleading*, London, 1853.

Saunders, Albert: *Maritime Law*, 2nd edition, London, 1920.

Senior, William: *Doctors' Commons and the Old Court of Admiralty*, London, 1922.

Setaro, F. C.: 'The Formative Years of American Admiralty', 5 *New York Law Forum* 9 (1959).

Smith, T. E.: *Law and Practice in Admiralty*, 4th edition, London, 1892.

Squibb, G. D.: *The High Court of Chivalry*, Oxford, 1959.

Talbot, G. F.: *Ashur Ware*, Address to the Maine Historical Society, 20 May 1887.

Temperley, R.: *The Merchant Shipping Acts*, Porges and Thomas ed., London, 1964 and supplement 1965.

Thompson, G. H. M.: *Admiralty Registrars*, McGuffie ed., London, 1958.

Twiss, Sir T., ed.: *Black Book of the Admiralty*, 4 volumes, London, 1871–6.

Ubbelohde, Carl: *The Vice-Admiralty Courts and the American Revolution*, Chapel Hill, North Carolina, 1960.

Van Heythuysen, F. M.: *An Essay upon Marine Evidence*, London, 1819.

Wendt, E. E.: *Papers on Maritime Legislation*, 3rd edition, London, 1888.

Who Was Who, Chicago, *1943 et seq.*

Who's Who, 1966, London, 1966.

'Why Abolish the Admiralty Court?', 177 *L.T.* 54 (1934).

Williams, R. G., and Bruce, Sir G.: *Jurisdiction and Practice of the English Courts in Admiralty Actions and Appeals*, 1st, 2nd & 3rd editions, London, 1868, 1886, 1902.

Wiswall, F. L., Jr: 'Admiralty: Procedural Unification in Retrospect and Prospect', *35 Brooklyn Law Review* 36 (1968); *161 New York Law Journal* 4, Nos. 15–17 (22–4 January 1969).

Yale, D. E. C.: 'A Historical Note on the Jurisdiction of the Admiralty in Ireland', 3 *Irish Jurist* (n.s.) 146 (1968).

[only writings referred to in the body of the work are listed]

INDEX OF SUBJECTS

INDEX OF PERSONS